LESSONS FROM EVICTION COURT

LESSONS FROM EVICTION COURT

How We Can End Our Housing Crisis

Fran Quigley

ILR PRESS

AN IMPRINT OF CORNELL UNIVERSITY PRESS

Ithaca and London

Copyright © 2025 by Cornell University

First published 2025 by Cornell University Press

Librarians: A CIP catalog record for this book is available from the Library of Congress.

ISBN 9781501782091 (hardcover)
ISBN 9781501782107 (paperback)
ISBN 9781501782114 (epub)
ISBN 9781501782121 (pdf)

For Ellen

Contents

Acknowledgments

With a title like *Lessons from Eviction Court*, some explanation is in order. According to my job description, I am the one who is supposed to be providing the lessons, especially to the law students who work with me advocating for people facing the loss of their homes. In truth, our clients provide most of the lessons, to the students and me both.

These working parents, children, seniors, and persons living with disabilities live every moment wondering if they will be thrown out of their homes. Common sense and multiple studies tell us that they endure enormous physical and emotional damage as a result.

But, with very few exceptions, our clients shoulder that crushing burden with remarkable grace. The stories of their struggles fill this book, since those struggles illustrate the many ways that we fail them and point out how we can do better. But our clients' strength deserves acknowledgment, too, along with my appreciation for how they inspire all of us who push for change. If we allies can be just a fraction as persistent and resilient as the people living with housing insecurity, together we will win the struggle to make housing a fully realized human right.

Speaking of how we can win, tenant union members and organizers every day show how we can end housing injustice. Moreover, they show how we can build human rights in every sector of society. Special thanks to Jessica Bellamy and Josh Poe of the Louisville Tenants Union and Tara Raghuveer of KC Tenants and the Tenant Union Federation, and the thousands of people at their sides.

I have learned so much from my students and colleagues at Indiana University McKinney School of Law, Indiana Legal Services, and the Indiana Justice Project. Judge Garland Graves and other respectful, dedicated judges and their staffs show us all how justice can be administered with compassion and wisdom. Housing justice advocates in Indiana and beyond, including the tenant navigators and volunteer court watchers we see in court each week, inspire and guide me and my students.

Years ago, my son Jack helped kick-start this book project with his excellent research on religious traditions supporting the human right to housing. My friend Bob Healey reads every word I write—poor guy. Bob was a constant source of encouragement throughout the writing of this book, as he has been in our court cases and in my previous book projects. The same holds true for my dear friend Dr. Joe Biggs. Professors Kathryn Sabbeth and Davida Finger have spent years advocating for tenants, practicing in eviction courts, and issuing important critiques of the process. They read this book in manuscript form and offered insightful suggestions and much-appreciated encouragement.

The grand finale of gratitude goes to my family. My life is immeasurably blessed by Sam, Katie, Jack, and Collin. All those blessings started with the beautiful, brilliant, and unfailingly kind Ellen, to whom this book is dedicated. Thank you with all my heart.

LESSONS FROM EVICTION COURT

INTRODUCTION

Carmen Jones nudged me in the arm, then pointed down at her cell phone screen. A text had just come in from a company that manages a half dozen rental properties on the far east side of Indianapolis.

"Your rental application has unfortunately been denied for one or more of the following reasons: Court filing from landlord on tenancy screening report."

As it happened, we were at that very moment in front of a judge who was conducting a hearing on that court filing: her landlord's demand that Carmen and her two children be evicted. Shortly after the constable delivered court papers to her door, Carmen and her children (I will not use clients' real names in this book) voluntarily left the apartment. But that did not stop the so-called "Scarlet E" of the eviction filing from following her.[1]

By the day of the court hearing, Carmen and the children were sleeping at an extended-stay motel, with Carmen leaving the room every morning to go to work. The cost of eighty-five dollars a night was clearly unsustainable, and some nights Carmen could not come up with the fee. On those nights, she and the kids slept in their car. But motels don't check tenant reports, and the landlords she applied to were rejecting her left and right. Many of the other motel residents were in the same situation.

After the hearing ended, one of my law students and I walked out in the hallway to talk for a few minutes with Carmen. But the court bailiff followed us out, summoning us back into the courtroom for Natasha Green's case.

The police had recently arrested Natasha's abuser, the father of her children. The arrest protected Natasha from his drunken beatings but also left her without

1

his income to help support their five kids. So Natasha took a job thirty-five miles away from home, working in a warehouse on the 6 p.m. to 4 a.m. shift, four nights a week. She has a rickety car and tenuous nighttime child care arrangements.

Natasha is struggling with lack of sleep—she does not have much help watching the kids during the day. But she hopes that she can keep all this going long enough to pull in the paychecks she needs to catch up on rent.

Tanya Lyons sits in court watching all this, waiting for her turn. Tanya's four-year-old son Amari is nestled into the crook of her arm, drawing with a highlighter on white paper the court reporter has given him. Two days ago, one of our law school clinic students had successfully argued that the judge should allow Tanya and Amari to stay in their home an extra month before eviction. But at 10 p.m. the night after the hearing, the home's power was cut off, presumably after a call to the utility company by the angry landlord.

So goes about twenty minutes in eviction court.

When we started our student practice program at Indiana University McKinney School of Law a decade ago, we called it the Health and Human Rights Clinic. The plan was for law students on the verge of graduation to gain experience by advocating for low-income clients who were seeking access to health care. At first, we spent most of our time helping clients appeal denials of their applications for Medicaid. But what experts call the social determinants of health kept poking up in our clients' lives.[2] There were red-tape cutoffs of food stamps for hungry households, shady employers not paying hardworking roofers and restaurant servers, unemployment benefits blocked by a system seemingly designed to prevent laid-off workers from getting stopgap help.

And, of course, housing.

There may be no more critical social determinant of health than whether a person is living in a safe, secure home. Decades of research tells us that each eviction causes damage not just to a family's finances, but also their physical and mental health.[3] Evictions are particularly harmful to the health of the children in these displaced households—and a household with young children is one of those most likely to face an eviction.[4]

During the first year of the COVID-19 pandemic, the combination of massive work income loss and rent taking up a huge chunk of the financial obligations of low-income families made one thing clear: a tsunami of evictions was coming, even as the US Centers for Disease Control moratorium held it back temporarily. Now, as I write this in late 2024, the number of evictions across the country is rising.[5] The latest census reports show over seven million households are behind on their rent, which means they are on track to join our clients lining up in court each day to fight to stay in their homes—or, more often, to hear what day the judge orders them to move.[6]

Fifty-five million people in the US live in households paying more than half their income for rent, and that spells trouble too.[7] These families may be balancing all their obligations now, but our clients' experience tells us that many are just a broken-down vehicle or a child's illness away from eviction court.

Lawyers and law students can't fix all this. But we can sometimes slow down the eviction process for tenants, buying them time to search for a safe place to move or uncover a temporary influx of cash to make rent. And we can push for fairness in a process that is notoriously dismissive of renters' rights. Like firefighters arriving at a home already engulfed in flames, we arrive too late to prevent the worst damage from happening. But we do have the tools to mitigate the harm, at least some of the time.[8]

So the Health and Human Rights Clinic became a housing clinic. This book shares the lessons we learned about how our nation should respond to our clients and the millions of others struggling to stay housed in your neighborhood and mine.

Full disclosure here: The first four chapters of this book are not uplifting. They describe the devastating impact of housing insecurity on families and individuals. They lay out how the US abandoned a once-promising approach to ensuring housing for all. These chapters also walk us through the shameful legacy of racism in US housing policies and practices and describe how we lavish government housing benefits for wealthy individuals and corporations while leaving low-income families out in the cold.

When it comes to the US housing crisis, it is tempting to despair. But we shouldn't, because we know how to fix this. The later chapters in this book show the way.

We learn in chapter 5 that we can prevent many evictions simply by no longer allowing our courts to operate as a fast and cheap collection tool for landlords. Research from Princeton's Eviction Lab shows that higher eviction filing fees, even in low-income states like Alabama, are associated with significantly lower eviction rates.[9] And there are fewer evictions in cities where the law requires landlords to show "good cause" before putting tenants out.[10]

In chapter 6, we learn that US cities like Houston, Milwaukee, and Denver, as well as international examples like Finland, prove that a "Housing First" approach can all but eliminate chronic homelessness. The most humane response to the needs of our sisters and brothers struggling with homelessness is to prioritize a safe, secure roof overhead as a human right, then addressing other social service needs. This Housing First process works, reducing the number of people who are unhoused and blocking the too-common path from homelessness to arrest and incarceration.

We also learn in chapter 6 that inclusionary zoning in cities like Santa Fe can blunt the forces of gentrification. Zoning codes should ensure that we can build affordable housing in areas where low-income working families, seniors, and others can access jobs, schools, health care, and public transportation.

For our clients and most other low-income families, housing costs are by far the highest expense in their household.[11] That means that income supports like child tax credits, maximized food stamps, and stimulus checks can keep these families housed. Emphatic proof of this approach came during the first years of the COVID pandemic, when expanded benefits pushed US poverty rates to the lowest they have been in recorded history—a remarkable achievement accomplished during an era of widespread joblessness and illness.[12]

In chapter 7, we see how two-hundred-plus US municipalities with rent control measures in place have prevented the price gouging that has led some of our clients to lose their homes in communities like ours in Indianapolis, which have no rent control. The longtime presence of rent control in many of our nation's most profitable real estate markets proves that reasonable price limits not only protect tenants, but they also guarantee landlords a fair return on their investment. These regulations do not slow housing development, either: New Jersey in particular has proved that housing construction can thrive and even boom in locations where both inclusionary zoning and rent control are the law.[13]

In chapter 8, we address the fact that millions of households, because of disability or low wages or both, have incomes that are too low to consistently afford market-rate housing. The good news is that there are many examples across the US and in other countries showing that public housing can be a safe, secure alternative. We can provide housing that is far less expensive than the for-profit market could ever offer, protecting our most vulnerable neighbors and allowing families to thrive.

Chapter 9 reviews the success stories from other nations proving that providing housing for all can be effective, affordable, and sustainable. We will see that many of the most highly praised cities in the world feature a great deal of subsidized housing, built on a foundation of legal and binding commitments to housing as a human right. The blueprints for success are there for us to follow.

Abundant, high-quality public housing. Rent control. Tenant protections. Of course, as our clients attest, none of that is the norm in the US today. So chapter 10 shows us how religious communities, who have played key roles in past social movements, can make an important contribution to the current housing movement, too. Strong scriptural and historical foundations are already in place calling for US religious communities to prioritize housing. Many already do so. More need to pitch in.

Finally, in chapters 11 and 12, we reveal what I think is the most promising development in US housing: the growing tenant movement.

History tells us that social change happens when those most affected are in the lead, so it is exciting to see that US tenants are pushing to the front of the line. Tenants across the country are mobilizing under the "Rent Is Too Damn High" banner. They are demanding a tenants' bill of rights that includes good-cause protections from eviction, mandates for livable housing conditions, and federal action on rent control.

These tenants are canvassing rental communities and trailer parks, occupying vacant buildings, and pushing ballot initiatives. And they are starting to rack up impressive victories. So chapters 11 and 12 tell their stories, with a particular focus on the vibrant, multiracial Louisville Tenants Union.

This movement needs all of us. So, on behalf of Carmen, Natasha, Tanya, and the millions of other Americans who are engaged in the daily struggle to keep a safe, secure roof over their heads, thank you for reading about their challenges. And thank you for reading about how we can end their suffering. I hope you will agree that we can—and we must—make their struggles a thing of the past.

THE VIEW FROM EVICTION COURT

At first, when my students and I stood up in front of eviction court judges to announce that we represented our clients on behalf of something called the Health and Human Rights Clinic, the name didn't sound quite right. After all, we were in eviction court, and all the cases we handled focused on housing. Should our clinic's name, a vestige of years working on access to health care programs, be reconsidered? Maybe we should call ourselves the Housing Clinic.

But, soon enough, we learned the old name still fit. We found that health problems cause housing problems, with illness and disability making it hard if not impossible to pay the rent on time.[1] Our client Gloria checked herself out of the hospital after thirty-seven days of treatment for COVID complications, to come to court hoping to prevent her and her paralyzed son from being evicted. Another client, Reginald, was in a car accident while driving to work, and his injuries kept him from collecting a paycheck for several weeks and caused him to fall behind on his rent.

We also learned the directional arrow goes the other way, too: bad housing leads to bad health. Felicia's children are sickened by the mold, rodent droppings, and sewage backups that her landlord won't address. Effie is a senior with multiple disabilities, and she struggles with her apartment's excessive heat in the summer and drafty cold in the winter.

When we meet our clients, they are in the thick of their eviction process, which by itself has well-documented negative health impacts. Evictions are affirmatively linked to a horrifying list of crises: premature birth, low birth weight, depression, suicide, hospitalizations, and the ultimate data point: all-cause mortality.[2] Evictions trigger a domino effect of higher costs of living, setbacks in employment, family breakdowns, and subsequent evictions.[3]

For many of our clients, their next stop after court will be doubling up with family and friends, often sleeping on floors. Those overcrowded, unhealthy housing conditions harm children in the short term and also lead to the kids experiencing long-term behavioral and physical health issues.[4] As Alieza Durana of the Eviction Lab at Princeton University told me, "Eviction is not just a condition of poverty; it is a major cause of it."[5]

We are witnesses to that causation. Julia recently came to court wearing the pale blue scrubs from her home health care job. She was there to beg the judge to reduce the garnishment siphoning from her already meager paycheck. The source of the garnishment was a six-year-old eviction judgment against Julia and her ex-husband, complete with court costs and the landlord's attorney fees. Julia's ex is long gone, and now she is facing another eviction because she has so little money left over for current rent. Like so many others, Julia left the courtroom in tears.

Our clients are not the only ones feeling the stress. Some of my students come from privileged backgrounds, and they struggle with the shock of seeing first-hand the despair of poverty in their community. For other students, their clients' trauma unearths painful memories from their own families' troubles. Clients cry; students cry.

During a class discussion, one student described a conversation with a client who was making plans for his family to live out of their car. The student stopped for a long moment, then spoke again. "This is just horrible. I don't know what else to say. This just sucks." No one replied.

He was right. For months after our eviction courts first returned to in-person sessions after COVID isolation measures, I went home from court each day with a throbbing migraine. Headaches and sleepless nights are still a regular feature of this work. They are reminders that our clients deal with pressure that is immeasurably more intense than anything I struggle with.

"They Can't Go Anywhere"

One of the most dispiriting aspects of the eviction court experience is realizing that our clients' suffering is inflicted on them by a handful of people who profit from their misery. The iconic mom-and-pop landlords still exist, but they are a vanishing breed. Most of our clients pay their rent to corporate landlords, who are also known as "institutional landlords," because sometimes their businesses are structured as massive partnerships and trusts. These mega-landlords own the majority of all US rental units, 80 percent-plus of the properties with twenty-five or more units, and are gobbling up single-family homes at a rapid pace.[6]

In eviction court, these corporate landlords' presence is even more dominant than these numbers suggest. A study by the Federal Reserve Bank showed that these mega-landlords evict more often and more quickly than smaller landlords.[7] A recent analysis of our local eviction records by the *Indianapolis Star* showed that a full 88 percent of the eviction cases were filed by corporate landlords.[8]

Many of these court filings are not even aimed at reclaiming the rental property from the tenants. As we discuss more in chapter 5, our clients' experience dovetails with the national research showing that many of these cases are so-called serial filings. Serial filings are multiple evictions filed on the same household in an effort to shake down the tenants for late rent.[9] At first glance, the court cases may seem like a costly annoyance for landlords. But they are not, because the landlord-written leases include provisions that require the tenants to pay several hundred dollars in court fees and penalties each time a case is filed. Matthew Desmond and Nathan Wilmers shows that landlords in low-income neighborhoods earn greater profit—on average $300 per month per apartment—than landlords in middle-class and rich neighborhoods.[10] Serial filings are one of the reasons why, along with the limited bargaining power of tenants with poor credit histories or the Scarlet E of past evictions.

Landlords don't try to hide the fact that their goal is to squeeze maximum profits out of renters. Bob Niccols, CEO of one of America's top corporate landlords, Monarch Investment and Management Group, gleefully told investors in the midst of the COVID pandemic that big rent hikes were coming. "We have an unprecedented opportunity . . . to really press rents," Niccols said. "Where are people going to go? They can't go anywhere."[11] Sure enough, the six biggest property management companies in the United States made a whopping $4.3 billion in profits the year after Niccols's prediction, citing "pricing power" and "strong rent growth" as the source of their windfalls.[12]

As you might imagine, mega-landlords are not eager to reduce their profits by devoting money and personnel to ensuring that their properties are well maintained. Studies have shown that corporate landlords are more likely to neglect pressing maintenance needs than smaller landlords.[13] (To be clear, smaller mom-and-pop landlords often exploit and abuse our clients, too. But they are far easier to track down for conditions complaints. Like most cities, ours does not have an effective landlord registry, so even finding out the true owners of some properties can be impossible.)[14]

In our community, tenants have endured several corporate landlord nightmares. One apartment complex with a murky out-of-state ownership group accumulated a stunning three thousand housing code violations in a six-year period, including eight fires in two years.[15] The same ownership group racked up hundreds more violations and an unpaid $1.3 billion water bill that caused eight-hundred-plus residents in another complex to have their water shut off.[16]

A few months later, we saw some of these same residents in court. They had withheld their rent because of the water shutoff, trash being allowed to accumulate, and multiple other problems. Once these tenants' rent was not submitted, the same landlord who could not be found to respond to poor conditions quickly emerged—to file evictions against them.

Sometimes, corporate landlord abuse is inflicted on a house-by-house basis. Investors have swooped down on communities to buy up single-family homes, which they often rent out even when they are in bad shape.[17] We have had clients in these homes live with several feet of standing water in their basement, no heat, major rodent infestation, and gaping holes in exterior walls and windows.

There is an industry term for the practice of investors buying a big stock of low-quality properties and renting them to desperate families: "milking."[18] The term is supposed to refer to the extraction of the remaining value of these homes. But our clients feel they are being drained dry, too. The largest corporate landlord of single-family homes in our community has been accused of milking thousands of properties by renting them out in poor condition and then neglecting maintenance.[19] The same company has been sued by our neighboring Midwest city of Cincinnati for repeated code violations and illegal eviction practices.[20]

My students and I find these single-family home rental cases to be particularly sad, because the corporate landlords are benefiting from the very same crisis many of them created. Our clients tell us they fled to these homes hoping to escape the filth and chaos of the multifamily complexes where they used to live. Some clients even signed exploitative rent-to-own contracts where the landlord-seller tries to pass off the trouble and expense of dealing with poor-condition homes as our clients' responsibility.[21]

Given the low quality of this rental housing, you might think that it is inexpensive. Usually, it's not. Landlords know that our clients and their neighbors have few options: many are branded with the Scarlet E of a past eviction or other poor credit history that disqualifies them from higher-quality rental properties. Others can't pay multiple months' advance rent and the big deposits or application fees those properties require.

So, landlords of low-quality housing capitalize on their tenants' limited options by charging surprisingly high rents. A study of our community showed that median rents in high-poverty areas were only 17 percent less than the overall community average.[22] Factor in the savings these landlords get from buying the properties on the cheap and dodging maintenance costs, and you understand how data have shown that landlords in poor neighborhoods can make double the profits of landlords in wealthier areas.[23]

"If We Get Evicted, We Lose Everything"

One day, Jessica and her family came to court in a panic. Jessica had contracted COVID and missed several weeks of work, which caused her to fall behind on the rent she owed to a mobile home park. She and her elderly mother and disabled brother lived together in the family home. All were facing eviction.

The good news was that Jessica and her family came to court with several folded and dog-eared money orders they had managed to cobble together over the past few weeks. The amount they had collected added up to the rent due. The bad news was that the landlords said they wouldn't dismiss the eviction case unless Jessica paid for their attorney's fees, too. Jessica agreed to do so. Oops, the attorney said, we forgot to add on court filing fees to the ledger. Under your lease, you have to pay those as well, he told her.

I was getting angry. This was more of a shakedown than negotiation. But Jessica saw no choice but to agree. "We'll just have to figure out how to get the money," she told me. "We can't risk getting evicted."

But the dismissal of this case didn't eliminate Jessica's risk. The landlord refused to let Jessica or any other park resident sign a long-term lease. They insisted on keeping everyone on month-to-month terms, meaning the residents can be forced out with as little as thirty days' notice.

For Jessica and her neighbors, that is an even more disastrous prospect than it is for our clients who live in traditional apartments or rented homes. Jessica and her mobile home park neighbors own their homes. Jessica paid $37,000 for hers fifteen years ago. Since then, she and her family have put thousands of dollars and countless hours into improvements, including an attached wooden deck on the back. But they don't own the land under their home, the so-called lot it sits on. For that space, the landlord charges them $470 per month.

The dirty secret about so-called mobile homes like Jessica's is that they are often not very mobile at all. It can cost as much as $14,000 to move a mobile home, assuming the home is sturdy enough to move at all and the owner finds another place to site it.[24] Jessica's home has sat on the lot for more than three decades, which means she is not at all confident it can be relocated intact. "If we get evicted, we lose everything we have worked for," she says.

Jessica is in a can't-win position, and her landlord knows it. In court we see mobile home park residents who report that park owners have refused to renew leases by the dozens. That leads the mobile home owners to abandon their houses, which the park owners snatch up and resell or lease.[25]

Jessica and her family are among the twenty-two million people—one in every fifteen people in the country—living in mobile homes, also known as manufactured housing.[26] Those homes are far cheaper to buy than traditional single-family homes, making them the largest source of unsubsidized affordable housing in the United States.[27] Like Jessica, most of those people own the homes—80 percent of manufactured housing is resident-owned.[28] But, like Jessica, many of those people are economically vulnerable. The median income of manufactured home owners is less than $35,000, half as much as the income of more traditional homeowners.[29]

Owning a manufactured home does not bring with it the same kind of stability associated with traditional homeownership. If the purchase was financed with a loan, that loan is likely a so-called chattel loan, with high interest rates and a shorter payoff period, terms that resemble a car loan more than a traditional home loan.[30] Lending companies factor in the instability caused when the land underneath a manufactured home is owned by someone else, making the home depreciate in value, nearly unheard of in traditional homes. The personal finance radio host Dave Ramsey calls manufactured homes "a car you can sleep in," bluntly declaring them a terrible investment.[31]

"Sell to the Masses, Eat with the Classes"

History shows that when low-income persons have a desperate need, exploiters will soon step in. As one mobile home park owner says, being the landlord for people like Jessica provides an enticing "sell to the masses, eat with the classes" opportunity.[32] These particular masses are all but forced to pay whatever price is charged. Frank Rolfe, whose 250 mobile home parks make him one of the top five owners in the industry, boasts, "We're like a Waffle House where everyone is chained to the booths."[33]

Rolfe and his partner also operate Mobile Home University, which provides training and materials to aspiring mobile home landlords. A feature of the pitch to sign up for their courses is the gun held to the head of residents like Jessica: "The fact that tenants can't afford the $5,000 it costs to move a mobile home keeps revenues stable and makes it easy to raise rents without losing any occupancy," says the testimonial on the Mobile Home University website.[34]

Some of the world's wealthiest people have noticed. Investment firms like Blackstone, Apollo Global Management, the Carlyle Group, and Stockbridge Capital Group all have bought large interests in mobile home parks.[35] Warren Buffett owns both the largest manufacturer of mobile homes and some of the largest holders of the high-interest mobile home purchase loans.[36] Equity Life-style Properties, a real estate investment trust founded by the multibillionaire

Sam Zell, who has been accused of "gouging grandma" via rent increases, is the largest mobile home park landlord in the country.[37]

For these wealthy investors, part of the attraction is that mobile home park landlords have far less obligations than landlords of traditional housing. All the maintenance and upkeep of the actual structures is the sole responsibility of the mobile home owners. Mobile home park investor Michael Torres told NPR in 2022, "It's just basically resurfacing roads and having a shared community center. You don't own walls and roofs." This largely passive income flow, added to the inability of Jessica and other tenants to easily move, makes being their landlord "the gold standard of investing in property," Torres says.[38]

Yet those park landlords often shirk even their minimal obligations. The NPR story and many others have chronicled neglected maintenance that led to flooding, power outages, and sewer backups in parks. That neglect is not exactly accidental: at least one landlord company gave its park managers bonuses based in part on keeping repair costs low. The bottom line, Rolfe claims, is that mobile home parks have the highest yield in real estate.[39]

Remarkably, the federal government is helping contribute to those profits. A 2021 NPR story unsubtly titled "How the Government Helps Investors Buy Mobile Home Parks, Raise Rent, and Evict People" revealed that the government-backed mortgage finance agencies Fannie Mae and Freddie Mac provide billions of dollars in low-interest loans that huge investment companies use to buy the parks.[40] The Lincoln Institute for Land Policy told the Associated Press that Freddie Mac, whose mission is to make housing more affordable, has provided nearly $10 billion in financing to purchase over nine hundred mobile home communities in the last decade.[41]

Worse, when a company spikes the rent in one set of parks, it improves the company's chances to get more government-backed loans, because those rent hikes boost the company's cash flow. "What's ironic about it is that one of the missions of Fannie Mae and Freddie Mac is to help preserve affordable housing," Lincoln Institute's George McCarthy told NPR. "And they're doing exactly the opposite by helping investors come in and make the most affordable housing in the United States less affordable all the time."

For me and my students, this housing injustice is painful to witness. For our clients, it is far more painful to endure. The good news is that there are ways to prevent the suffering we see every week, and models to follow that are proven to be effective. Most of this book will be devoted to showing how our housing system can be far, far better. But first, it helps to show how we got into this mess. The next three chapters will explain.

HOW WE ABANDONED AFFORDABLE HOUSING

How would it look for the US to make and keep a commitment to treating housing as a human right, not just a commodity? We don't have to rely on our imagination to come up with an answer. In chapter 9, we will look at wonderful current examples in places like Vienna, Singapore, and Helsinki, where communities ensure housing for all. But we don't have to leave the shores of the United States for proof that we can do much, much better than we do now. That is because the US once made a highly effective commitment to housing all our people.

After the Great Depression and through the 1970s, very few people in our country were homeless. Those who were homeless mostly were older men living in cheap hotels, so-called flophouses. Many experts predicted that even that level of homelessness would be eliminated by the end of the 1970s.[1]

Why did we not have the housing problem then that we see now? Simple: we sincerely tried to address it. Back in 1949, the American Housing Act set out the goal of ensuring a "decent home in a suitable living environment for every American family." That language echoed the Universal Declaration of Human Rights, signed by the US the year before. For a few decades, we took that goal seriously. Recognizing that affordable housing cannot be left to the for-profit market, we made the required significant government investment. In the mid-1970s, the US devoted 1.4 percent of our gross domestic product to federal interventions in affordable housing. Today, our commitment is less than a fifth of that, only 0.25 percent.[2]

During the Great Depression, the US created the Home Owners Loan Corporation (HOLC) and the Federal Housing Administration (FHA). These agencies and the Veterans Administration purchased, insured, and issued mortgages to protect at-risk homeowners. They also provided millions of others with opportunities to buy houses through significantly lower down payments and interest rates—often with monthly payments that were less expensive than renting.[3]

Many historians consider the FHA to be our nation's most impactful government agency for the half-century between 1930 and 1980.[4] (At least, it made a profound impact on white people: as we will see in chapter 3, these transformative homeownership programs were largely off-limits to Americans of color.) In the 1960s and 1970s, home purchase support was buttressed by rent support programs, along with the creation of the Department of Housing and Urban Development (HUD).[5]

Then . . . we abandoned those commitments. In the early 1980s, President Ronald Reagan and a compliant US Congress slashed funding for affordable housing by nearly 80 percent.[6] At the same time, persons living in state hospitals were deinstitutionalized, benefits for persons living with disabilities were cut, and eligibility for those benefits was so tightly restricted that hundreds of thousands of people lost the only income they had.[7]

A dark era had begun. As Western Regional Advocacy Project director Paul Boden said, "Racism, poverty, and addiction all existed before 1982. What did not exist was a homeless shelter."[8] While Reagan famously claimed that many people are "homeless by choice," the choice was his, not theirs.[9] Urban policy scholar Peter Dreier puts it bluntly: "Every park bench in America—everywhere a homeless person sleeps—should have Ronald Reagan's name on it."[10]

A review of US housing policy over the past four decades is frustrating and depressing. Opportunities were missed, backward steps were taken. People suffer as a result. Where did we go wrong?

The Slashing of Affordable Housing Investment

As we discuss more in chapter 8, public housing is a necessary, proven response to the needs of our clients and millions of other Americans who cannot afford market-rate housing. But since 1996 there have been zero dollars spent in HUD funding for new public housing.[11] That neglect has been piled on top of the flawed foundation of US public housing created by the 1937 Housing Act. That legislation provided too little funding for high-quality housing construction, especially in the segregated units built for Black renters. And it included no support for necessary maintenance costs.[12]

Hawaii state senator Stanley Chang, a supporter of public and social housing, calls the 1937 Housing Act the "original sin" of federal involvement in housing. "That is when private developers forced income restrictions for every unit to make sure that the middle class and the upper middle class would never be able to live in public housing," Chang told me in an interview.

"Eighty-seven years later, public housing is still restricted to the poor. The old saying in Washington is that a program for the poor is a poor program. And that is indeed what has happened. You don't have large scale buy-in from the public at large on public housing the way that you do for programs like Medicare and Social Security, which benefit everybody and therefore receive support from everybody."[13]

The fiscal starvation of public housing led to severe maintenance problems and an inevitable decline in available units.[14] Opponents of public housing have cynically used the deterioration of public housing stock to claim public housing in the US has failed, and then to justify their attempts to destroy it.[15] They succeeded in passing severely damaging legislation like the 1998 Quality Housing and Work Responsibility Act, which was part of the Clinton administration's "end welfare as we know it" cuts to federal antipoverty programs. The result: there are only 958,000 public housing units today, compared to more than 1.3 million a quarter century ago.[16]

Victor Bach, senior housing policy analyst at the Community Service Society in New York City, told Human Rights Watch that the current support for public housing is merely "starvation funding."[17] That underfunding has led to an estimated $70 billion in repair needs for public housing in the US.[18] As conditions deteriorate, demolitions follow, with ten-thousand-plus desperately needed public housing units being demolished each year.[19]

These policy choices did not occur in a vacuum. From its very beginning, public housing in the US was hamstrung by political compromises forced by real estate lobbyists who wanted public housing to fail, teaming up with southern senators determined to maintain segregation.[20] Then, throughout the second half of the twentieth century, the real estate industry lobbied against more public housing being created, pushed for inferior design and construction materials, supported the demolition of existing public housing, and joined with white communities to oppose the placement of public housing anywhere except neighborhoods that mostly included people of color.[21]

Sociologist Daniel Aldana Cohen and economist Mark Paul have chronicled the real estate industry's successful lobbying effort. Their account mirrors Hawaii state senator Chang's conclusion. "Back in 1937, the real estate industry successfully repelled the efforts of the Labor Housing Conference and the New Deal's Public Works Administration to create social housing in the United States that would look much like the successful model still used today in Vienna—mixed-use, mixed-income, and high quality," Cohen and Paul have written. "This, after all, was the real estate industry's nightmare: A viable public housing option that could undermine the private sector's ability to rake in massive profits."[22]

Housing researchers Gianpaolo Baiocchi and H. Jacob Carlson have summed it up: "The failures of public housing can be traced to early sabotage, chronic under-funding, and segregationist logic."[23] The influence of the for-profit real estate industry continues to this day. Pointing out that global real estate is a $200-trillion-plus industry constituting 60 percent of the world's assets, urban planner Samuel Stein refers to the US and other countries as "real estate states."[24]

The success of the private real estate industry and the accompanying struggles of public housing were not inevitable. As will be described in chapters 8 and 9, there are several public housing success stories in US, thriving communities that have managed to survive institutional neglect. And public housing is both prevalent and successful in other nations where it enjoys both adequate funding and political support.

Yet, in the eviction courts where we work, the human cost of the abandonment of US public housing is on full display. Virtually all our clients are low-income and thus technically eligible for a federal housing subsidy that would cap their housing costs at 30 percent of their income.[25] It is hard to overstate how impactful this subsidy is. Consider that households with a low-wage or disability income of $1,200 per month would pay less than $400 for a public housing apartment, compared to the $1,000 or more they pay in the private market now. A federal housing subsidy also comes with a guarantee of substantially more renter protections from arbitrary evictions and rent spikes than tenants have in the private housing market.[26]

But our clients almost never have a federal housing subsidy. They are among the unfortunate 75 percent of Americans eligible for the subsidy but unable to get it because the program is so underfunded.[27] In class, we describe this quest for a housing subsidy as the cruelest musical chairs game: three of every four people lose out.

If they could, our clients would eagerly join a waiting list for a subsidized unit. But the average family waits two and a half years on subsidized-housing waiting lists.[28] A recent survey of forty-four housing agencies revealed more than 737,000 households on waiting lists, with some lists closed for more than a decade.[29] The New York City Housing Authority last opened its waiting list in 2006.[30] The delay can reach the point of absurdity: one Chicago woman recently had her name come to the top of the waiting list—twenty-nine years after applying.[31]

The Privatization of Affordable Housing

As we will see in chapter 4, wealthy individuals and corporations reap a bounty of government-provided benefits from high-end or market-rate housing.

Sometimes they receive the benefits for living in the housing, often by investing in it and renting it out. Remarkably, our current US affordable housing programs direct many of their investments not directly to persons in need of housing but to private landlords and investors seeking to maximize profit off housing for the poor.

During the Nixon administration in the 1970s, the US began to switch our affordable housing dollars away from public housing. Instead, the plan was to subsidize for-profit landlords via direct payments and tax breaks in return for providing some housing to low-income renters.[32] This diversion of affordable housing dollars to for-profit entities is virtually unheard of anywhere else in the world. Most nations take the logical, efficient approach of directing their affordable housing investments to government or nonprofit organizations.[33]

This practice, and the broader dismantling of affordable housing programs, began during the Nixon administration and then accelerated in earnest under Ronald Reagan. But Democrat presidents inflicted grievous damage, too. When Bill Clinton enabled public housing agencies to tear down developments without replacing units, he was fulfilling the destiny envisioned by President Jimmy Carter's HUD secretary, Patricia Harris, in 1976: "I would rather have people in the marketplace purchasing their own shelter—with the encouragement that this would give to private development at all levels—than have the government put up the kind of public housing monstrosities . . . that we've had in the past. We should make it clear that we are abandoning the whole notion of public housing."[34]

Powerful forces may have wanted to abolish public housing, but they never abandoned the use of affordable housing tax dollars to enrich the wealthy. While public housing has been undermined and scaled back, there remains a robust pipeline of affordable housing subsidies to for-profit landlords, chiefly through the Section 8 voucher and project-based programs. In the voucher program, technically called housing choice vouchers but widely known as Section 8 vouchers, low-income renters are provided with vouchers they can use to find housing in the private rental market.[35] If a landlord agrees to the arrangement, the federal government will pay the difference between market rent and 30 percent of the renter's income—the same rent obligation that a public housing resident has.[36]

But the voucher program relies on the self-interest of for-profit landlords, which often makes the promise of vouchers an empty one. As many as 30 percent of households who receive vouchers end up forfeiting them because private landlords will refuse to accept "Section 8" tenants.[37] Sometimes the landlord refusal is due to discrimination. Sometimes they say no because the HUD determination of fair market rate is lower than what landlords believe they can collect from nonsubsidized tenants.[38] In those situations, desperate tenants sometimes agree to pay rents higher than the HUD fair market amount, causing nearly half of all voucher holders to still be in the "rent-burdened" category.[39]

When we first saw our client Belinda, her years on a waiting list had finally led to her receiving one of the coveted vouchers. But Belinda was still sleeping on a friend's floor because she could not find a landlord to accept her voucher. Most states, including ours, do not prohibit a landlord from simply refusing to accept tenants with housing vouchers: in those states, 77 percent of landlords reject voucher-holders.[40] Belinda never did find a landlord willing to accept her, so her voucher expired. The last time we connected with her, Belinda was homeless.

HUD does not maintain data on the landlords who benefit from the $19 billion per year spent on vouchers, but analysis by the Poverty and Race Research and Action Council suggests that many of those vouchers directly fund large, for-profit landlords.[41] Similar direct payments to for-profit landlords occur in the Project-Based Section 8 program, where the subsidy is connected to the unit, not the tenant. Most of these property owners are for-profit entities who can convert to market-rate housing at the end of their HUD contracts. They often do so, leaving nearly half of the tenants without their previous subsidy.[42] Just north of Indianapolis, a senior living complex refused to renew its Section 8 contract, forcing out more than one hundred seniors.[43]

The Emergency Rental Assistance program, $47 billion allotted in 2020 and 2021 in response to the COVID pandemic, mimicked the process of the HUD programs, delivering most of its benefits to for-profit landlords.[44] The money was delivered with no strings attached, not even the promise of decent living conditions for renters. Time and again in court, we saw some of the most notorious slumlords in our community raking in tens of thousands of dollars in government rent dollars.

"The chief benefactors of public capital are private capitalists," California Assembly member Alex Lee told me in an interview. "They are the ones who try to delude policy makers and the public that housing is fueled by the private market. But by and large, when it comes to suburban sprawl or affordable housing, so much of housing is supported by public financing. And it's not efficient public financing. We basically send money off to private entities, then kiss it goodbye."[45]

A "Better-Than-Nothing Gimmick"

The congressionally mandated freeze on public housing development has been in effect since 1998. That has left the Low-Income Housing Tax Credit (LIHTC) program as the one program remaining that funds the creation of new, so-called affordable housing (more on the meaning of "so-called" affordable housing below).

A full 90 percent of new affordable housing is built via the LIHTC program.[46] That makes LIHTC the US government's chief tool for creating new affordable housing.[47]

But this affordable housing tool is a dull and ineffective one. As housing researcher Alyssa Katz has written, LIHTC is "a better-than-nothing gimmick that helps the poor by rewarding the rich."[48] Unfortunately, the reward for the rich is far more impressive than the help provided to the poor.

Here is how LIHTC works: The program offers developers a ten-year tax credit if they invest in the development of housing that guarantees a certain number of affordable units.[49] The credit is allocated by the federal government to the states, which administer the programs. Most LIHTC properties, including 78 percent of the LIHTC apartments built between 1987 and 2013, were developed by for-profit companies.[50] Even when the developers are nonprofit, the LIHTC model pushes them into funding arrangements with for-profit investors, who buy the credits to reduce their tax liability. Simply put, LIHTC is a tax shelter scheme for wealthy corporations.

Those LIHTC investors include the notorious Blackstone Group, a multinational private equity corporation that is the US's largest landlord.[51] The United Nations' special rapporteur for housing has accused Blackstone of "wreaking havoc" on the global housing market with aggressive evictions, inflated rents, and unreasonably high fees for ordinary maintenance.[52] In 2018, Blackstone spent more than $6 million fighting a California ballot initiative to permit rent control.[53] This is who is receiving our government housing dollars.

No matter who is benefiting from the tax credits, LIHTC is a poor substitute for public housing. I call the affordable housing reference in LIHTC's name "so-called" because the program often leads to rents much higher than other subsidized housing. Federally subsidized housing via public housing, vouchers, or Section 8 tie maximum allowable rents to the tenants' income: if a tenant makes only $967 in a Supplemental Security Income check, that tenant's rent is less than $300.

But LIHTC rents, tied to area median income, are significantly more expensive, which means less than half of LIHTC households are extremely low-income.[54] And among the few poor renters in LIHTC buildings, many can only afford to live there because they are using housing choice vouchers or other assistance to help pay their rent.[55]

Not only is LIHTC support for affordable housing units limited in its immediate impact, but it often is quite temporary. Affordability requirements on LIHTC developments expire after thirty years, and some owners can opt out of affordability restrictions after just fifteen years.[56] Many of those developments are switched to market-rate housing after the restrictions end, an ominous sign, since more than 138,000 LIHTC units will come to the end of their affordability periods by 2025.[57]

For taxpayers, who lose $10 billion in forgone tax revenue annually due to LIHTC, this is an expensive way to produce housing.[58] For example, the cost of developing each LIHTC housing unit in California is a whopping $480,000.[59] The overall return on US taxpayer investment is unjustifiable.

In fact, even LIHTC's "better-than-nothing" label may be an overstatement: one study published in the *Journal of Housing Economics* concluded that at least some of LIHTC-funded housing would have been created even without the government subsidy.[60] LIHTC housing can even make the situation worse for low-income households by fueling housing price inflation and further spurring the speculation that makes housing scarce and expensive.[61] Frustrated legislators like Stanley Chang and Alex Lee call LIHTC "legalized theft of government assets."[62] Even the Congressional Budget Office has admitted that the LIHTC program is "more suited to the needs of investors than poor renters."[63]

So much for the American Housing Act's 1949 commitment to ensuring a "decent home in a suitable living environment for every American family." But it is important not to paint too rosy a picture of the old days in affordable housing. Even when US government dollars were flowing much more freely to meet housing needs, there was a dam of racism blocking most of that support from reaching persons of color. That is the topic of chapter 3.

"WE HAVE TO ADDRESS THE RACISM"

Early in each semester, after the students have been to court three or four times, I ask them to guess the racial composition of the township where we do most of our work. Their responses usually range from 70 percent to 90 percent Black. That is a reasonable estimate, since it matches the population of the tenants who sign in with the court clerk and take their seats on the gray metal folding chairs outside the courtroom.

But the Black population of the area is only 37 percent.[1]

The scenes in our courts are not unique to our community. Across the country, Black families are far more likely to be evicted than whites, with Black women with children the most likely family group to be losing their home.[2] Although less than 20 percent of renters in this country are Black, over half of all eviction filings target Black residents.[3] Nearly one of every five Black or Hispanic children has experienced eviction by age fifteen.[4] Black people are significantly overrepresented among our country's homeless population. And they are at proportionately greater risk of returning to homelessness when they do get housed.[5]

As we explain in chapter 4, homeownership in the US often provides a basketful of tangible financial benefits. These include significant tax breaks and growing equity—the average US home gained almost $150,000 in value over the past ten years—not to mention the advantages of predictable monthly payments and living-space autonomy that are denied most renters.[6] While 74 percent of white American households reap those benefits by owning their own home, only 46 percent of Black households do.[7]

In recent years, that gap has only grown wider.[8] Even when Black Americans do own their own home, lower home valuations and predatory lending practices in minority neighborhoods contribute to Black homeowners having far less equity in their homes compared to the average white homeowner.[9]

This is important. For most American households, the value of our homes makes up most of our wealth.[10] That means the homeownership and equity gap has implications far beyond the status of the roof over the family's head: the average net wealth for white households is almost eight times the wealth for Black households.[11]

As part of my research for this book, I spoke with Apryl Lewis, an organizer for Action NC (North Carolina). Lewis's work focuses on housing justice, a topic she knows all too well: as a single mom, she had to scramble several times to keep from being evicted, despite working two and sometimes three jobs. Lewis and Action NC organize in support of eviction moratoriums, tenants' rights, more affordable housing development, and rent control. But those reforms alone would not fully reach the root of the crisis, Lewis says. "A lot of the problems with housing have not improved since the Jim Crow era," she says. "To address housing, we have to address the racism."

Many others have written more and better on this topic than I could ever aspire to. Richard Rothstein's book *Color of Law: A Forgotten History of How Our Government Segregated America* is legendary.[12] Keeanga-Yamahtta Taylor's *Race for Profit: How Banks and the Real Estate Industry Undermined Black Homeownership* deserves to be.[13] A strong one-stop summary of our multicentury legacy of US racism in housing and other core facets of daily life is provided in the first fourteen pages of US Supreme Court justice Ketanji Brown Jackson's dissenting opinion in the 2023 affirmative action decision, *Students for Fair Admissions, Inc. v. President and Fellows of Harvard College.*[14]

I recommend those sources for a deeper dive into this critical topic. But I can summarize our nation's housing-racism problems here in six facts:

1. The Systemic Theft of Black Labor Has Created Housing Disparities

Of course, the impetus for the seismic suffering inflicted on generations of Black Americans via slavery was the theft of their labor. For nearly two and a half centuries, Black people in this country were forced to build wealth for white slaveholders and the nation at large. They succeeded in spectacular fashion. By the middle of the nineteenth century, cotton picked in slave states was not only the number one export product in the United States—it exceeded all other exports combined.[15] The Mississippi River Valley had more millionaires per capita than any other region in the nation.[16] Yet enslaved Blacks gained nothing from their contribution to this bonanza, while whites built wealth that continues to benefit their families today.[17]

The end of the Civil War did not stop the exploitation of Black labor. In the communities where freed Black people had been living, land was the critical source of income and wealth. But white southerners would largely refuse to sell land to Black people. Sometimes, the so-called Black Codes that predated Jim Crow laws legally prohibited them from doing so.[18]

For the few formerly enslaved Black people who were able to buy rural land in the South, that land was often taken from them by a combination of violence, swindling, and corruption. "A war waged by deed of title" led to the dispossession of 98 percent of Black agricultural landowners in America, Vann R. Newkirk II wrote in a 2019 *Atlantic* article. Newkirk described how the federal government enabled the theft by allowing racist and corrupt local officials to control the much-needed federal money from the US Department of Agriculture, despite those officials being elected in areas where Black people were blocked from voting.[19]

Without land of their own to farm, Black people found they had limited options for survival. Black Code laws blocked Black people from pursuing many occupations and sentenced them to chain gangs if they did not fulfill onerous labor contracts with whites.[20] For many Black people, the only remaining path to survival was to return to working for the same whites who once enslaved them, this time as a sharecropper. Fraudulent bookkeeping regularly left the working Black people owing more to the white farmer than their wages would cover.[21] As Justice Jackson wrote, sharecropping was "de facto reenslavement."[22]

Some Black people managed to escape sharecropping for wage employment, largely in the northern states. Yet they did not escape government-created discrimination in the workplace. In the 1930s, Congress and the Franklin Roosevelt administration passed into law revolutionary New Deal protections for workers, including a minimum wage guarantee, Social Security old-age insurance, the right to organize into unions, and unemployment compensation. But those laws exempted agricultural workers, domestic workers, and tipped workers, professions disproportionately filled by persons of color. Nearly two-thirds of Black workers were blocked from these new benefits.[23]

As National Employment Law Project executive director Rebecca Dixon told Congress in 2021, "These exclusions did not accidentally deny Black people and other workers of color the rights and protections given to white workers. Congress intentionally excluded whole categories of workers from vital protections in order to deny Black people the opportunity for economic and social freedom and to preserve a system where employers could profit from racist exploitation."[24]

Many of those workplace protection exclusions remain, as does their disproportionate negative effect on the income of workers of color. Less formalized discrimination in the workplace continues as well: one in four Black workers report having been treated unfairly in the past year in hiring, pay, or promotion because of their race.[25]

The effect of generations of employment racism is that Blacks in the US on average earn 25 percent less than whites in hourly earnings—a gap that has increased in the past forty years.[26] Gaps in educational level—themselves deeply impacted by racism in schooling and opportunities—contribute to the wage difference.[27] But they don't explain all of it. College-educated Black men still earn only 80 percent of the wages of college-educated white men.[28]

There is a clear connection between today's housing insecurity and the generations of theft and undervaluing of Black labor. Obviously, it is imperative for any household to earn enough money each month to pay rent. Lower incomes also mean less opportunity to accumulate the savings needed to put a down payment on a home. Many of our clients pay far more each month in rent than they would for a comparable home's mortgage payment, a common situation for renters.[29] But they lack the down payment needed to qualify for a mortgage—and the generous benefits that our government provides to homeowners.

2. Our Government Housing Policy Has Benefited Whites and Excluded Blacks

As with employment, our government has long used its housing laws and dollars to favor the prospects of whites while actively suppressing the aspirations of persons of color, particular Black people.

As we discussed in chapter 2, our current housing crisis should not obscure the fact that the US has in the past achieved massive successes with government housing programs. Starting in the mid-nineteenth century, the Homestead Acts gave away hundreds of millions of acres of public land, nearly 10 percent of all the land in US. "The Homestead Acts were unquestionably the most extensive, radical, redistributive governmental policy in US history," historian Keri Leigh Merritt says. Merritt estimates that a quarter of the US population are descendants of Homestead Act recipients and thus the beneficiaries of the wealth built through this government program.[30]

As we saw in chapter 2, the US created the Home Owners Loan Corporation (HOLC) and the Federal Housing Administration (FHA) during the Great

Depression. These agencies purchased, insured, and issued mortgages to protect at-risk homeowners and provided others with opportunities to buy houses through significantly lower down payments and interest rates.[31] After World War II, the Veterans Administration guaranteed mortgages for tens of millions of returning veterans.[32]

This government support set the stage for US homeowners to enjoy the predictability of a thirty-year, fixed-rate mortgage, an advantage unheard of in other nations.[33] Recognizing the core role that home equity plays in US family asset-building, this mid-twentieth-century era of huge government support for home-ownership is widely acknowledged to be the greatest mass opportunity for wealth accumulation in the nation's history.[34]

But not all people were provided that opportunity. These programs both de facto and de jure operated with a "Whites Only" sign on their entrance. Only a few thousand of the 1.6 million families who received land through the Homestead Acts were Black.[35] To guide its loan decisions, the HOLC created, and the FHA later adopted, color-coded maps of neighborhoods. On those maps, the color red indicated neighborhoods where Black people lived—and thus an allegedly risky mortgage investment. "Redlining" led to decades of these federal agencies refusing to provide the same support for Black homeownership as whites enjoyed. By so doing, our government dramatically widened the wealth gap already created by slavery, the Black Codes, and Jim Crow.[36]

Often, the federal government couched its discrimination in terms of alleged concerns about default on the home loans. Other times, no one bothered to disguise the racism. Rothstein writes about a 1941 plan to sell suburban New Jersey property to a dozen middle-class Black families with good credit ratings. The FHA refused to sign off, stating flatly, "No loans will be given to colored developments."[37]

Under the federal government's redlining practices, a single Black household could taint an entire neighborhood as unworthy of investment. This provided an economic incentive for whites to block Black people from living in their communities. One white homeowner in mid-century Levittown, Pennsylvania, said that a new Black neighbor was "probably a nice guy, but every time I look at him I see $2,000 drop off the value of my house."[38]

The government-favored neighborhoods typically avoided any risk of redlining by adopting restrictive covenants that blocked the sale or renting of homes to Black persons. State and local governments routinely supported and enforced these covenants, and the US Supreme Court in 1926 ruled they were legal. These covenants were also endorsed by the FHA in the form of higher mortgage approvals for communities that adopted racist covenants.[39]

The bottom line: our government is guilty of massive housing racism, and the impact is quantifiable. Between 1934 and 1962, 98 percent of the hundreds of millions of dollars in family-transforming FHA loans went to whites.[40] In New York and northern New Jersey, of the sixty-seven thousand VA-insured mortgages, fewer than one hundred went to non-whites. In many communities across the South, the percentage of loans to non-whites was even lower.[41]

In 1948, in the case of *Shelley v. Kraemer*, the US Supreme Court finally ruled that states could not enforce racially restrictive housing covenants.[42] The pervasive impact of those covenants was memorably demonstrated by three of the nine Supreme Court justices being forced to recuse themselves from the *Shelley* case: each of them owned property that was subject to restrictive covenants.

After the *Shelley* decision, massive segregation did not stop. Many communities simply substituted their overtly racist covenants with rules that limited neighborhoods to single-family homes with large lot sizes and parking restrictions. These exclusionary zoning rules had the same effect as the racist covenants they replaced: most persons of color were barred from the communities. Sociologist Matthew Desmond calls exclusionary zoning "our politer, quieter means of promoting segregation." In most areas of our country, it is fully legal. Exclusionary zoning's effects and efforts to eliminate it are discussed more in chapter 6.[43]

3. Predatory Housing Practices Disproportionately Harm Black Americans

When racist government housing practices prevented Black families from obtaining the household stability and financial advantages from homeownership that whites received, a crew of shady actors stepped in to take advantage. The seminal account of this nefarious government-capital partnership is Keeanga-Yamahtta Taylor's *Race for Profit: How Banks and the Real Estate Industry Undermined Black Homeownership*.[44] Blocked from FHA and other government-backed loans, Black and brown people who sought the advantages of homeownership had no choice but to enter into deeply exploitative purchase agreements and/or loans. Taylor calls the phenomenon "predatory inclusion."[45]

That predation often came in the form of home contract purchases, sometimes known as rent-to-own or land sales contracts. These forms of contract purchases are still widespread in communities where access to favorable credit is not available. The common denominator among them is that the contract terms are skewed at all turns in favor of the seller.[46] The purchaser has to provide a large down payment and make high monthly payments but is denied any equity until the contract is completed. The seller retains the deed. If a single payment is late or missed, the seller promptly strips the purchaser of both the home and the purchaser's investment in it—and often resells the house to yet another contract purchaser.[47]

One analysis by researchers from Duke University and the University of Illinois–Chicago estimated that these contracts accounted for as many as 95 percent of homes sold to Black families in Chicago during the 1950s and 1960s. Contract prices were routinely marked up more than 80 percent from the true value of the homes, and Blacks paid almost $600 more per month in current dollars than they would have under a conventional mortgage. The researchers estimated that these rapacious housing contracts stripped Black families in Chicago of as much as $4 billion in wealth they would have accumulated under conventional mortgage purchases.[48]

For many of the Black families who could get a mortgage, the exploitation continued. As of the beginning of the twenty-first century, Black homeowners were 50 percent more likely than their white peers to be holding a subprime loan, which features higher payments and interest rates that can spike significantly.[49] These loans' predatory terms set the stage for Black victimization in the 2008 foreclosure crisis, when more than half of the wealth accumulated in US Black and brown communities was devoured.[50] In 2012, Wells Fargo Bank, the largest residential home mortgage originator in the United States, paid $184 million to settle a Justice Department suit alleging that during 2004–2009 it pushed Blacks and Hispanics into predatory loans even when they qualified for more favorable terms.[51] The year before, Bank of America's Countrywide Financial had settled similar litigation for $355 million.[52]

Again, the government was complicit in this outcome: the US had for decades prior to 2008 been deregulating the banking and finance industries, incentivizing subprime mortgage lending.[53] And when the crash happened in 2008, the government sold foreclosed homes to private equity corporations at discount prices.[54]

The saga continues. Just as wage gaps and exclusionary zoning ordinances endure as more veiled successors to the overt racism of past generations, government-sanctioned racial capitalism in the housing market is alive and well. Federal government and Brookings Institution research estimates that, controlling for other factors like housing and neighborhood quality, homes in Black neighborhoods are typically valued at 23 percent less than similar homes in white neighborhoods. That disparity robs an average of $48,000 in value from each of these Black neighborhood homes. That leaves their owners vulnerable to the latest iteration of real estate exploitation: mass purchases of single-family homes by investors.[55]

The record-breaking surge of investor home purchases is heavily concentrated in Black-majority neighborhoods. Analysis of single-family home sales by Georgia Tech researchers revealed that in some Black neighborhoods, 76 percent of purchases were by investors.[56] An analyst from the realty company Redfin explained why to the *Washington Post*: "We know historically that places where minorities live are undervalued or lower priced."[57]

Racism's impact on valuations causes investors to identify these homes as bargains to buy and then rent or flip. Multiple investigations and lawsuits report investors are using deceptive practices and targeting elderly or desperate homeowners, with the goal of buying the houses at a fraction of their value.[58]

In eviction court, we see the result of these predatory practices. Locked out of the value of homeownership, Black families are more than twice as likely to be renters as white families.[59] That does not mean their housing is inexpensive: many of our clients are paying more each month in rent than the lawyers representing them do for their own home mortgages.

Black families are not only more likely to rent, but they are also more likely than white renters to live in substandard conditions.[60] The typical scenario we see is a renting client who lives in an unsafe, unhealthy home and has been unable to reach anyone representing the landlord to request repairs. Why? Because the landlords are out-of-state investors motivated to keep maintenance and staffing costs as low as possible.[61] And where did these absentee landlords get the houses our clients rent from them? Often, they snatched up these now-rented homes from a Black homeowner.[62]

4. Urban "Development" Disproportionately Harms Black Americans

The eviction court where we work is located on the far east side of Indianapolis. When I was growing up in this community a half century ago, the far east side was much more predominately white than it is today. But this became the side of town where many Black families ended up after the gentrification of strong Black neighborhoods in the center of our city, along with the bulldozing of entire blocks of Black communities to make way for interstate highways, an urban university campus, and a medical complex.[63] The campus where I teach and the urban highway loop I travel to get to court are both built on the land of displaced Black families.

Our clients' parents and grandparents used to live in stable communities in the center of our city.[64] Their descendants now live at the city edges, clinging to apartments infested with rodents and rental homes where mold spreads and the wiring may be deadly. Sometimes they lose their grip on even those sketchy homes: 54 percent of our community's homeless individuals are Black, almost double the Black overall population by percentage.[65]

Across urban America, this is a sadly familiar story. Starting with the 1949 Housing Act, the federal government spent over $13 billion on a series of programs informally known as urban renewal.[66] In Black neighborhoods, the programs were more commonly known as "Negro removal."[67] And for good reason: Black Americans made up the majority of the quarter-million families displaced by urban renewal, even though Blacks made up less than 15 percent of the nation's population at the time.[68]

For example, the largest dislocation project was Cincinnati's Kenyon Barr, where 97 percent of the nearly five thousand families who lost their homes were Black. As University of Pennsylvania historian Brent Cebul has written, displaced renting families sometimes received relocation assistance of just a few hundred dollars. Other times, they received only a flyer listing the names of real estate brokers.[69]

Like with labor theft, redlining, and predatory lending, Black victimization led to white profit. As was the case in many cities, our city's Black displacement led to our urban areas being reshaped into "meds and eds" complexes that are now easily accessible by the newly built highways, which allowed white suburbanites to smoothly commute to the new high-paying jobs.[70] Local historian and activist Wildstyle Paschall wrote for *New America* about the leveling of the Indiana Avenue community anchored by thriving Black-owned businesses, including Madam C. J. Walker's beauty supplies empire, and hundreds of acres of multi-generational Black neighborhoods:

> The destruction of the Indiana Avenue neighborhoods amounts to the decimation of 100 years of Black neighborhoods and culture. Many one-time Indiana Avenue–area Black homeowners and business owners couldn't relocate for the price of their original investments. And so business owners became employees, homeowners became tenants, and both groups were robbed of their ability to leave intergenerational capacity, stability, or wealth to their children. . . . And it happened as a result of a plan coordinated by universities, hospitals, city leaders and state government. All of these are public institutions, making it a cruel twist of irony that the Black community had helped finance their own annihilation simply by participating in the American economy.[71]

Urban renewal did not take every neighborhood from the Black communities. But the ones left standing were often highly segregated and stripped of access to public and private services like health clinics, good-paying jobs, and grocery stores.[72] That segregation also leaves the Black communities as easy targets for the environmental racism of so-called "sacrifice zones" where toxic-waste dumps, chemical plants, and landfills proliferate.[73] Black families being forced into substandard housing has led to Black children having on average twice the level of lead in their blood, exposure that often has severe consequences for cognitive development.[74]

5. Public Housing's Struggles Are Rooted in Racism

From its beginning, racism harmed our nation's public housing system. Public housing complexes were routinely segregated by design, with the units designated for Black residents built with cheap, inferior materials.[75] Federal agencies allowed local governments to site public housing in segregated, poor Black neighborhoods, in part a response to the for-profit real estate industry's efforts to limit the appeal of public housing for whites.[76]

For example, 98 percent of the public housing units built in Chicago over a fifteen-year period in the 1950s and 1960s were placed in all-Black neighborhoods.[77] A 1984 investigation by the *Dallas Morning News* covering forty-seven metropolitan areas revealed that nearly all public housing was segregated by race, with Black housing projects lacking in amenities that white projects enjoyed.[78]

That intentional segregation, along with the greater housing and income opportunities for white households, has led to the US public housing population being disproportionately Black. Forty-three percent of household heads in public housing are Black, with another 26 percent Latino or Hispanic.[79] This means public housing is and has been especially important for Black families, leaving those families grievously damaged by the systemic demolition, underfunding, and neglect of public housing.

We discuss more fully in chapter 8 how the US government and local agencies have destroyed well over one hundred thousand public housing units and left many of those that remain in a dangerous and unhealthy state of disrepair. What was the motivation behind this abandonment of public housing? Urban planning professor Edward Goetz conducts a thorough analysis of the public housing crises in Chicago, Atlanta, and New Orleans in his book *New Deal Ruins: Race, Economic Justice, and Public Housing Policy*. Goetz finds a clear answer: "In these cities the full-scale attack on public housing was employed as a means of eliminating entire communities of poor Black residents."[80]

When Goetz widened his scope beyond those three cities, he found that Black public housing residents across the nation are far more likely to be displaced than white residents of public housing.[81] Through the demolition and neglect of public housing, we are repeating urban renewal's sin by targeting the elimination of Black homes.

6. We Can Make Things Right, If We Want To

There is a good reason this discussion of racism's impact on housing started with income and wealth. The scarce supply of subsidized housing in this nation means that most households of all races depend on the private, for-profit market to secure a roof over their heads. In our eviction defense work, our clients' housing emergencies usually could be solved with an infusion of cash. That means we can make an enormous impact in our housing crisis by erasing the racial wage and income gaps, which would immediately boost our Black clients' abilities to find safe, decent housing.

In chapter 6, we explore the possible non-housing remedies for our housing crisis. Beyond just increasing wages, this approach means stepping away from the US's outsize reliance on the value of our homes as the family safety net. Instead, a robust national pension, disability support, and health care system should provide that security.[82] Keeanga-Yamahtta Taylor focused her landmark book *Race for Profit* on the way our housing system has benefited whites and abused Black people. But she does not see the remedy for this toxic legacy coming through housing reforms alone:

> The real issue here is how the insistence on homeownership as the solution to economic or racial inequality actually leaves African Americans behind.... This shouldn't be interpreted as accepting the limits imposed by discrimination or the marginalization of African Americans. Instead, it is a plea that we do not leave the quality of people's lives in the supposedly invisible hand of the market economy. Instead of relying on the home as an asset to secure retirement or weather an unforeseen health emergency, government should play a larger role in providing retirement benefits or healthcare to ensure consistent and equitable public welfare.[83]

Housing-specific reforms are called for, too. The FHA and VA et al. proved convincingly that our government can promote stable housing at enormous scale. We should launch similar efforts again—this time, minus the racism. In fact, we should start affirmatively undoing the effects of housing racism. One current program that is widely praised is the US Department of Agriculture's 502 Direct Loan Program, which provides guaranteed, low-interest loans to first-time homebuyers.[84] It is a good approach, but the 502 program's focus on rural homebuyers raises echoes of the white-benefiting housing programs that dominated the last century. A similar effort should target the Black communities that have been left out of past government homeownership programs.[85]

The long legacy of US housing racism has led to multiple reparations proposals that focus on housing subsidies for Black Americans. Seattle, Santa Monica, and Berkeley, California, all have proposals in various stages that are designed to help provide affordable homes for Black residents.[86] In 2022, the city of Evanston, Illinois, took one of the most tangible reparations steps yet, giving $25,000 housing vouchers to six-hundred-plus Black residents.

A larger, broader Evanston reparations program is planned, but the local Black community deliberately chose housing to be its priority. "Our harm report showed that housing is an area in which we were harmed and stripped away of wealth and opportunity," said Robin Rue Summons, chairperson of the city's reparations committee. "So we've started with housing."[87] We should all follow their lead.

HOUSING SOCIALISM FOR THE RICH

Robert comes to court with his right eye twitching, and he is compulsively stretching and rotating his neck. He tells us that he is nervous and afraid in a way that he has not been in years: Robert is in real danger of becoming homeless.

Robert's monthly disability check is less than a thousand dollars. For several years, he has somehow managed to make his rent payment on the first of each month, even as the amount due steadily rose to $875. His clothes are mostly threadbare; he has a circuit of three or four food pantries he visits at rotating weeks of the month. He kept this precarious financial balance going until he learned that his niece with type 1 diabetes could not afford her insulin. Robert gave her $300, which left him short on his rent at the start of the month. Six days later, his landlord filed to evict him.

There are many ways that our nation and community fail Robert. Even if he was physically able to earn money by working, it would jeopardize his disability check. Since that check is designed by law to be his sole income, why does it add up to far less than any conceivable calculation of the cost of living? And why does the only wealthy nation in the world without universal health care require Robert to be the funder of necessary medical treatment for his niece?

If we measure by its impact on the cost of his monthly survival, the most profound way we fail Robert is in housing. His low income means he easily qualifies for a federal housing subsidy. As we discussed in chapter 2, that subsidy could take the form of a voucher he can use in the private rental market. Or it could mean a subsidized apartment in public housing or a privately owned complex with a government contract. No matter its form, the terms of the subsidy are the same: Robert would be required to pay 30 percent of his income for rent, and the federal government would cover the rest.[1] For Robert, his monthly $875 rent would shrink to a little over $300.

A complete game changer.

But Robert does not receive a housing subsidy. Instead, he is one of the losers in our nation's cruel housing musical chairs game, where only one of every four people with incomes low enough to qualify for a federal housing subsidy get any assistance at all.[2] By refusing to properly fund our US housing programs, we force the unlucky 75 percent to spend half their income or even more on market-rate, for-profit housing.[3] This adds up to sixteen million households who are eligible for subsidized housing but are instead forced to scrape together enough each month to pay a for-profit landlord. It is a shaky arrangement, and it too often collapses into chaos when a car breaks down, work shifts are missed because a child gets sick—or an expensive prescription needs to be filled.[4]

The losers in the cruel musical chairs game are among the eight million households in the US behind on their rent, a number that disproportionately includes mothers with young children, seniors, and persons with disabilities.[5] For many of them, the road ends with an appearance in front of a judge, waiting to hear what day they will be ordered to move from their homes.

As we will see in chapter 9, grim scenes like these are unthinkable in the many nations where all who qualify for housing assistance receive it. Even in the US, we do not play this cruel game with programs like Medicaid and SNAP (food stamps), where eligibility equals an entitlement to receive the benefit.[6] The contrast is on display outside the courtroom where we work, where a worker funded by government dollars sits behind a table and colorful signs, inviting the people getting evicted to sign up for our state's version of Medicaid.

It is easy to say that Robert and all those who are eligible for subsidized housing should receive it. But housing is not cheap. Ensuring that all in need are safely housed will cost money. Is it even possible for the US government to afford the cost of making housing a fully realized human right?

Yes.

We know we can afford to do this because our government already devotes tens of billions of dollars each year to subsidizing housing, more than enough to ensure a home for Robert and others who need it the most. The problem is that we devote most of our housing subsidies to the benefit of those who need it the least. Rev. Martin Luther King Jr. said long ago about the US, "We all too often have socialism for the rich and rugged free market capitalism for the poor."[7] In housing, Dr. King's words ring true.

Most people would say that the United States has the free market economic system Dr. King invoked. But housing in this country does not remotely resemble an unfettered market. Federal, state, and local governments have eagerly assumed roles as major players in the housing business. The problem is that the government's heavy hand in housing is typically placed on the scales on the side of the wealthy. Over the past decade, corporations have seized on significant tax breaks to dramatically increase their holdings of both multiunit rental properties and residential homes.[8] We have already learned that institutional owners— corporations or limited liability companies—now own most US rental units overall and 80 percent-plus of the properties with twenty-five or more units.[9]

As our clients living in corporate-owned housing can attest, this is a problem. Compared to smaller landlords, corporations are demonstrably more eager to evict and less responsive to maintenance needs.[10] We already saw in chapter 1 that tenants struggle with out-of-state landlords that leave mold unaddressed, broken appliances and windows unrepaired, trash not picked up, and sometimes even fail to pay for water and other essential services.[11]

Yet our government provides a boatload of loopholes and tax breaks that allow the wealthiest landlords and homeowners to make billions of dollars from housing, all while their neighbors like Robert are homeless or barely hang on to a rented unit. With housing by far the largest cost for most households, this contrast between how we treat landlords and tenants is a big contributor to the fact that the highest-income 1 percent in the US are now wealthier than they have been at any time in the past eighty years.[12]

This chapter will pull back the curtain on our shameful approach to housing funding, especially the socialism-for-the-rich abuses baked into our tax laws. And we will review the commonsense steps that will fix this.

California billionaire Geoffrey Palmer explained in a 2015 interview why he chose to focus his business on real estate: "Quite simply, I don't like paying taxes!"[13]

Palmer chose wisely. In that same interview, he claimed that his firm had not paid federal taxes in thirty years. A better-known real estate billionaire, Donald Trump, also avoided paying any federal taxes for most of the years examined in a 2019 investigation by the *New York Times*.[14] Consider also Stephen Ross, a former tax lawyer who became one of the 200 richest people in the world and owner of the Miami Dolphins NFL football team. Ross made $1.5 billion in real estate income from 2008 to 2017 yet did not pay a penny in federal income tax over those years.[15] "If you're looking to get richer while telling the tax man you're getting poorer, it's hard to beat real estate development," concluded a 2021 ProPublica report on Ross's and others' tax avoidance.[16]

How does our government allow this to happen? To break down the process, we will examine the enormous tax gifts provided to landlords in the context of a hypothetical couple, Steve and Sally Slumlord. We will say the Slumlords own a multifamily residential housing complex, Dilapadia, which was worth $10 million when they took out a loan to buy it.

Pass-Throughs

First, the Slumlords do not own Dilapadia in their own names. Instead, their accountant and attorney have set them up with a limited liability corporation, LLC, which holds the title to Dilapadia. This is the norm, with the ownership of most multifamily real estate structured as an LLC, partnership, or "S" corporation. Those arrangements provide the Slumlords with the benefits of corporate protection, meaning they usually cannot be held personally responsible for the business's debts. Yet the arrangements also allow the rental income from the entity to "pass through" to the Slumlords or other beneficiaries personally, without any assessment of the corporate income tax that is charged against other forms of corporations. A true "have your cake and eat it too" deal, courtesy of United States tax laws.

Avoiding both corporate tax and personal liability is already a huge gift our government gives to the Slumlords. But the gifts keep on coming, because the Slumlords are also allowed to deduct 20 percent of Dilapadia's pass-through income each year. Similar pass-through benefits are provided to Real Estate Investment Trusts, REITS, which distribute their income to shareholders. Huge hedge funds and private equity firms like Blackstone have exploited these loopholes to create REITS that now own over a million US rental units, including an increasing number of single-family homes.[17]

The pass-through income deduction is estimated to provide $50 billion worth of benefits each year, almost solely to the richest among us.[18] Alex Schwartz, author of the seminal book *Housing Policy in the United States*, calls these benefits "tax expenditures": while the government does not write a check to the Slumlords, the government gives them the same value by sacrificing money that otherwise the Slumlords would owe in taxes.[19] According to the Congressional Joint Committee on Taxation, over 60 percent of the pass-through deduction's benefits go to the top 1 percent wealthiest Americans.[20]

Let us look at Tammy Tenant, who lives at Dilapadia, or Maggie Manager, who works there. Tammy and Maggie get no such break on the taxes they pay on the income they earn from their hard work. But the Slumlords get these benefits on their "passive income": money they make just for sitting around as owners. The former chief of staff of the Joint Committee on Taxation, Edward Kleinbard, calls the pass-through deduction the "worst tax idea ever. . . . It simply excuses the affluent from taxes imposed on the rest of us."[21]

Depreciation and Tycoon Love

"I love depreciation," Donald Trump admitted during a 2016 presidential debate.[22] No wonder. It is one of the most impactful tax breaks that Trump and other real estate tycoons receive. Trump's fellow real estate tycoon Geoffrey Palmer attributes his three decades of tax avoidance to "the magic of depreciation."[23]

It is a magic trick that benefits the Slumlords as well. On top of the 20 percent pass-through deduction they receive, they also get to deduct the $10 million cost of Dilapadia in proportional amounts over the course of 27.5 years. That is the period during which the law says a multifamily residential building depreciates down to zero value. So the Slumlords get to take an automatic $362,000 deduction from their taxable income each year.

They also get to deduct the cost of doing business, like the fees paid to the accountants and lawyers that set up their LLC, Maggie Manager's and others' salaries, maintenance costs, etc. And they can depreciate the cost of capital improvements to Dilapadia, such as a new roof.

Of course, despite the IRS deduction formula, Dilapadia's value after twenty-seven years is clearly not zero. In fact, Dilapadia's worth is likely to have increased a great deal, since that has been the case for most multifamily housing in the US.[24] So, if they sell Dilapadia, the Slumlords would in theory owe taxes on the difference between the sale price and the depreciated value. This is called "recapture" of the depreciation benefits provided over the years: if the Slumlords sell for $20 million and they have taken all their depreciation, the "recapture" would mean they owe taxes on all of that $20 million. But, spoiler alert: our tax laws have provided the Slumlords with paths to avoid this recapture, too.

Capital Gains and "Voluntary" Taxes

Both the increase in the value of Dilapadia and the pass-through income from it are classified as capital gains. Wealthy people like the Slumlords make most of their income through sources like capital gains and other forms of pass-throughs.[25] By contrast, most working people never see much capital gains in our bank accounts: nearly 70 percent of capital gains in the US are received by the wealthiest 1 percent.[26]

Our tax laws provide these wealthy few with a breathtaking array of benefits on their capital gains income. First, their investment income is taxed at a lower rate than the equivalent amount of employment income, again rewarding the Slumlords for making money passively—while penalizing Tammy and Maggie for earning their money via hard work.[27] Second, capital gains from the increase in Dilapadia's value are not taxed when they occur: the Slumlords pay taxes on their gains only if they sell the property. That means there is a huge amount of untaxed wealth sitting around in this country. Capital gains that have not yet been taxed make up over one-third of the assets of the wealthiest 1 percent of US households.[28]

So the Slumlords have the luxury of choosing an opportune time to sell. For example, they can sell during a year when they have capital losses to offset the gains, thus reducing or even eliminating any tax bill. Those of us who pay taxes on our working income are not so fortunate. Consider the IRS's reaction if Tammy or Maggie—or you or I—announced, "I choose to delay paying my payroll taxes for the foreseeable future, thank you very much."

Finally, and best of all for the Slumlords, there are easy ways to not just delay paying capital gains taxes, but to avoid them altogether. So easy, in fact, that the Center on Budget and Policy Priorities calls capital gains taxes "effectively voluntary."[29] We will review some of the paths to capital gains tax avoidance.

Buy, Borrow, Die: Tax-Free Cash to Spend

We know that Dilapadia likely increases in value even as the Slumlords get to claim depreciation deductions each year. But, since they are not selling Dilapadia, that increased value is just a paper figure that provides no immediate benefit to the Slumlords. Right? Wrong. Not only can the Slumlords borrow money against Dilapadia's increased worth, but the loan proceeds are not counted as taxable income. The Slumlords even get to deduct the costs of securing that loan, plus the interest they pay on it.

Real estate pros call this "the harvest." It is stage two of the real estate tax avoidance strategy known as "Buy, Borrow, Die."[30] (More about the final-act "Die" stage three later.)

One real estate tax adviser who enthusiastically touts the benefits of this cash-by-borrowing approach admits the quiet part out loud: Tammy Tenant will foot the bill for the Slumlords. "Over time, your tenants pay the loan off for you. You get to keep the property, which hopefully keeps appreciating for you, and the rents rise with time, even as your mortgage payment remains fixed," writes the DPW Certified Public Accountants firm. "And when you pay off the loan in full, guess what? You can turn around and do it all over again, borrowing more cash against your property and letting your tenants pay that loan off, too."[31]

As a longtime real estate joke has it, "I must be rich, because I owe millions." What is not so humorous for the rest of us is that those millions owed can and do pay for lavish lifestyles for landlords, funded by their tenants and other taxpayers.[32]

Home Cooking with State and Local Tax Breaks and Funding

Maggie Manager purchased a two-bedroom bungalow a few years ago. Each year, she receives a bill for property taxes she owes. Those taxes, which help pay for local schools, public safety, and road maintenance, are based on the value of Maggie's home. But her wealthy bosses may pay a lower rate for those same property taxes.

The Slumlords' property tax bill for Dilapadia may be reduced by abatements or PILOTs (payments in lieu of taxes) provided by local government in return for promising to develop or improve property. For example, the City of New York's 421a program gave $1.7 billion per year in tax abatements to developers and owners, more than the city spent on low-income housing.[33] Another example: the massive REIT Mid-America Apartment Community, whose one-hundred-thousand-plus units make it one of the largest landlords in the nation, received $3.8 million in tax-increment financing (TIF) subsidies for projects in Texas.[34] The Lincoln Institute for Land Policy estimates that property tax incentives for businesses cost local governments as much as $10 billion each year.[35]

Why are the Slumlords so extremely successful in negotiating down their local tax obligations and wrangling subsidies from state and local governments? Because they can and do hire the best lobbyists and attorneys to advocate for them—and then deduct those professionals' bills from their tax obligations. Poor Maggie cannot compete with that. But, hey, someone needs to pay for the fire trucks, right?

Being Rich and Owning a Home

The Slumlords own two homes, a mansion in Poshville and a beach house on Sandy Acres. Being homeowners qualifies them for tax breaks that their Dilapadia renters like Tammy Tenant do not receive. The Slumlords can claim a deduction on the mortgage interest they pay on both homes on loans that total up to $750,000. They can deduct the property taxes they pay up to $10,000, and they can sell the homes without paying capital gains on amounts up to a half-million dollars. Together, these tax breaks benefit homeowners more than $30 billion each year.[36] Government homeownership subsidies are a big contributor to the startling fact that the richest American families rake in nearly 40 percent more in government benefits each year than the poorest families.[37]

That contrast is alarming, but calling out homeownership subsidies can be a tricky business in the United States. Intertwined with this government largesse are powerful cultural and marketing forces that elevate homeownership: nearly three-quarters of Americans say owning a home is a higher measure of achievement than having a successful career, raising a family, or earning a college degree.[38]

As Alex Schwartz writes, "Regardless of political affiliation, race, ethnicity, or class, virtually all Americans regard homeownership very positively. Not owning a home is unimaginable to countless homeowners and achieving homeownership is a vital goal for many renters. . . . Homeownership is widely considered essential to achieving the 'American Dream.'"[39]

As we saw in chapter 3, beginning with the New Deal, our government began heavily subsidizing home purchases—for white people, at least.[40] The Trump-pushed 2017 tax reform made mortgage interest and property tax deductions largely benefits taken by the wealthiest only. But the exemption of up to $500,000 tax-free income for married couples selling their home is still a huge benefit to homeowners across income brackets.[41] With the average US home gaining almost $150,000 in value over the past ten years, it is understandable that most Americans see homeownership as a no-brainer financial investment.[42]

Homeownership provides other benefits, too. Schwartz's analysis and ongoing survey data show the same thing we see with our renter clients: nearly all of them would prefer the stability and autonomy of owning the roof over their heads.[43] And for good reason, given that so many of their landlords have refused to make basic repairs, retaliate when the tenants complain, and force displacement by refusing to renew leases for arbitrary reasons.

So, whenever I criticize government support for homeownership, our clients' desire to own their own homes gives me pause. Would stopping the subsidies now be like pulling up the ladder to economic and housing security, right after multiple generations of white people have safely scaled the top rung? After all, as discussed in chapter 3 and chronicled in Richard Rothstein's *Color of Law* and elsewhere, the US white middle class was created in significant part by government-subsidized home purchases that were largely off-limits to Blacks and other persons of color.[44]

As we have seen, those racist housing policies are a big reason why there is such a startling contrast in Census data on wealth by race.[45] With most US households holding a majority of our wealth in our home, Black households have on average just $9,567 in net worth, compared to white households that enjoy an average net worth of $171,700.[46] Rather than cutting off the flow of homeowner benefits, perhaps we should beef up enforcement of the Fair Housing Act? Perhaps we should pursue housing reparations or other race-conscious funding programs so that Blacks can finally get the same homeownership boost we have already handed to white households?[47]

The problem with this approach is that even our generous government subsidies do not ensure that homeownership benefits everyone. For several reasons, including racist home valuation practices, the Black-white wealth discrepancy does not get erased when Black households own their homes. Even when factors like schools, commute times, and crime rates are factored in, homes in Black-majority neighborhoods are worth much less than comparable homes in white-majority neighborhoods.[48] And Black home purchasers were the biggest casualties of the mortgage abuses of the early 2000s and the foreclosures that followed.[49]

We saw in chapter 3 that Keeanga-Yamahtta Taylor, author of *Race for Profit*, calls the abuses that use the powerful lure of homeownership "predatory inclusion."[50] These schemes are more American nightmare than dream, even after the foreclosure crisis led to tightened mortgage regulations. In our clinic, we still see low- and middle-income renters who are being exploited by rent-to-own arrangements. We also see mobile home purchases where, as we discussed in chapter 1, the requirement of leasing the land where the home is situated can be disastrous for the homeowners.[51]

The elevation of homeownership hurts society more broadly, too. For the disproportionately white households that do benefit financially from homeownership, their fiscal reliance on the value of their homes too often motivates toxic behavior. Racial discrimination in home lending and sales was driven not just by governments and lenders; it was fueled in significant part by white homeowners fearing the loss of their nest egg because of integration. Those same forces still motivate aggressive NIMBY (not in my back yard) resistance to affordable housing across the country.[52] As historian Rick Perlstein has written, "A home-owning American working class . . . [behaves] like a bourgeoisie—more interested in preserving home values than extending the circle of social solidarity. . . . A social democracy that depended on homeownership was always a social democracy poised to swallow itself."[53]

In a nation with limited public pensions and a tattered safety net, individuals' and families' laser focus on preserving home value is quite predictable. Since homeownership is by far the top source of US family wealth, Canadian writer Dan Darrah says that our houses provide a "fig leaf" that covers for our lack of universal social and economic rights. "Neoliberal governments have been happy to let the home function not just as a place to live but also a retirement plan," he writes.[54]

But that fig leaf is too small to obscure the inequities in the US economy—even in housing. In theory, since Maggie Manager owns her own home, she can benefit from these tax breaks, too. But, like most people with incomes below $200,000, she is unlikely to claim itemized deductions. That means most of the benefits of the mortgage interest and property tax deductions are enjoyed by the wealthiest 20 percent of households.[55]

Other nations have shown that it is possible to deemphasize homeownership while achieving universal housing access.[56] "We've very much been brainwashed into thinking that homeownership provides stability that rentership can't," says Jenny Schuetz of the Brookings Institution. "[But] we could create that sort of long-term stability of payment for renters, which would allow them to stay in neighborhoods for longer and to put down roots and be part of the community without being pushed out by financial circumstances."[57]

Instead, as Schuetz and other housing experts have concluded, our current mortgage interest deduction does not effectively incentivize homeownership, especially for first-time home buyers. Instead, it only encourages already wealthy people like the Slumlords to buy more expensive homes.[58]

Zones of Opportunity—for the Rich

The 2017 Tax Cuts and Jobs Act (TCJA) was a bonanza for landlords. Besides preserving previous real estate tax breaks like depreciation and pass-throughs, the TCJA gifted real estate investors with a new path to avoiding capital gains taxes: opportunity zones.

The pitch for the opportunity zones scheme sounds great. It encourages investors like the Slumlords to take capital gains earned from the sale of property like Dilapadia and invest them in areas where the community has significant needs for development. Senator Tim Scott of South Carolina, who promoted the legislation, claims the program "provides needy communities with a new tool and a level playing field when competing for investment. . . . Opportunity Zones are already credited with spurring economic development, job creation, revitalization, and new opportunities for countless Americans."[59]

Under this scheme, the tax breaks for the Slumlords are enormous: if they keep their investments in the zones in place for ten years, they get a permanent exemption from all the capital gains they make on those investments. Even if they hold the investment for a shorter time, they still get tax deferrals or reductions. The Joint Committee on Taxation estimates that opportunity zones will cut these investors' tax burdens by $3.5 billion a year.[60]

But this is not government money well spent. The definition of what areas count as opportunity zones is far too broad, and the guidelines for who benefits from the investments are far too loose. Not-so-low-income areas can receive opportunity zone–qualifying investments. Even investments in truly low-income areas may be subsidizing gentrification rather than helping the current residents in need. Investigations into the opportunity zones scheme have revealed that untaxed money is invested in expensive hotels and high-rent apartment buildings, student housing at elite universities, and even luxury condominiums at a superyacht marina.[61]

This program provides attractive tax-avoidance options for the Slumlords but not much benefit to those in need. As Samantha Jacoby of the Center on Budget and Policy Priorities has written in her analysis of opportunity zones, "The direct tax benefits of opportunity zones will flow overwhelmingly to wealthy investors, but the tax break might not do much to help low-income communities, and it could even harm some current residents of such communities."[62]

Like-Kind of a Scam—1031 Exchanges

The 2017 tax law was not all good news for rich people. It closed a loophole that had allowed individuals and firms to avoid taxes on the sale of assets by using the sale proceeds to buy something similar, such as selling one antique car and buying another. But when shutting off this practice, the TCJA preserved a single form of this "like-kind," or 1031, exchange. You guessed it: real estate.

That means the Slumlords can still sell Dilapadia for a net profit and pay zero taxes on that profit. They just need to use that sale money to buy another piece of real estate, say Dilapadia II, within six months. These exchanges can go on indefinitely, all while the Slumlords take out loans against the properties' value to assure them a generous cash flow.

Those like-kind exchange delays mean the deferral of taxes owed—often on tens of millions of dollars in gained value—goes on indefinitely, too. These like-kind swaps benefit real estate investors—and cost taxpayers—in an amount estimated to be $10 billion each year.[63]

Not Avoiding Death but Still Avoiding Taxes: Stepped-Up Basis and Estate Tax Exemptions

The Slumlords can delay paying taxes indefinitely. But, alas, they cannot live forever. When they die, the government will finally collect their long-deferred taxes on their real estate gains, right?

Nope. Stage three of the "Buy, Borrow, Die" tax-avoidance strategy kicks in.

Let's say Dilapadia doubled in value from $10 million to $20 million during the Slumlords' ownership, a predictable increase in worth for multifamily housing.[64] Remember that they avoided paying any taxes on that increase in value, since the assessment of those capital gains taxes does not occur until a sale happens. Now, as it turns out, the Slumlords' capital gains died with them, thanks to the "stepped-up basis" tax break.

For estate tax purposes, the value of Dilapadia is "stepped up" to its worth at the time of the Slumlords' deaths. All the capital gains accrued during their lifetime are wiped out, so the estate does not owe any taxes on them. They disappear, never to be taxed. The stepped-up basis rule on capital gains benefits wealthy heirs in an amount as much as $53 billion each year.[65]

Combined with the huge federal estate tax exemption of nearly $26 million for a couple like the Slumlords, the Slumlord heirs will take over full benefits of Dilapadia without paying a penny of tax. This may seem outrageous, but it happens quite often: less than one-tenth of 1 percent of estates owe any federal tax at all.[66]

With all these breaks to wealthy heirs, it should come as no surprise that as much as 60 percent of all wealth in the US is inherited.[67] Much of those unearned riches come in the form of tax-protected real estate. While Tammy Tenant and Maggie Manager pay taxes on the money they earn with their hard labor, the Slumlords avoided taxes during their lifetime. And the Slumlord Juniors will become rich the old-fashioned way: they will inherit it. As Justin Miller, national wealth strategist at the investment banking company BNY Mellon, told the *New York Times* for a 2019 article on real estate tax breaks, "You're almost allowing the creation of a royal class of families."[68]

How We Fix This

The Center on Budget and Policy Priorities flatly states, "Much of the income of the well-off never appears on their tax returns."[69] It is no wonder that the wealth of billionaires has skyrocketed even while evictions and emergency shelter requests are rising.[70]

But these landlord tax breaks are the result of political choices, and those choices can be reconsidered. Along with the Center on Budget and Policy Priorities (which graciously provided advice for this chapter) and Patriotic Millionaires (whose terrific book, *Tax the Rich! How Lies, Loopholes, and Lobbyists Make the Rich Even Richer*, was cowritten by my wonderful son Sam Quigley), the Economic Policy Institute and others have long called for the repeal or major restructuring of the loopholes we have discussed here.[71] They call for the elimination or vast reductions in pass-through deductions, opportunity zones, stepped-up basis, like-kind exchanges, and estate tax exemptions. US Senate Finance

Committee chair Ron Wyden has proposed a billionaires income tax to terminate many of the tax avoidance schemes that benefit wealthy investors.[72]

Beyond cutting back on tax breaks for wealthy landlords, advocates at the national and local levels like People's Action and Center for Popular Democracy push to switch our approach completely: use tax policy to deter toxic real estate investor behavior and raise funds for affordable housing.

Among their proposals are to impose extra taxes on investors who buy housing not for much-needed shelter but instead for speculation or tax-avoidance purposes.[73] Wealthy investors are known to buy condominiums to sit empty, operating as so-called "safe deposit boxes in the sky." The result is some cities have more vacant units than they do unhoused persons.[74] Nationally, there are twenty-eight vacant homes for every one person experiencing homelessness.[75]

We can address this by imposing a hefty charge on profits made from selling a home without making any capital improvements. A flipping tax can charge for quick turnarounds by home purchasers. Blight/vacancy taxes and taxes on high-dollar real estate transactions are possible, too. They were among the popular proposals that won approval from voters in the November 2022 elections, including a "mansion tax" Los Angeles voters imposed on high-dollar transactions.[76]

At the federal level, multiple members of Congress have introduced legislation like the Stop Wall Street Landlords Act and the Stop Predatory Investing Act.[77] This legislation would block wealthy investors from claiming some deductions on their ownership of single-family homes, impose a transfer tax on their purchase of single-family homes they are buying solely for investment purposes, and incentivize the investors to sell the homes back to community members. We will see in chapter 9 that housing success stories like Vienna's were built on tax policies like these, including significant taxes on luxury goods and unused land, along with overall progressive tax rates that demanded greater contributions from the wealthy.[78]

In tax policy, we get the behavior we reward. Do we want to have a housing policy that helps our client Robert instead of real estate billionaires? Do we want to see housing as a fully realized human right for all instead of a tool for windfall profits for a select few? If so, we must fix the tax policies that got us here.

HOW WE FIX THIS—PUMP THE BRAKES ON OUR EVICTION MACHINE

"Do you want to pay and stay?"

That is one of the first questions that we train our law students to ask tenants on the day of their eviction hearing. It is the question we asked Lisa, who two months earlier had found herself unable to pay the rent for herself and her eighteen-month-old son. "I'm not going to lie," Lisa told us when explaining her situation. "My mom died, and I was really struggling. I just stopped going into work for a while."

When Lisa did not pay her rent on the first of the month, her landlord filed an eviction lawsuit. But by the time she came to court, Lisa was back at work. If this eviction case could be resolved, she had several more months remaining on her lease. Thus, the pay-and-stay question.

As you read this, a variation of that question is being asked in eviction courts across the country. Likely, it is a question posed even more often in informal conversations between landlords and tenants in the days leading up to a court hearing. The scenarios are like Lisa's: the tenant was unable to pay the rent on time, and the landlord responded by filing an eviction case in court, sometimes as soon as the day after the rent was due.

Yet the landlord is typically happy to let the tenant "stay" if they "pay." With a catch: the payment owed is no longer just the rent. It now includes court filing fees, late fees, and often attorney's fees, adding hundreds of dollars to the total the tenant was already struggling to come up with.

That makes a pay-and-stay arrangement for tenants like Lisa a rough deal. But it is a deal they often take, since the alternative is a court order and police action that uproots their family from their home. Lisa knew this, so she agreed to pay the landlord the rent and all the add-on fees. At least she and her son would not have to move on short notice. "I don't have anywhere else to go," she told us.

There is no comprehensive national data on the pay-and-stay phenomenon, but my and others' experience suggests that nearly half of all eviction filings end up this way. That guess is bolstered by a couple of recent studies of eviction filings, including an analysis of eight million court records by a team that included the legendary Matthew Desmond, sociologist and Pulitzer Prize–winning author of the book *Evicted*.[1]

These studies, and the scenes we witness in court each week, all point to a fundamental problem: our government runs a cheap but ruthlessly efficient collection and repossession machine for the benefit of landlords, particularly corporate landlords. But with that problem comes an opportunity. Since we the people run this eviction machine, we can decide to pump the brakes.

Fast, Cheap, and Easy

My home state of Indiana has one of the nation's highest eviction rates.[2] Evictions here are caused by our affordable housing crisis, of course. But other states with far fewer evictions have a housing crisis, too. We evict more often in our state because our lawmakers and courts choose to make evictions remarkably fast (as quickly as five days after a case is filed), cheap (as little as $104 for a landlord to file a case), and easy (most tenants don't have lawyers, most judges here say unsafe conditions are not an excuse for nonpayment, and our state has neither rent control blocking big rate hikes nor a good-cause requirement for a landlord refusing to renew a lease).[3] Indiana has fewer legal protections for tenants than many other states, but nearly all states make eviction filing a snap, as Desmond and colleagues found in their study of court records from dozens of jurisdictions across the country.

The beneficiaries of the government eviction mill are corporate landlords.[4] As we mentioned in chapter 1, these mega-companies file for eviction much more quickly than the vanishing breed of mom-and-pop landlords—nearly 90 percent of our local eviction filings come from corporations.[5]

We know that the pay-and-stay deal can be very expensive for tenants like Lisa. For landlords, though, it works great. In fact, many eviction court filings are not intended to result in eviction at all. Instead, the landlords are taking advantage of the fast-cheap-easy system to shake down their tenants for rent and fees. As reported in the journal *Social Forces*, Desmond et al.'s data showed that almost half the cases they reviewed were "serial filings," multiple evictions filed on the same household.[6]

Sure enough, the attorney for Lisa's landlord happily agreed to allow her to pay and stay. He says that a strong majority of the cases he files end up this way. He also admits to one of the tactics he and other landlord attorneys use when competing for the lucrative business provided by corporate landlords: they promise to file eviction cases as quickly as possible. The sooner the case is filed, the sooner the extra fees start accruing, and the sooner the tenants feel the court-provided pressure to pay up.[7]

This scheme is fully legal. But after Desmond et al. reviewed records and interviewed dozens of property managers, attorneys, and court officials, they concluded that our courts are being exploited:

> In these interactions between owners and tenants, civil courts are not neutral arbiters. We found market actors to be responsive to lax regulation and more than willing to use the courts to collect rent and fees. Courts with low barriers to eviction are frequently contracted by property owners to manage and discipline tenants. In this way, those courts act more like an extension of the residential rental business than an impartial arbitrator between landlords and tenants.[8]

Courts acting as "an extension of the residential rental business" and helping "manage and discipline tenants" does not mesh well with what our students learn in other classes about the constitutional guarantees of due process of law. Desmond et al. estimated that an eviction filing added an average of $180 in fines and fees to the typical renter household. They say that number is likely conservative, and I agree. It is quite a bit lower than the costs we see late-paying tenants shouldering, with typical attorney's fees alone totaling $300 and more.

While Desmond et al. relied mostly on a mega-data review, housing researchers Philip Garboden and Eva Rosen published an analysis based on interviews with 120-plus randomly selected landlords and property managers in Baltimore, Dallas, and Cleveland. Their results, reported in the journal *City and Community*, lined up with Desmond et al.'s:

> The process of repeated ("serial") filing for eviction and charging late fees, even on tenants who are expected to eventually pay their rent, is used by some landlords as an additional revenue source. . . . Far from a trivial fee, larger landlords and property managers use these fees as a

secondary source of income, encouraging them to file for eviction on tenants whom they fully expect to pay their rent and remain in a unit. This strategy was described by a number of respondents.[9]

When it came to describing the role our government plays in this process, Garboden and Rosen were even blunter than Desmond et al.:

> Filing costs a modest fee, and initiates a legal process that leverages the power of the state both symbolically and physically to encourage the tenant to pay her late rent. . . . The transformation of an economic transaction from rent to debt is as much a moral shift as an economic one, legitimizing more direct state intervention in the process than other forms of contract enforcement. This intervention is, of course, ultimately material—in its final stage, a law enforcement official will come to a tenant's home and bodily remove her from the premises if the threat has not prompted her to find the money to pay.[10]

Law professor Kathryn Sabbeth, who like me works with law students to advocate for tenants facing eviction, has analyzed eviction courts' role in the US housing system. Sabbeth points out that the work of removing people from their homes is often assigned to small claims courts. In small claims courts, filing fees are a fraction of the cost of other civil litigation, and tenants are expected to respond much more quickly than other civil litigants. This cheap and fast practice endures despite an eviction being what she rightly identifies as "fairly significant injunctive relief." Sabbeth concluded that the fast/cheap/easy process for evicting tenants is an intentionally created tool to maximize landlords' ability to control tenants and extract their wealth: "Short timeframes that rush cases to judgment make the courts less like fora for application of the rule of law and more like asset collection devices or means for forcible removal."[11]

Like Sabbeth, Garboden and Rosen point out that the smooth path to action and collection that our courts provide to landlords is a luxury not enjoyed by other creditors. Landlords know it. The researchers found that landlords were aware of their privilege, so they eagerly used the court system to jump the line in front of tenants' other obligations like utilities, food, health care, etc.: "The landlords in our sample are nearly unanimous in their assessments of the power of this [court case] tool to prompt a tenant to pay back rent. They recognize that poor tenants generally have a number of competing financial demands. . . . But landlords feel they need the threat of eviction in order for their debt to achieve prominence over their tenant's other expenses."[12]

Yet even when the landlords' only purpose of filing for eviction is to collect rent, that does not mean the harm to the tenant goes away when the case does. As we discussed in the introduction, the moment their landlords filed the eviction claim in court, tenants are branded with the dreaded "Scarlet E."[13] Even before tenants know a case has been filed against them, a publicly available court record has been created showing they have an eviction filing.[14]

A tenant's next prospective landlord is likely to check court records or get a screening company's report that references the court record. For many landlords, that information leads to an automatic rejection of the tenant application—no matter the outcome of the case.[15]

So our client Sarah and her two children wasted hundreds of dollars in rental application fees only to be turned down each time because of a past eviction filing. Then they were forced into an extended-stay motel that accepts "bad credit" tenants in return for far-higher costs and no lease protections.[16] After Charles and Autumn were evicted, they paid a whopping $2,500 a month for a hotel room where they and their five children stretched out onto every available bed and floor space to sleep. They also paid another $200 each month for a storage unit to hold the family's belongings.

Pumping the Brakes

Landlords taking advantage of a court system designed for their benefit is not exactly shocking news. For them, the decision to exploit the judicial system is a no-brainer. But it raises a question for the rest of us: Should our government be providing landlords with a VIP path to court orders and police enforcement that other court parties cannot access?

No, says our law school clinic student Steve Nisi in an article published in the journal of the Indiana State Bar Association.[17] (Adam Mueller, executive director of the wonderful Indiana Justice Project, and I are listed as coauthors, but Steve did the majority of the work making this excellent argument.) Steve makes the same point law professor Kathryn Sabbeth does: the cliché that the wheels of justice move slowly is usually quite true—except when it comes to evictions. Our courts provide no such fast track to collecting and enforcing other forms of debt: "Imagine a homeowner who got down on their luck and failed to make a mortgage payment," Steve writes. "It would be absurd if the bank came to court ten days after the missed payment, seeking immediate possession of the home. But landlords can."[18]

Beyond this unparalleled speed, the typical court order requiring tenants to leave their home—with the police power of the state at the ready to enforce the order—is an extraordinary benefit to landlords. It is a judicial outcome that other creditors can almost never obtain, especially without years of litigation.

That outcome is so rare because of a basic presumption of the law that has been in place for generations: courts are supposed to strongly favor awarding only money damages instead of what is called equitable relief—a judge ordering parties to do a specific act.

Not so with evictions. "Indiana law is clear that an ascertainable economic loss in the form of damages is an adequate remedy at law that rarely warrants equitable relief," Steve writes. "Yet evictions of tenants from their homes for contract breaches are the opposite of rare, being ordered by the thousands each year across the state."[19]

The Indiana Justice Project focuses on the harm evictions causes to mothers, pregnant women, and young children. So Steve worked with Adam to lay out the data showing that these tenants are disproportionately subjected to evictions. Moms and children are also likely to experience serious physical and psychological harm when they are displaced. I can reveal here a bit of the back-scenes conversation as this article was being written: the working title called for courts hearing eviction cases to "Slow the F— Down!"

Slower, More Expensive, More Difficult

The article's title changed, but its theme did not. Desmond et al. agreed, concluding their analysis of millions of serial eviction filings by highlighting two policy options: we could slow down the eviction process, or we could increase filing fees.

We should do both. And we should make court eviction orders more difficult for landlord to obtain, too. Here is how that can happen:

Not So Fast

As Steve Nisi points out, the warp-speed pace of evictions is a huge anomaly in our civil justice system. Two years ago, our clinic, along with the Notre Dame Clinical Law Center and the Indiana Justice Project, published a report calling for court rules to make an eviction filing in response to late rent a last resort, not the first step we now allow it to be.[20] We outlined a path to do that, including requiring that landlords and tenants engage in mediation before an eviction case can be filed.

This "press pause" rule would have lots of precedent. For example, our local county courts require mandatory mediation for parties who seek civil jury trials, post-divorce-decree litigation, or two hours or more of court time for contested family law hearings.[21] In home foreclosure actions in our state, settlement conferences are mandatory.[22] The court rule we called for would require landlords, before they could file for eviction, to show that they have complied with pre-filing steps, likely with exceptions if the landlord can demonstrate the property has been abandoned or actively harmed.

This kind of a rule would stop the current practice of some landlords rushing to court for a "gotcha" case filing within days of a tenant being late on rent. The delay we request would be short, but it could make a big difference: anyone working with struggling tenants can tell you that a little additional time is often precious. Even an extra week or two before an eviction case is filed could be the time needed for another paycheck or a tax refund to arrive, or a relative or social service agency to come through with the rent owed. Any one of these developments can prevent homelessness.

Not So Cheap

Desmond et al. and Garboden and Rosen all agree on an obvious and tangible barrier to serial eviction filing: increase the fees the court charges to file these cases. They are right. Another study showed that higher fees resulted in both fewer eviction filings and fewer eviction orders, even in low-income states like Alabama.[23] Sure enough, the landlords Garboden and Rosen interviewed made it clear that inexpensive filing fees motivated them to, as Garboden and Rosen write, "leverage the police power of the state." If our governments are going to operate a for-hire collection and enforcement apparatus, we can at least make it less of a bargain. We should also block landlords from passing on the cost of those filing fees to their tenants.[24]

Not So Easy

Steve Nisi says that the default remedy for a landlord seeking rent money should be a court order that compels tenants to pay what they owe, not a judge's mandate forcing them out of their home. That is hardly a radical idea, since orders to pay are the result in almost every other contract case—and landlord-tenant disputes are contract cases. Why should we use our courts and police to routinely displace families from their homes?

Similarly, why should we let landlords use the power of government without accounting for themselves to that same government through a landlord registry? Our clients, like tenants across the country, often struggle to discover which corporation is the owner of the building where they live. Those landlords are particularly hard to find when pressing maintenance needs come up. Most US cities and states do not have a robust landlord registration system, which would be enormously valuable in tracking down and sanctioning bad housing actors.[25]

In addition, our communities should protect tenants by requiring a landlord to show good cause—sometimes known as "just cause"—for refusing to renew their leases.[26] In our state and most others, landlords can simply displace tenants when their lease has expired, without having to state any reason at all. That unchecked landlord power not only disrupts tenants' sense of continuity and security; it operates as a powerful deterrent when tenants consider reporting bad housing conditions.

One client of ours, Jeffrey, came to court with a dilemma that many clients have presented. Jeffrey showed us photos of two-feet-deep standing water in his rental home basement, a broken door, and exposed electrical outlets, all of which his landlord refused to repair. But Jeffrey is on a month-to-month lease that his landlord can at any time choose to stop renewing, so Jeffrey has never complained to the local health department about the conditions. "I know he [the landlord] will just put me out if I file a complaint, and I can't afford to just up and move to another place," Jeffrey says. Research on the positive impact of good-cause protections in California, which is among six states that require a reason for the landlord to evict or not renew leases, shows that those laws would protect Jeffrey's stability and safety.[27]

Do you remember the dilemma faced in chapter 1 by our client Jessica and other mobile home owners, who can be evicted from the lot their home sits on even when it is impractical or impossible for them to move their home? States like Oregon and Delaware recognize the unique vulnerability of mobile home lot renters like Jessica. Those states require lot owners to renew leases unless there is good cause not to do so, like nonpayment of rent or breaking reasonable rules.[28] Investors who own parks know the significance of these protections, which is why park ownership groups openly advise prospective landlords to avoid "tenant-friendly" states.[29]

As we will discuss in chapter 7, we should also limit rent spikes via rent control rules. We should adopt "clean hands" requirements to block landlords with housing code violations from evicting tenants. And we should allow tenants to demonstrate that poor housing conditions are a defense to nonpayment of rent.[30] Eviction case filings should be sealed from public view, blocking the damages caused by the "Scarlet E." California and Colorado automatically do just that when eviction cases are filed.[31]

Tenants, including mobile home lot tenants, should have the right of first refusal to buy the property if it is for sale. Remember from chapter 1 about the favorable loan support the federal government provides to corporate purchasers of multifamily homes through government-sponsored entities Fannie Mae and Freddie Mac? That government support should be readily available to tenant cooperatives that want to buy their housing or the land it sits on.[32]

Since we control the eviction machine, we can even decide to shut it down during times of health, economic, or weather emergencies. We exercised this power to great effect with the Centers for Disease Control's COVID-triggered eviction moratorium, which prevented more than 1.5 million evictions, saving families and communities untold disease spread and suffering.[33]

All these legal protections for tenants are needed, but without enforcement they will only be paper tigers. So we also need to fix the fact that 90 percent of tenants go to eviction court without an attorney, while landlords virtually always have a lawyer.[34] When our state's supreme court chief justice visited a local small claims court to observe its eviction docket, she watched 275 cases: in not one instance was a tenant represented by counsel. "They all faced the judge and opposing lawyer alone," Chief Justice Loretta Rush said afterward. "That is not the model of a legal system where the poor, disadvantaged, and vulnerable are protected."[35] We need to follow the lead of the communities that have ensured that tenants have a lawyer by their side when the very roof over the family's head is at stake.[36]

Tenant advocates often package these protections together and label them as a Tenants' Bill of Rights.[37] That phrasing is on target, since these changes would ensure that the due process of law finally applies to tenants as well as landlords. And that would go a long way toward pumping the brakes on our runaway government eviction machine.

HOW WE FIX THIS—HOUSING FIRST AND BEYOND

As we will see in chapters 9 and 10, most nations, most religious traditions, and most Americans individually believe that housing is a human right. Of course, a human right cannot be withheld just because a homeless family does not have enough cash on hand to ensure the desired profits of a private landlord. So chapter 7 will review rent control, which limits those profits. And chapter 8 will make the case for dramatically expanding our public and social nonprofit housing, escaping the profit-seeking trap altogether.

Other important policy fixes will help move us forward on the road to guaranteed housing for all. In this chapter, we review four of them: "Housing First," inclusionary zoning, policies to prevent reckless speculation in housing, and universal housing vouchers.

Housing First

On my visit to Motels4Now, I learned that afternoons there are rarely boring.

In the parking lot outside the former Knights Inn in South Bend, Indiana, a young woman and an older man are engaged in a bitter argument. At times, the back-and-forth calms, only to loudly reconvene in one of the rooms or behind the building. The young woman, Clara (I will not use residents' real names here), issues a series of colorful, detailed threats and defies anyone to stop her from carrying them out. "I heard the cops are coming!" she yells. "Where are they? I ain't afraid!"

Soon after, a city police officer does drive up, but by then Clara has left. The police officer pulls away, ignoring the man riding his bicycle in tiny circles in the middle of the parking lot and the woman who emerges from one of the rooms every few minutes to levy rapid-fire accusations to no one in particular. A heavily bearded man takes it all in from his spot in a stained beige recliner next to the dumpster, while drinking from a twenty-five-ounce can of Hurricane High Gravity malt liquor. A small pile of empties is at his feet.

Another man hurriedly walking across the parking lot is greeted by Motels4Now director Sheila McCarthy, who welcomes him back from a short jail stint for violating his probation as a sex offender. McCarthy returns to the staff office, two motel rooms with the separating wall knocked out. Across from a stack of Narcan is a chart on the wall noting the body's safe injection sites. Desperation can trump discretion, though: one of the residents was recently treated for a large injection-created abscess in her neck.[1]

Motels4Now is a low-barrier shelter in the tradition of Housing First, meaning that residents do not have to demonstrate sobriety or medication compliance to be able to stay. The staff estimates that nearly all the 115 residents are dealing with at least one severe mental illness, often including substance use disorder. About 80 percent have lived on the streets for a year or more. Few can consistently keep any employment besides occasional one-off jobs. More than half of the current residents are on their second stay here, usually because they have been asked to leave during previous stays.[2] "Violence is about the only thing that will cause someone to have to go immediately," McCarthy says.

The challenges are on high-volume display, but McCarthy points out the less obvious signs of success. A group of older men sit and talk in mismatched chairs they have set up on the narrow sidewalk in front of their rooms. On the far right is Lawrence, who lived outdoors for eighteen years before he was invited to move to Motels4Now. There was an adjustment period. Lawrence at first did not want to spend the night indoors, and then he struggled to break his habit of hoarding food. But now he is settling in, and regularly getting medical care for the first time in four decades. "It is a myth that people prefer to be homeless if they have an alternative that allows them safety and respect," McCarthy says.

Motels4Now's most impressive success stories are no longer on site. More than three-quarters of former residents, more than five hundred people in total, now live in stable long-term housing. Those who have not yet joined them are on the same path, McCarthy insists, even as they deal with profound challenges exacerbated by years on the streets. She points to the office wall opposite the safe injection poster where a print made by a local artist reads, "Housing is Healing." "You can see when our repeat guests come back, they are a little better each time,"

McCarthy says. "It is visibly transformative for them to have a roof over their heads."

McCarthy picks an unlikely example: Clara, the young woman who was just threatening a fellow resident. Overall, Clara's stay was much more peaceful than her past times at Motels4Now, McCarthy says. Like all the others who have been asked to leave, Clara was assured that she has been automatically placed on the waiting list for a return stay. When her name gets to the top of that list, Clara will be welcomed back.

"It Is the Right Thing to Do Because It Works"

Filmmaker Don Sawyer, a longtime advocate for homeless people and director of the award-winning documentary *Under the Bridge: The Criminalization of Homelessness*, says Motels4Now's unconditional commitment to providing shelter and security is the foundation of the Housing First philosophy. "The record shows conclusively that this is not just the right thing to do because it gives them dignity—it is the right thing to do because it works," Sawyer told me in an interview. "For the first time in years for some of them, people can lock their own door, put their things away, and find a little bit of calm where they can safely breathe, where they can safely think. And that usually allows them to move toward stability."

Indeed, more than two dozen studies and high-profile success stories from Houston to Helsinki have shown that Housing First can quickly and relatively inexpensively end homelessness.[3] Sawyer also points out that immediate shelter programs that use motels or hotels provide a far safer and healthier response than congregate shelters. Studies from the University of Washington and the Yale School of Public Health have shown that motel shelters lead to improved health and social outcomes.[4]

Like many other motel- or hotel-based programs, Motels4Now grew out of COVID-19 pandemic necessity. In the summer of 2020, the virus forced the closure of South Bend's congregate facilities. Tent encampments popped up on the edge of downtown for the first time, quickly swelling to a population of more than one hundred people, all living without access to clean water or sanitation. When some of those people developed COVID and were subsequently quarantined by city officials at local motels, it became clear that the motel rooms could respond to the broader need. Yet it was just as clear that some of the encampment residents struggled with mental illnesses and addictions that would prevent them from complying with traditional shelter rules.

This was not news to the members of the St. Peter Claver Catholic Worker community in South Bend. Founded in 2003 in the tradition of the movement created by Dorothy Day and Peter Maurin seventy years earlier, the Workers in South Bend created Our Lady of the Road, which offered the homeless community a place to take showers, do laundry, eat a meal, and simply sit and rest.

Volunteers at Our Lady of the Road had known many of the tent city residents for years. Moved by the visible tent city crisis in 2020, the group's supporters donated funds to cover the cost of more motel rooms. Soon after, local government officials offered CARES Act dollars to rent out the entire Knights Inn by the airport if Our Lady of the Road agreed to run the operation. McCarthy, a longtime Catholic Worker who had earned her PhD in theology at Notre Dame, was enlisted to lead the Motels4Now team.

During its three-plus years of service, Motels4Now has welcomed over seven hundred residents, with the average stay lasting about four months. Most residents live with a roommate in the seventy-four rooms spread across three single-story buildings. Another local ministry provides meals, security is on site around the clock, and community mental health providers have an office in the motel.

Motels4Now explicitly avoids proselytizing to its residents. There is no "pray to stay" requirement like what some programs maintain. But there is an undeniable religious undertone to the approach.

"I could not do this work now without first spending so many years at the Worker," McCarthy says. Her seven years at the Catholic Worker had provided her with plenty of time to get to know members of the homeless community who did their laundry and ate breakfast at Our Lady of the Road. McCarthy, who also teaches classes at the nearby Westville Correctional Facility, says the Worker training dovetails perfectly with the low-barrier and Housing First philosophy. "The Catholic Worker teaches you to see people without judgment, to love people without attachment, and let them be who they are without projecting your disappointment onto them," she says.

Eliana Armounfelder, Motels4Now's head of housing, agrees, citing the legendary Matthew 25 admonition: I was hungry, and you gave me something to eat; I was thirsty, and you gave me something to drink; I was a stranger and you invited me in. "A low-barrier commitment to shelter is the same as Jesus's approach, because it was his mission to be with the people that others shun," Armounfelder says. "When our guests have been kicked out of virtually every other setting, accompanying them is clearly what the Gospels tell us to do."

McCarthy puts on her theologian hat to point out that this commitment to unconditional love and service is by no means an exclusively Christian concept. The Quran mandates care for the poor, and the Torah repeats no less than thirty-six times the commandment to welcome the stranger.[5] McCarthy notes that the Hindu "namaste" greeting connotes the same divinity-in-every-person belief that animates Matthew 25. (We will discuss in chapter 10 the multifaith commitment to housing as a human right.)

Beyond tangible housing and support services, that philosophy manifests itself at Motels4Now in less measurable ways. The staff call their work "accompaniment," not case management. Residents are considered honored guests and addressed as such. "Both Housing First and the Gospels have the same mandate: we give unconditional positive regard for our guests because we see Christ in them," McCarthy says.

"We Are Not Giving Up on Them"

As the "4Now" portion of the program's name acknowledges, converted motel rooms are not the ultimate solution for the residents. Our Lady of the Road has obtained funding from the City of South Bend and the state mental health agency to build both a new low-barrier intake center and an adjacent facility for permanent supportive housing. Until then, long-term housing for most Motels4Now residents will have to come from a combination of federal subsidies and private landlords that are willing to accept them.

Armounfelder's role is to help residents search for that housing and assist with the often overwhelming details of applying for and retaining the government subsidy. With help, many residents can obtain housing choice vouchers, once known as Section 8 vouchers, which cap their rent at 30 percent of their income, with the federal government paying the rest. The subsidy is critical for the many Motels4Now residents living on a monthly SSI disability check that is less than $1,000, an amount that would barely cover market-rate rent and leave nothing for other daily needs.

But obtaining a voucher is only half the battle, as private landlords often refuse to accept tenants who rely on vouchers.[6] This is where Armounfelder and colleagues step in, building relationships with local landlords and promising to assist if there are ever problems with tenants who are former Motels4Now residents. Armounfelder also helps with the intimidating process of keeping the vouchers, most notably the document-intense annual recertification process with the local public housing agency. "We do not end our relationship with our guests when they move out of the motel," she says. About 80 percent of the motel residents who have moved into permanent housing have stayed there.

Teddy hopes to soon join that number. He spends most days walking the streets of South Bend. With his unruly, graying beard, dirty clothes, and his speech sometimes an unintelligible mumble, Teddy fits every stereotype of a homeless person. But he is not. When Teddy relaxes with a drink after a long workday, he does so at his home—Motels4Now.

It just happens that Teddy's workday consists of him pulling on a reflective vest and walking up to five miles pushing a shopping cart he fills with aluminum cans, which he redeems for thirty-five cents a pound. Then his post-work relaxation commences in that stained beige recliner next to the dumpster across from his room at Motels4Now. "My boss gave me the rest of the day off," he jokes. "And he can't fire me, because he knows that would make the whole business go under."

Teddy has been asked to leave Motels4Now a time or two before for fighting, conflicts which he is happy to describe blow by blow. But he has been welcomed back, and a relative has agreed to serve as the payee for his monthly disability check. Teddy is on track to soon secure a voucher and apartment of his own. Although some Motels4Now residents arrive fresh from an eviction or a hospital bed or jail cell, Teddy is among the majority of current residents who are on their second or more stay. That recidivism may seem like a failure. Not to McCarthy. "When people have been on the street for years, struggling with so many mental health and addiction challenges, the healing can take a while," she says.

Linda too is a return resident. She is very thin and has deep, weathered creases running vertically down her cheeks. Linda's best guess is that she has been at Motels4Now three times, but she is not sure. "The people here are mostly nice," she says. Then she pauses and cocks her head to the side a bit. "Some of them get on my nerves sometimes, though, if we're being honest."

McCarthy hears that and smiles. Linda's and other residents' annoyance is often directed at the Motels4Now staff. One of Catholic Worker founder Dorothy Day's favorite quotes came from Dostoevsky's *The Brothers Karamazov*, when a wise monk counsels a would-be do-gooder. The woman wants to serve the poor but fears that she will not receive the warm fuzzies of gratitude in return. The monk affirmed her fears. "Love in action is a harsh and dreadful thing compared with love in dreams," he said.

The analysis holds up, McCarthy says. "We are up front with our staff that you need to expect to be verbally abused sometimes," she says. "We all just have to understand that our guests are expressing the hurt that they feel after years of people and systems letting them down, and they are transmitting that pain toward us."

Technically, neither Linda nor Teddy nor any other Motels4Now resident has ever been kicked out. Instead, they are asked to "take a break." Like Clara today, they are automatically put on the waiting list for future openings. And while they wait, they remain welcome at the affiliated Our Lady of the Road café and laundromat. "We want to assure people that we are not giving up on them," McCarthy says.

After three years of Motels4Now's operation, local service providers, police, and business owners all agree that South Bend's visible homeless population has been sharply reduced.[7] The number has dwindled so much that the Motels4Now team can identify virtually every unhoused person they see. "Most of those on the streets have been with us before and will soon be back, or they are newly homeless and they will head our way or find another option," McCarthy says. "It is no exaggeration to say that we have ended long-term homelessness in our community."

Which, McCarthy admits, surprised her. "Starting out, I knew this was the morally right thing to do. And intellectually, I believed in the concept," she says. "But the fact that four of every five guests we have ever had are now either safe at our motel or on to more permanent housing? I did not think it was possible that this many people could get this much better after years of dwelling in such brokenness."

The lesson, she says, is that there is no reason the US cannot join other nations, some of them with far less resources than ours, that have all but eliminated homelessness. "Other communities and programs don't have to do it the same way we do, of course," she says. "But the experience here does show that this works. It can completely transform not just individual lives but a whole community."

Housing First and the Hidden Homeless

Each night, our client Barbara and her four children spread out blankets and lie down, head to foot, on the floor of her sister's living room. Barbara is not sure how long this arrangement can last. Her sister and husband have two kids of their own, and they are worried their landlord will hear about them packing nine people into their two-bedroom apartment.

Kevin and Samantha and their infant daughter sleep in their Ford Focus, then take turns watching the baby while the other one works a shift at a fast-food restaurant. They arrive early for their shifts so they can spend time in the restaurant bathroom trying to bathe themselves the best they can.

After she was evicted, Melissa slept in a neighbor's garden shed. The neighbor charged her rent to do so.

Here in the US, the Department of Housing and Urban Development estimates more than a half million people are homeless each night. That is widely considered to be a significant undercount. Even so, it is a number so large it equals the entire population of Kansas City, Missouri.[8] For most of us, the visible evidence of this crisis comes from seeing in-the-street struggles of people like the Motels4Now residents who are chronically homeless. But most homelessness is more hidden.

Why do our clients experience homelessness? For most, it is simply because they cannot afford rent. Research from the US Government Accounting Office shows that for every $100 in average rent increases, there is a 9 percent spike in homelessness.[9] Barbara, Kevin, Samantha, and Melissa can attest to the truth of that.

They are not alone. A comprehensive study of the homeless population of California, the largest such sampling in the past thirty years, found that homeless persons' median income the month before they became unhoused was only $960.[10] For them, just like for the people who are unhoused because of mental health issues, Housing First works. Providing a safe, secure roof overhead immediately, then addressing other social service needs, is the most humane response to the needs of all our housing-insecure sisters and brothers.

As Motels4Now's track record proves, it is also the most effective response, reducing the number of people who are unhoused and blocking the too-common path from homelessness to arrest and incarceration. That same survey of homeless persons showed that nine of every ten unhoused people felt they would have been able to stave off homelessness if they had access to a voucher for affordable housing.[11]

Housing First is not "Housing Only."[12] The Housing First model adds in wraparound services that can include psychiatric and substance abuse treatment when needed.[13] The comprehensive Housing First approach connects deeply to the conversations we will have in chapters 9 and 10: housing is a human right, and it is immoral to create conditions people must meet in order to have a safe, secure roof over their head. Beyond immoral, it should be illegal, too. It is in Finland, where Section 19 of the Finnish Constitution guarantees housing and is the impetus for that country's enormously successful Housing First program.[14]

Housing First may seem like a no-brainer approach to the problem of homelessness, but it was not always the norm. Until the early 2000s, the consensus among government funders and service providers was that unhoused persons should be required to "earn" a shot at permanent housing. They cleared that barrier by first living in transitional, nonpermanent housing, and completing treatment and/or employment training.

But that "housing readiness" approach rarely worked. So, in the 1990s, the New York City organization Pathways to Housing replaced it with Housing First. It proved to be far more successful in both getting people with psychiatric disabilities into housing and keeping them there.[15]

As multiple studies verified Pathway's success with Housing First, it gained excited, bipartisan support from policymakers. President George W. Bush's homelessness czar was a fan, as was President Donald Trump's first secretary of housing and urban development, Dr. Ben Carson.[16] Housing First was the centerpiece of the Biden-Harris administration's approach to homelessness.[17]

But today, Housing First faces two significant challenges. First, it is being attacked by right-wing politicians and commentators who label it as a failed liberal policy approach that makes cities more dangerous. The critics include the activist Christopher Rufo, who also helped elevate critical race theory into a reliable political target, and commentators like Tucker Carlson.[18] The partisan motivation behind these attacks is revealed by their focus on homelessness in Democrat-governed California and by claiming addiction is the cause of the crisis—even though homelessness in California and beyond is proven to be largely fueled by the inability to afford stable housing.[19]

To me, the labeling of homelessness as largely an addiction or mental health issue is deeply frustrating. As someone who each week stands alongside people who are on the brink of homelessness, I can attest that their plight is rarely caused by mental health issues. Their main problem is a lot simpler than that, and a lot easier to solve: they can't afford their rent! And even though people like our clients are not as visible as the Motels4Now future residents on the streets struggling with mental health challenges, studies show time and again that people like our clients are the majority of people facing homelessness in our nation.[20] In 2023, the Pew Charitable Trusts summarized decades of academic research on this question: "Housing costs explain far more of the difference in rates of homelessness than variables such as substance use disorder, mental health, weather, the strength of the social safety net, poverty, or economic conditions. Some vulnerabilities strongly influence which people are susceptible to homelessness, but research has repeatedly concluded that these factors play only a minor role in driving rates of homelessness compared with the role of housing costs."[21]

Beyond the mischaracterization of the causes of homelessness, Housing First programs face a second challenge, too. This one comes from a less obvious source. Many Housing First supporters undercut its effectiveness by watering down the program, reducing costs by not offering the wraparound services that have proved to be critical to participants staying housed. Unfortunately, the Biden-Harris administration was among those who have attempted to achieve Housing First success on the cheap, reducing federal spending on supportive services like drug treatment and health care.[22]

Half-baked Housing First efforts can be incredibly damaging, producing the kind of underwhelming outcomes that both perpetuate the cycle of homelessness and fuel cynical criticism of the overall approach. That criticism is also bolstered by the mixed evidence on the cost savings of Housing First: although Housing First significantly reduces costly emergency health and law enforcement interventions triggered by chronic homelessness, there is no denying that up-front housing costs are not cheap.[23]

But political noise and funding debates should not distract us from the most important outcome of Housing First: it gets people housed, and it effectively helps them stay that way. I rarely agree with Trump administration officials, but Ben Carson was right on target when he said in 2017,

> For years, there has been a growing mountain of data showing that a Housing First approach works to reduce not only costs to taxpayers but the human toll as well. The evidence is clear. . . . Once we give people a stable place to live, it becomes much easier to provide mental and physical health treatment, education and job training—essential rungs on the ladder out of homelessness. . . . We can say without hesitation that we know how to end homelessness.[24]

The "mountain of data" Carson refers to started with the multiple studies, including randomized control trials, which showed the Pathways to Housing turn-of-the-century approach achieved better results than anything tried before.[25] Similar results have followed from US cities like Houston, Milwaukee, Denver, and Santa Clara, California.[26]

The most widespread evidence of Housing First's impact comes from its remarkable success reducing veterans' homelessness by over half. That outcome was made possible by the fact that the VA—like Motels4Now and some other programs—does Housing First right, providing access to VA health care and other programs to buttress the housing provided.[27] Housing First has worked just as well in nations like Canada, Finland, Australia, and multiple European countries.[28] We can do that here, too. And there is a plan to do so: former Representative Cori Bush, who has herself experienced homelessness along with her children, along with multiple other members of Congress introduced "Housing Justice for All" legislation that would create a national-level Housing First program.[29]

Inclusionary Zoning

Still wearing olive-green scrubs, Phyllis comes to court straight from her shift as a medical assistant at a local hospital. She faces eviction because her frustration finally led her to withhold her rent from her apartment complex.

More than two months ago, Phyllis and her teenage daughter both smelled gas in their apartment. The complex, whose corporate ownership had changed twice in the past three years, did not respond to their maintenance calls. So Phyllis reached out to the local utility company, who sent out a service technician. He found multiple leaks in the apartment appliances and immediately cut off the gas supply.

Phyllis renewed her calls, texts, and emails to the apartment complex. Now, seven weeks later, the apartment complex has still not fixed the leaks. All the while, Phyllis and her daughter have been without hot water to bathe and cannot use their cooking stove.

There is a list of other health and safety concerns Phyllis and other residents have about the complex—we have represented other clients there with complaints about mold, security, and leaks. But like most of the other complex residents we have represented, Phyllis does not want to move. At first, that surprised me and my students. But Phyllis answered our question about moving with a question of her own: "Where else are we going to go?"

We do not have a good answer. The national vacancy rate in rental units was less than 5 percent in 2022, and the rate is similar in our community.[30] Lower-rent housing is in even higher demand.

There seems to be an obvious solution. We should build more affordable housing or rehabilitate the many vacant units that exist throughout the nation, especially near jobs like Phyllis's and good schools that her daughter can attend. Brookings Institution housing expert Jenny Schuetz explains how that would work: "In places where land costs are high, the easiest way to reduce per-unit housing costs is to build more homes on a single land parcel," Schuetz writes. "Stacking small apartments vertically, even in relatively low-rise buildings, can substantially lower the per-unit cost of each home."[31]

Simple, right? If only it were not illegal.

For three-quarters of the land zoned for housing in major US cities, the only housing allowed to be built on that land are single-family houses, often with required minimum lot sizes that ensure they are spread far apart.[32] The resulting US landscape of automobile-dependent, sprawling metropolitan areas comes to us courtesy of our practice of allowing local communities to pass their own laws controlling the use of land. Those laws—Matthew Desmond calls the term "municipal zoning ordinance" the most soulless phrase in the English language—create a de facto moat separating Phyllis and other limited-income people from many of the most desirable neighborhoods across the country.[33] The *New York Times* calls single-family zoning "practically gospel in America."[34]

The usual academic term for these laws is exclusionary zoning. But some call it "snob zoning."[35]

The snob zoning label may not be fair. As we discussed in chapter 4, we live in a nation where we provide limited retirement and disability protections but huge tax breaks for homeowners. That leaves the value of a home as the chief source of income security for those fortunate enough to buy one.[36] So nervous homeowners vote for zoning restrictions that perpetuate housing scarcity, which increases their nest-egg homes' value but shuts Phyllis out of options. Phyllis is not the only one who loses out: a generational conflict has emerged where baby boomers who want exclusivity to increase their investment are angering a younger generation who cannot find affordable housing.[37]

Economist William Fischel coined the term "homevoter" to describe the powerful bloc of residents in every community who are laser-focused on supporting laws and practices that protect and increase their home values.[38] Little wonder, since the average US homeowner has over $270,000 in home equity.[39] Exclusionary zoning has been called a form of home-value insurance.[40] Surveys show most Americans support more public housing; they just do not want it in their own neighborhood.[41] The homeownership influence on policy support is dramatic: voters who receive a mortgage interest deduction—as we saw in chapter 4, a deeply impactful form of government subsidy—on average oppose more investment in public housing. At the same time, self-identified conservative renters are more likely than self-identified liberal homeowners to support affordable housing being built nearby.[42]

And, as we saw in chapter 3, there is a far more sinister history of exclusionary zoning that reaches beyond family economics. After the US Supreme Court in 1917 struck down zoning exclusion by race, that same court nine years later upheld exclusion by house type.[43] The stage was set to impose rules restricting neighborhoods to single-family homes and large lot sizes as substitutes for the rules that once prevented Black people and other persons of color from the same communities. In Atlanta, for example, neighborhood zoning district names were simply changed from white to "dwelling house" and from colored to "apartment house."[44] Exclusionary zoning weaponizes our enormous wealth and income gaps by race, causing US neighborhoods to remain nearly as segregated now as they were when the Fair Housing Act was passed in 1968.[45]

We are not helpless to overcome these barriers to creating more affordable housing for Phyllis and others like her. Cities like Louisville, Minneapolis, Boston, and Seattle, along with states like New Jersey, California, and Oregon, are creating land-use policies that push back against exclusionary zoning.[46] Since it will always be an uphill battle to persuade local communities to open their zoning processes in a homeownership economy and culture, state and national-level approaches are called for, too.[47] The Biden-Harris administration proposed providing extra funding to localities that adopt inclusionary zoning to facilitate affordable housing development.[48]

Along with a carrot like this, there should be sticks: cities and states that are hungry for federal funds for highways and mass transit should be required to dismantle their exclusionary zoning restrictions.[49] Inclusionary zoning alone cannot solve our affordable housing crisis. As we will explain in chapter 8, market solutions can never fully address the significant needs of households who cannot afford market-rate rent. But fixing our zoning laws is clearly a step in the right direction.

Discouraging Housing Speculation

We know from chapter 4 that US policies too often treat housing as a tool for profiteering instead of a human right, especially by adopting tax policies that subsidize rich individuals and corporate landlords. The result is toxic: global equity firms and other super-wealthy entities gobble up rental properties, then spike rents, neglect maintenance, and often turn around and sell the properties soon thereafter.[50] Charles was a recent client who kept track of the different property management companies overseeing his complex: he counted five property managers in just two years, with at least two ownership changes in that period as well. Charles's calls about a caved-in ceiling in his apartment were routed to out-of-state call centers. Weeks went by before anyone showed up to fix his ceiling.

Just like with exclusionary zoning, we have the tools to stop this. Our local, state, and federal governments should slam shut the tax loopholes that reward corporate, speculative property purchasers. Instead, we should aggressively tax speculators that keep properties vacant and/or flip properties.[51]

For example, a land value uplift tax can impose a hefty charge on profits made from selling a home without making any capital improvements.[52] A flipping tax can charge for quick turnarounds by home purchasers; blight/vacancy taxes can impose significant costs to the speculative practices that damage a community. Land value taxes can discourage investors from hoarding vacant or unused properties, forcing them to either develop the property for housing or sell to someone who will.[53] The revenue from all these taxes should be devoted to creating more affordable housing.[54]

Equally justified is a tax on high-value property transactions, with the revenue going to create more affordable housing.[55] At least seven states and some cities have progressive transfer taxes that increase with the sale price of the property.[56] Los Angeles voters in 2022 overwhelmingly approved a "mansion tax," Measure ULA, that imposes extra taxes on the sale of property worth over $5 million. The money generated by this new tax goes to building affordable housing and providing rental or cash subsidies to low-income older people and people living with disabilities.[57]

Beyond tax policy, we have other tools to discourage housing speculation. Our governments must divest their pension funds from speculative real estate. We should increase transparency requirements of real estate investors, and we should regulate campaign finance to limit real estate speculators' outsize influence on our political process.[58] The federal government can make a big dent in real estate speculation by banning rent securitization—the bundling of rental property assets together to sell as bonds—and limiting the same securitization of mortgages, too.[59]

Universal Housing Vouchers

As we learned in chapter 4, the tenants we see lined up in eviction court are almost always losers in the cruel musical chairs game our nation plays with housing assistance: only one of every four people with incomes low enough to qualify for federal housing subsidy get the help they need.[60] In some communities, the gap is even larger. In central Indiana where our clients live, there are over 118,000 households with incomes low enough to be eligible for vouchers, while only a little over 11,000 vouchers are available.[61] The local public housing agency that administers the program long ago closed its vouchers waiting list.

The fast, logical, and humane response to this travesty is to make housing subsidies available to all who qualify. A "universal voucher" approach would triple the number of housing choice (Section 8) vouchers that can be used to find private rental units for which the federal government helps pay rent.[62] This approach would mirror how we already administer programs like Medicaid and SNAP (food stamps), so-called entitlement programs where eligibility guarantees access.[63] It would be a step in the direction of popular, successful universal-access programs like public schools and Medicare.

A universal voucher program was a campaign promise made in 2020 by President Biden, and it is the subject of legislation pending in the US House of Representatives.[64] Polling in 2020 showed a strong majority of voters support universal vouchers, including a majority of Republican voters.[65] The Urban Institute has estimated this expansion can be accomplished for $62 billion per year—a sum far lower than the revenue forgone by the federal government via the many corporate landlord and wealthy homeowner tax breaks listed in chapter 4.[66] Further, the cost of universal vouchers would be a mere fraction of the US military budget.[67]

In chapter 8, we will discuss why the long-term solution for our housing crisis must center on the de-privatization of affordable housing. But, in the short term, the urgency of the housing crisis and the limited public housing supply mean that we need to expand the voucher program. University of Pennsylvania researchers have called for this expansion to include "project-based" vouchers tied to particular units. Those vouchers would ensure those property owners a guaranteed source of income they can use to ensure good maintenance and necessary rehabilitation. Of course, we need to accompany a voucher expansion with inclusionary zoning measures that ensure multifamily housing is welcome across communities.[68]

Unavoidably, this fast expansion of rental assistance will reward for-profit landlords. But we cannot allow those private landlords to discriminate against prospective tenants who hold federal housing vouchers. We need a federal ban on that practice, which would follow the lead of the eleven states and fifty-plus cities that have already adopted "source of income" antidiscrimination laws.[69]

This source-of-income discrimination ban is critical to voucher expansion. A social worker friend recently referred Sarah to our clinic, hoping that we had some housing suggestions for her. Sarah, seven months pregnant and with a two-year-old already, was one of the fortunate few who had a housing choice voucher—the local waiting list has been closed for years.[70] But Sarah was growing desperate: her current landlord wanted to stop accepting voucher tenants at the end of her lease, and she could not find another landlord to accept her as a voucher tenant. If she did not find a voucher-accepting landlord soon, Sarah would forfeit her voucher.

As we saw in chapter 2 with our client Belinda, Sarah's situation is common: the voucher program's reliance on the self-interest of for-profit landlords means that the promise of vouchers is often an empty one. As many as 30 percent of those who receive vouchers end up forfeiting them because private landlords will refuse to accept Section 8 tenants.[71] Refusing to rent to Sarah, Belinda, or other prospective tenants because they hold vouchers should be as illegal as refusing to rent to prospective tenants because of their race or religion.

Beyond Housing

The tsunami of struggle that engulfed Brenda's life swept her up and deposited her in eviction court. First, her husband Jared suffered injuries in a car accident that left him quadriplegic, which compels the family to spend extra money on a rental house with wider doorways and hallways to accommodate his wheelchair. Now, Jared has been hospitalized for surgeries and then complications in recovery. Because Jared is in the hospital, his disability checks have stopped coming to the home.

During the limited time she is not caring for Jared or their young son, Brenda puts in shifts at a home health care agency. But that has not been enough to pay the higher-than-usual rent. She is picking up extra hours at a child care center, but the rent and the late fees and court and attorney's fees are starting to pile up.

Brenda's story has unique details, as do the stories of all our clients. But the stories almost always share a common theme: the family simply does not have enough money to pay the rent. In 2023, the largest study of homeless people in decades confirmed what reams of previous research have shown: an effective response to the needs of people who have too little money is to give them money. Even small amounts of financial assistance are enormously effective at helping people stay safely housed.[72]

Yet millions of Americans teeter on the edge of becoming unhoused. Census figures show 12.5 million households report being behind on either their rent or mortgage payments.[73] Thirty-eight million people in this country live below the poverty level, which means they do not have enough income to meet their essential needs.[74] Eighteen million of those endure so-called "deep poverty," trying to survive on incomes below $13,000 for a family of four.[75]

Beyond the lack of affordable housing, how did we get here? Well, many of our clients are home care workers like Brenda. Others are restaurant cooks and servers, or child care providers, or retail workers. As we will discuss more in chapter 12, the US pays our service-sector workers less than any other industrialized nation.[76] We have a very low federal minimum wage and laws that restrict unionization.[77]

Compared to these similar nations, our safety net does not do a good job protecting for income loss, child care, health care and disability needs.[78] For this we can thank decades of demonizing of the poor—recall Ronald Reagan's mythical "welfare queen" and Bill Clinton's promise to "end welfare as we know it."[79] This was always a lie: people receiving assistance spend less than the rest of us on nonessential items like alcohol and entertainment, both in real dollars and proportionally.[80] Racism is intertwined within this contempt for the poor, with most Americans inaccurately believing that most welfare recipients are Black.[81]

Despite these headwinds, a year and a half before Brenda faced eviction, she and nearly every one of the other seventy-three people on that day's eviction docket were safely housed. They were making ends meet thanks in large part to a combination of stimulus checks, extended unemployment benefits, expanded child tax credit, and maximized food stamps, all instituted as a response to the COVID pandemic.

Together with a national eviction moratorium, we extended a lifeline to tens of millions of Americans. The Eviction Lab at Princeton University estimates that these programs prevented more than three million eviction cases.[82] More broadly, we achieved the remarkable result of reducing poverty rates during a pandemic. In fact, the percentage of Americans in poverty reached the lowest level in a half century.[83]

The Center on Budget and Policy Priorities says that just one component of our COVID response, the American Rescue Plan of 2021, may be the most effective antipoverty legislation since the New Deal in 1935.[84] For the first time, the

US's shared prosperity began to resemble that of other industrialized nations where housing is a human right and subsistence needs like health care and child care are guaranteed.

Then, one by one, we let all these effective programs drift away. The extended unemployment benefits ended in September 2021; the expanded child tax credit was not renewed for 2022. Food stamps reverted to their previous level.[85]

For a while, one program remained: Emergency Rental Assistance. In two segments, Congress approved $46 billion in rental assistance to be distributed by cities and states. If renters had endured pandemic-related financial hardship and their incomes were below 80 percent of their area's median income, they could get funds delivered directly to their landlords or sometimes to the renters themselves.

For many of our clients, housing costs take up nearly all their monthly income, especially if they live with a disability or have extensive child care obligations. So it was no surprise that these clients and millions of others flocked to the emergency rental assistance program. The Joint Center for Housing Studies at Harvard University documented that almost one in four renters with annual incomes below $25,000 applied to the program.[86] Analysis by the US Department of Housing and Urban Development shows that the program kept millions from becoming homeless.[87]

We can attest to that. For Elise, who has been unable to work much while caring for a sister living with severe disabilities; for Courtney, who shuttles between two fast-food jobs while finding off-hours child care for her toddler son; for James, who missed seven weeks of work after being injured on the job—the rental assistance program kept them all housed.

Now it is gone, too.

Once the programs started drifting away, eviction filings quickly rose to prepandemic levels.[88] Indianapolis's version of emergency rental assistance, called IndyRent, hung on longer than many similar programs. But it too ended, just one day before Brenda was summoned to court. When she got there, the sign outside the courtroom with the four-foot blue arrow directing people to Rental Assistance was still up. But it did not point to anything.

Brenda's court date was early December, and the judge ordered families to move out of their home by December 22. In the hallway after their hearings, we told them they likely have a few extra days beyond the official move-out date. Neither landlords nor constables like the optics of putting families out of their homes around Christmas.

But their eviction day is coming. Not so long ago, our country saw the struggles of Brenda and the other families lined up in court, and we pulled them up to a place of safety. But then we let go of that rope.

HOW WE FIX THIS—RENT CONTROL

Ashley comes to court because she hears that free lawyers and law students are there, and she needs some legal advice. The good news is that Ashley does not have an eviction filed against her yet. The bad news is that our state's laws do not protect her from facing an eviction, likely very soon.

Ashley simply wants to stay in her rented home. Her kids attend the local school, her apartment is close to her two jobs providing home health care, and she has some neighbors that she trusts. One of them is a single mom, too, and she watches Ashley's daughter and son sometimes when Ashley can't find a sitter.

Ashley makes only $13.50 per hour at her jobs, and the hours can be unpredictable. But she always prioritizes paying her $900 monthly rent, and she has been making things work during a challenging time.

With her current lease set to expire next month, Ashley expected that the rent would go up. She has been thinking about how she may be able to squeeze out an extra $50 or so each month—skip a few more meals, maybe beg for a few extra work hours. Then she got the notice from her landlord: she was welcome to renew her lease, but the monthly rent would be a whopping $300 more than what she pays now.

"Is there anything I can do about this?" Ashley asks us.

"The Rent Is Too Damn High" is a national rallying cry for good reason.[1] In a country where Ashley's is one of forty-four million households renting their home, rents in recent years have been rising far faster than wages and faster than overall inflation.[2] This pattern continues a disturbing trend: in the first fifteen years of the twenty-first century, median rents increased 50 percent, adjusted for inflation, even as household incomes did not increase at all.[3] In our city of Indianapolis, rents went up almost 31 percent in 2022 alone.[4]

The huge increases that Ashley and other renters are facing are in part caused by high occupancy rates and large demand for rental housing.[5] But an even bigger influence is the effect of corporate landlords tightening their grip on the nation's rental market. As we learned in chapter 1, institutional owners—corporations or limited liability companies—now own most of all US rental units and 80 percent-plus of the properties with twenty-five or more units.[6] Many of them use anticompetitive algorithms that keep rents artificially high.[7] In 2024, the US Department of Justice and eight attorneys general sued RealPage, the company that deploys these algorithms for the benefit of their landlord clients, for antitrust violations. "Americans should not have to pay more in rent because a company has found a new way to scheme with landlords to break the law," said Attorney General Merrick B. Garland when filing the lawsuit.[8]

These mega-landlords are aware of what that kind of market control lets them get away with. Remember from chapter 1 the chilling words in 2021 from Bob Niccols, CEO of one of America's top corporate landlords, when he bragged about plans to spike rents: "Where are people going to go? They can't go anywhere."[9] Following Niccols's pronouncement, the six biggest property management companies in the United States collected $4.3 billion in profits the next year.[10]

We have already seen that housing is easily the top cost for most households, especially renter households like Ashley's.[11] That means when mega-landlords "press rents," a term corporate landlords like to use when they talk to investors, they create broad, toxic impacts. Many renters go without food. Ashley admits doing that several times. Others delay medical care, or have their utilities shut off. As the saying goes, "the rent eats first."[12]

Sometimes, these desperate measures are still not enough: as of mid-2024, over seven million households were behind on their rent and thus in imminent risk of adding to the already rising number of evictions.[13] Ashley came to talk to lawyers and law students because she does not want to join that group.

But we can't help her.

Our state has not yet adopted the most immediately meaningful policy to confront our housing crisis: rent control, sometimes known as rent stabilization or rent caps. Rent control is government-imposed limitations on the amount landlords can charge for rent. Almost all current rent control programs allow for regular rent increases, often a significant percentage plus an increase that reflects inflation. For example, the state of Oregon's rent control allowed landlords to increase their rent in 2024 by 10 percent.[14]

So rent control guarantees landlords a fair return on their investment while also protecting tenants like Ashley from price gouging. Yet most states are like ours and allow landlords to spike up the rent as high as they wish. That free hand for landlords comes after their lobbyist industry has spent hundreds of millions of dollars spewing false claims about rent control in ad campaigns and in media appearances. In too many of those media appearances, baseless allegations about rent control go unchallenged.[15] Not here, though.[16] This chapter takes on all those lies and summarizes the dozen best arguments in support of rent control:

1. Rent Control Provides Relief That Is Fast

The long-term answer to our US crisis is for us to move away from the commodification of housing and instead embrace housing as a human right guaranteed to all. As we will see in chapter 8, that means far more public housing and other forms of social housing, along with much better maintenance of the public housing we already have. We will see in chapter 9 that these are solutions proven to be effective in other nations and in our own past US practices. We just discussed in chapter 6 one necessary step on that path: universal vouchers, guaranteeing housing assistance for all who are eligible, the same way the US already does with food, medical assistance, and public schooling.[17] All these non-market policy reforms are imperative in a nation where millions of Americans—including a lot of the single parents and persons living with disabilities whom we see in court—simply cannot afford market-rate rent.[18]

But these non-market fixes will take time to implement, and Ashley and the tenants we see in eviction court each week need immediate relief. The remedies others support with more enthusiasm than I do, such as a big increase in housing construction, which would in theory lead to lower costs overall, will not be immediate, either.[19] (More on this "filtering" theory, where more housing supply would lead to lower costs, in chapter 8.) In the current reality, the only housing option for Ashley and most renters is to find a home in the private, for-profit rental market. That means the response that best addresses their monthly struggle right now is limiting the cost of for-profit rent.

Part of the reason rent control can move so fast is that it carries little cost to taxpayers. Rent control administration is performed by government agencies, some of whom fund themselves with small fees charged to landlords. The modest cost governments incur to administer rent control is more than offset by avoiding the high government expenses associated with housing insecurity, such as homeless services, eviction proceedings, and health care interventions.[20]

2. Rent Control Provides Relief That Is Vast

The most comprehensive, well-structured report on rent control I have seen was written by researchers Amee Chew and Sarah Treuhaft and published by Policy Link, the Center for Popular Democracy, and the Right to the City Alliance. Chew and Treuhaft summarize the case for rent control perfectly: "Rent control is the most immediate solution to address the affordability crisis—its speed and scale, cost-effectiveness, and ability to protect a huge swath of low-income and marginalized renters are unrivaled."[21]

The breadth of rent control's impact is demonstrably true. In cities with active rent control, the number of households with stabilized rents far exceeds households living in public and subsidized housing.[22] So when landlord lobbyists attempt to water down rent control's impact, it is important to resist. Often these lobbyists argue for exempting from controls some rental property, like single-family homes or mobile homes. But those exemptions disproportionately harm struggling rural renters.[23] So-called vacancy decontrol, a loophole that allows landlords to spike rents between tenants, is problematic too, since it creates a strong incentive for unjustified evictions.[24]

Most importantly, we should not limit rent control because rent control works, and works well. Landlord lobbyists have been able to sow popular confusion about the impact rent control has on new housing construction and whether the poorest renters benefit the most, issues we will address in arguments 6 and 9 below. But even the landlord lobbyists can't quarrel with the data showing that rent control effectively addresses the pressing crisis experienced by Ashley and millions of others: simply put, rent control lowers the cost of housing compared to unregulated housing.[25]

The price of for-profit housing, even when controlled, is still too high for the many renters we see in eviction court who have severely limited incomes because of disability and family obligations. For them, non-market housing is a necessity. But, as these same clients tell us all the time, every dollar reduced from their rent puts them a dollar closer to the safety and security they need and deserve.

Speaking of security, the evidence is extremely solid that rent control leads to tenants staying in their homes for a longer time. That is a benefit so important that it deserves two of its own arguments:

3. Built to Last, Part 1: Rent Control Brings Stability to Households

For families who have been battered and displaced by big annual rent hikes, rent control allows them to take a deep breath, put down roots, and reap the benefits of a stable living arrangement. The evidence on this point is conclusive: under rent control, tenants stay in their homes significantly longer, even in neighborhoods that are being gentrified.[26] Rent control disproportionately benefits those who need it most, especially Black-led households, households with children, and elderly renters—the households most likely to be displaced when costs are not controlled.[27]

As we saw in chapter 4, US tax policy provides to homeowners generous tax benefits that renters do not enjoy, part of the reason why homeownership is so often portrayed as the essence of the American dream. Even beyond tax benefits, renters' desire for homeownership is fully rational, because homeownership promises stability that renting in an unregulated environment cannot match. In our work, we routinely see families being displaced because their landlords increased their rent by huge amounts, refused to renew leases because of a desire to remodel and charge higher costs, or sold the home out from under their tenants. Along with good-cause requirements for evictions and other renter protections discussed in chapter 5, rent control would provide renters with the stability that homeowners already enjoy.

Research has shown that housing stability is linked to longer tenures at jobs and improved educational outcomes for children.[28] Other studies show that a student loses three to six months of education with each family move.[29] Housing stability has a particularly positive impact on health. Research conclusively confirms what common sense already tells us: frequent moves and housing instability harm children's and adults' physical and mental well-being, leading to increased hospitalizations, worse mental health, reduced ability to escape domestic violence situations, decreased access to medications and healthy food, and spikes in depression and anxiety.[30]

We can do better. As Rutgers University economist Mark Paul has pointed out, we already do—for wealthier homeowners. The long-term fixed-rate mortgage was created by the US government to provide housing cost control. "Homeowners, who skew white and rich, benefit tremendously from the government's rules, regulations, and subsidies that allow them to pay a fixed monthly sum for housing over 30 years," Paul says. "It's high time for the government to extend these benefits—and the economic security that comes with them—by adopting rent control to cover all people in the United States."[31]

4. Built to Last, Part 2: Rent Control Brings Stability to Communities

The value of rent control extends beyond the walls of the homes of those whose costs are regulated. Renters who stay in their homes for longer periods are more likely to be civically engaged, an outcome that has powerful anticrime effects.[32] Children staying in the same school longer reduces the need for additional educational intervention.[33] Economically, renters with controlled rent costs can afford to spend more money in their community, boosting local businesses in a way that remotely located real estate speculators of those same houses do not.[34]

Without rent control, much-needed service-sector and caregiving workers are forced by high rents in cities to live far from urban centers, often compelling them to rely on cars instead of mass transit for their commutes.[35] Under rent control, these workers can live in neighborhoods close to those jobs. When they do not face difficult commutes and work near their children's schools and care centers, these workers' carbon footprint is reduced while their capacity to be productive and reliable employees goes way up.

5. Rent Control Has a Long, Successful History

In addition to being a common practice in other nations that have avoided housing crises as acute as that in the US, rent control has a long and successful history in our country.[36] Fair rent committees were established in over 150 cities during World War I, and were followed by rent control systems that covered 80 percent of all rental housing during World War II.[37] Tenant advocacy during the second half of the twentieth century led to rent control being applied in nearly two hundred cities.[38]

US courts, including the US Supreme Court in a 1988 decision written by the conservative chief justice William Rehnquist, have repeatedly confirmed that rent control is fully legal.[39] As the US Second Circuit Court of Appeals wrote in 2023 affirming the dismissal of landlords' lawsuit challenging New York's rent stabilization law, "Among other reasons, the [New York law] was enacted to permit low- and moderate-income people to reside in New York City—when they otherwise could not afford to do so. It is beyond dispute that neighborhood continuity and stability are valid bases for enacting a law."[40]

As our courts keep repeating, our government represents the people. That means the government has a strong legal interest in preventing private companies—who benefit heavily from government programs like infrastructure, research and development, and public safety—from price gouging us on the cost of a good that is necessary for our survival.[41] When those companies exploit people who must have access to that essential good, those companies can undercut the entire economic system and all our antipoverty efforts.

For example, increases in wages and benefits like the Earned Income Tax Credit, designed to support working families, can instead be gobbled up by landlords via rent spikes. Since 1985, rent increases have exceeded wage growth by over 300 percent.[42] And renters like our clients often pay far more per month to landlords than they would if they were buying the homes and paying mortgages.[43]

Policymakers and voters realize this. We have had multiple forms of US price controls past and present, starting with limits on the price of staples imposed by the colonial governments and the earliest states in the US.[44] Current price controls include regulations on the amount companies can charge for goods like electricity, water, gas, and prescription drugs.[45] Sweeping price controls on food and other necessities were imposed during wartime on multiple occasions.[46] The Richard Nixon administration in the 1970s instituted price controls, including rent control.[47] And broad price controls are being proposed again today in Congress and by a coalition of economists.[48]

The two-hundred-plus municipalities in the US that impose some kind of rent control include large cities like New York, Los Angeles, St. Paul, Minnesota, and Washington, DC, along with smaller communities like Los Gatos, California, and dozens of small towns and townships in New Jersey.[49] New rent control laws are being passed every year, especially via voter referendums.[50] Oregon adopted statewide rent control, joining the District of Columbia. And multiple rent control campaigns are active in other states and at the national level.[51]

6. Landlord Lobbyists Claim That Rent Control Depresses Housing Supply; the Evidence Says Otherwise

It comes as no surprise that the National Multifamily Housing Council, whose membership includes large corporate landlords like Blackstone and Starwood Capital Group, fiercely resists rent control. The core of its lobbying and marketing attack is summarized on its website: "Rather than improving the availability of affordable housing, rent control has exacerbated shortages."[52] The National Association of Realtors, which led the nation with $84 million spent on lobbying in 2020, has chimed in, claiming rent control deters incentives to build more housing.[53]

This is a self-interested rehashing of an Economics 101 argument: the lower the price of a good, the less incentive that for-profit providers will have to produce that good. Historically, many economists have subscribed to that very school of thought. The late Swedish economist Assar Lindbeck is often quoted saying that rent control is the most efficient way to destroy a city, "next to bombing."[54]

It is a dramatic image, and a superficially compelling argument. Many media outlets parrot this landlord lobbyist argument as an established fact.[55] But it is not true. It turns out there is good reason why Econ 101 is the beginning of the discipline's study and not its capstone.

As housing writer Jerusalem Desmas noted in a 2021 *Vox* article explaining why she switched from a rent control critic to supporter, the same raise-price/reduce-supply formula was once the basis for conventional economics wisdom resisting increases in the minimum wage. Then the data came in: actual analysis of minimum wage increases debunked the idea that that they significantly reduced the number of jobs available.[56] The simplistic critique of raising lower-end salaries failed to consider variables that benefited job growth and maintenance, including how lower-wage workers (like renters) boost their local economies by spending their extra salaries closer to home.[57] Employees who make higher wages also stay on the job longer, increasing efficiency in the workplace.[58] With the data now plentiful, increases in the minimum wage enjoy widespread support among economists.[59]

Similarly, criticism of rent control fails to consider the entire picture. As a 2019 report from the Urban Institute said, "Rent control's poor reputation in the economics literature has tended to rely more on models than on case studies or observed impacts."[60] Just as the critique of minimum wage increases dissolved as true empirical results rolled in, the landlord lobby's sky-is-falling predictions of reduced housing supply are proving to be untrue. As a July 2023 letter from thirty-two economists to the Biden administration arguing for rent control on government-backed rental properties said, "The economics 101 model that predicts rent regulations will have negative effects on the housing sector is being proven wrong by empirical studies that better analyze real world dynamics."[61]

Predictably, landlord lobbyists still cite studies that appear to support their argument that rent control will depress housing supply, including a widely criticized Stanford University analysis written by researchers with ties to the landlord industry.[62] Some of that quoted analysis is knocking down a straw man of strict rent ceilings with no increases. A report commissioned and distributed by the National Association of Realtors, one of the leading landlord lobbying organizations, admits that many economists who are supposedly anti–rent control are in fact opposing only those rent price ceilings, not the system of controlled increases contemplated by all current rent control proposals.[63]

So it is not surprising that, when housing researchers from the University of California Berkeley, the University of Minnesota, UCLA, and the University of Southern California have reviewed the evidence, they concluded, as the UC Berkeley report flatly states, the argument that "rent control has negative effects on the development of new housing are generally not supported by the research."[64]

Studies of rent control in New Jersey, Los Angeles, Washington, DC, Boston, and the Bay Area show no significant impact of rent control on construction rates.[65] The summary, according to City University of New York economics professor J. W. Mason: "Contrary to the predictions of the simple supply-and-demand model, none of these studies have found evidence that introducing or strengthening rent regulations reduces new housing construction, or that eliminating rent regulation increases construction."

Yet, Mason pointed out, there was one clear impact of rent control. "Most of these studies do, however, find that rent control is effective at holding down rents."[66] Which, we need to remember, is the core aim of rent control: responding to the crisis caused by the rent being too damn high.

On the question of housing supply, rent control not only does not have a negative effect, but it could also actually have a very positive impact. Rent control would block landlords and developers from generating huge profits by spiking rent prices—as they have recently, with average rent rising nearly 20 percent during 2021–2023 amid the widespread allegations of price-fixing.[67] So economists like University of Southern California's Gary Painter say that rent control will spur rental housing owners to change their approach. "Developers have to go to a Plan B if they want to make more money," Painter says. "Build more units."[68]

That result is particularly appealing, given that an enormous contributor to the current US housing supply problem is the overdevelopment of luxury housing and landlords keeping units vacant in search of higher rents.[69] As Painter says, rent limits would push market forces away from higher-end construction toward the needed affordable housing. A study of the effects of New Jersey's rent control implementation showed that landlords were indeed motivated post–rent control to create more rental units.[70]

The historical record shows the same. New York City's most robust periods of building occurred during the 1920s and the mid-twentieth century—when rent control regulations were strictly enforced.[71] After the landlord lobby persuaded Massachusetts voters to repeal rent control in 1994, the lobbyists' construction-depressing claims were proven to be untrue: multifamily housing construction did not significantly increase.[72] Rents went way up, though, as did evictions.[73] All of which suggests that the landlord lobby's continued anti–rent control argument is more about protecting their price gouging profits than increasing supply.

7. Landlord Lobbyists' Claims That Rent Control Harms Housing Conditions Don't Hold Up

In court, landlords consistently tell us that what they most covet is long-term, reliable renters who take care of the property. Those tenants reduce landlords' costs significantly, because they allow landlords to avoid the headaches and expense of turnover and avoidable maintenance.

Since rent control is proven to boost tenant stability, it is ironic that landlord lobbyists like the National Apartment Association and the National Association of Realtors claim that rent control will reduce the quality of rental housing.[74] These lobbyists' argument is that rent control discourages landlord investment in maintenance and improvements. Putting aside the ethical issues invoked by landlords saying they will refuse to maintain their rental properties if their profits are not unlimited, simple enforcement of existing housing codes should remedy any issues with landlords neglecting to keep up their properties.

As for improvements, landlords of rent-controlled units often find their tenants to be willing partners in home maintenance and remodeling.[75] These tenants' longer and more secure tenure motivates them to make their own improvements to the homes they plan to occupy for many years. Our renter clients will often show us photos of the additions and repairs they made on the property they called home for several years. As University of Virginia economist Edgar Olsen concluded after reviewing the data: "There is no basis for economists' strongly held belief that rent control leads to worse maintenance."[76]

You know who is aware that rent control can lead to improved conditions? Landlord lobbyists. In a comprehensive 154-page report on rent control prepared in 2017 for the National Association of Realtors, law professor Valerie Werness states the following: "In some cases, rent control may increase long-term tenants' incentives to renovate individual units. Common sense says that a tenant who knows he or she will be in the premises for a longer term is more likely to be willing to invest sweat equity and their own money into improving a unit. . . . As a side note, a 1988 study found no basis whatsoever for economists' assertions that rent control leads to worse maintenance."[77]

Kudos to Professor Werness for her integrity in writing a report for an organization that vehemently resists rent control. Professor Werness also acknowledges other key evidence in support of rent control:

- Removal of rent control in Massachusetts spiked rents and evictions.
- Rent control effectively limits rent increases and promotes household and neighborhood stability, especially in gentrifying neighborhoods.
- Rent control that allows for limited increases can exceed landlord costs and may not even reduce landlord profits.
- Evidence from New York and New Jersey does not support the landlord lobbyist argument that rent control depresses new construction.

The report is available on the NAR website, at least for the moment. If the reader can't find it, let me know. I downloaded a copy in the likely event that the landlord lobbyists decide to remove it.

8. Rent Control Moves the Needle toward Housing Being a Human Right, Not Just a Commodity

For me, housing policy priorities are shaped by the grim reality my students and I see each week in eviction courts. As I have described, we see single moms juggling multiple low-wage jobs and sick kids. We see people living with significant disabilities and fixed, very low incomes. For them, the private for-profit housing market will never consistently meet their needs, nor will it meet the needs of millions of others like them. As housing experts like Alex Schwartz and Kirk McClure have written, these people simply cannot afford housing costs that cover private landlords' own expenses, even with a limited profit.[78]

For these clients of ours, subsidized housing, not rent control, is the long-term answer. The permanent solution will be to stop the outrage we discussed in chapter 4, where our government spends more resources supporting wealthy homeowners and landlords than we spend on housing subsidies for the poor. We can and should provide universal vouchers covering all who are eligible, and we can and should build far more public housing and refurbish the public housing we already have—more on this in chapter 8. In chapter 9, we will talk about how other nations' governments promise in their constitutions and statutes that housing is a human right, and they fulfill that promise. We will learn that, even here in the US, we did a far better job housing our people before the 1980s. So, it can be done.

But first we need to get there. The "Overton Window," the idea that there is a spectrum of possible policy approaches that are widely acceptable to the public, is real.[79] So is the fact that the window can be shifted by adopting interim policies that move toward reforms outside the current mainstream political agenda. By recognizing that it is disastrous and immoral to allow a person or entity to extract every possible penny from someone else's dire need for shelter, rent control shifts that window of acceptable policy toward acceptance of housing as a human right. Rent control is not a substitute for greatly expanding our housing subsidies, but it is a step in that direction.

9. Rent Control Helps Those Who Need It the Most

In its court brief supporting landlord lobbyists' recent unsuccessful challenge of New York City's rent stabilization law, the National Association of Realtors gave voice to a claim about rent control's impact that is regularly levied by the

NAR, the National Multifamily Housing Council, and the National Apartment Association: "Rent control frequently benefits the wealthy while doing little to help the poor."[80]

If true, this conclusion would certainly be ironic. Who knew that wealthy landlord lobbyists are the parties truly concerned about the poor, while organizations led and supported by low-income tenants foolishly push for rent control? But the claim of outsize benefits for wealthy renters is not true. It has been refuted by a consensus of housing scholars, as evidenced by the formal court response to this NAR brief filed on behalf of multiple housing law and policy professors. These scholars label the NAR claim "simply false."[81] Amee Chew and Sarah Treuhaft's 2019 report cites two dozen studies to support the same, unequivocal conclusion: "Rent control disproportionately benefits low-income tenants, seniors, people of color, women-headed households, persons living with disability and chronic illness, families with children, and others who have the least choice in the rental market and are most susceptible to rent gouging, harassment, eviction, and displacement."[82]

It is particularly important to note that those studies show that rent control benefits households of color, most of whom are renters.[83] After our discussion in chapter 3 about the generations of housing racism in the form of government-supported redlining, demolition of Black neighborhoods, displacement, and predatory lending, we know that our nation has much to make up for.[84] Rent control is not the full remedy to that injustice, but its disproportionate benefit to households of color puts us on the right path.

10. Rent Control Helping the Non-poor Is a Feature, Not a Bug

We know that the National Association of Realtors' argument that rent control mostly helps the wealthy grossly overshoots the mark. But there is some truth underneath the histrionics: rent control does provide some benefit to people who are not poor. And that is a good thing.

History shows us that means-tested government programs that are accessible only to the poor are doomed to be perpetual targets of political attacks and middle- and upper-class resentment.[85] That has led to cutbacks in programs like SNAP (food stamps), Temporary Assistance to Needy Families (TANF), and child tax credits.[86] As the saying goes, programs for the poor are poor programs. Compare the political vulnerability of those programs with universal benefits like Social Security, the so-called "third rail of US politics"—touch it and you die.[87] Or look at another universal program, Medicare, so popular that health care reform debates in the early 2000s featured seniors paradoxically demanding that "government, keep your hands off my Medicare."[88]

Similarly, social movement history shows that a core requirement for a successful movement is a broad base of popular support.[89] That base often includes higher-income people who are more likely to be politically active and influential.[90] Forty-four million households in the US—more than a third of the population—rent their homes, and some of these renters are middle income and higher.[91] Renters form the majority of people in many of our largest cities, and there are millions of rural renting households as well.[92] So it should be no surprise that rent control proposals that will benefit people across the income spectrum have been receiving a winning level of popular support.

11. Rent Control Is Winning Support across the Country

As noted in argument 5, rent control has a long and impactful history in the US. That history is still being made, with rent control in place currently in 182 municipalities and the state of Oregon and the District of Columbia.[93] Across states and municipalities, there is a flurry of ongoing rent control activity, including vibrant campaigns in California, Florida, and Michigan.[94]

In 2021, St. Paul, Minnesota, voters approved a rent control ordinance.[95] That same year, Boston mayor Michelle Wu was elected on a platform of rent control, which enjoyed a two-to-one level of support among likely voters in a 2023 Boston poll.[96] A 2019 Data for Progress poll showed similar national-level majority support for rent control.[97]

In Illinois, the Lift the Ban campaign is pushing to reverse the 1997 statewide ban on rent control.[98] The adoption of rent control laws that target mobile home parks, such as the successful campaign in Humboldt County, California, suggests there is fertile ground for a powerful coalition. Millions of rural renters can find common cause with residents in urban areas.[99]

One of the most impressive recent victories for rent control occurred in November 2020, when 57 percent of Portland, Maine, voters handed a big victory to a rent control measure. The successful campaign was a dramatic reversal from a nearly two-to-one defeat of a similar proposal three years earlier, a change that organizers credited to organizing by a coalition of housing, environmental, and labor advocates.[100] Momentum seems to be building across the country, with the November 2022 midterm elections featuring rent control victories in multiple cities in Maine, California, and Florida.[101] A *Bloomberg News* headline after the midterm election said it well: "As Housing Costs Spike, Voters Look for Hope in Rent Control."[102]

At the national level, as we will learn more in chapter 11, tenant unions led a coalition of two-hundred-plus organizations calling on the Biden-Harris administration to impose rent control on all properties financed by government-backed mortgages, a measure that would apply to one of every four rental units in the country.[103] They are also demanding that the US require all states and cities that seek coveted Community Development Block Grants commit to rent control. Similarly, the national community organizing coalition Center for Popular Democracy calls for rent control at a national level.[104]

This tenant union campaign has brought hundreds of tenants to both the White House and Congress, calling for an executive order that would slow sky-rocketing rent increases. Tenant, housing, and legal advocacy groups even drafted the order for Biden to sign.[105] In 2024, Biden did order a rent cap on Low-Income Housing Tax Credit housing, a partial victory that showed the potential for federal action controlling rents.[106]

Aggressive federal action would reflect the changed renting landscape. Tenants who once dealt with mom-and-pop local landlords are now forced to confront the power of national and even multinational corporations. A 2021 Brookings Institution report showed that nine in ten rental units are owned either by businesses or individuals in wealthier households.[107] "Increasingly the real estate market is run by institutional investors who have consolidated the market," Tara Raghuveer, director of KC Tenants in Kansas City and the Tenant Union Federation, said in one of our several interviews. "These are multi-state or even multi-national actors that can't be effectively regulated by local or state policy alone."

These corporate landlords turn to the federal government to prop up their operations, Raghuveer pointed out. "The business model of many of these real estate investors is to get government-backed mortgages through Fannie Mae or Freddie Mac, or a tax credit from the Treasury Department or support from HUD or the Department of Agriculture," she said. "So, we see it as an absolute necessity that the federal government actually use those public subsidies and financing as leverage to increase the power position of the tenant relative to the landlord." We will dive deeper into this campaign in chapters 11 and 12.

12. Responsible Landlords Don't Need to Fear Rent Control

Landlord lobbyists have sliced off a chunk of tenants' rents to fund desperate fights against rent control proposals. Analysis from the California-based advocacy group Housing Is a Human Right tallies up over $175 million spent by landlord lobbyists in that state alone fighting against rent control proposals.[108] Those lobbyists have also filed expensive court actions trying to stop rent control laws, citing the perpetually rejected argument that government rent regulation amounts to an uncompensated taking that violates the Fifth Amendment.[109] Landlord lobbyists prop up the American Legislative Exchange Council (ALEC) model legislation designed to block cities from passing rent control laws, and the industry spent over $100 million in federal lobbying alone in 2020 and 2021.[110]

This landlord money has had an impact. In California, statewide ballot proposals to expand rent control have been defeated, in large part due to expensive and misleading ad campaigns by landlord lobbyists.[111] The ALEC-drafted legislation that preempts cities from passing rent control has passed in thirty-seven states.[112] In the 1990s, landlord lobbyists funded successful efforts to repeal rent control in Massachusetts and weaken it in New York City.[113] After St. Paul voters in 2021 voted to limit rent increases, the city council caved into landlord and developer pressure to override the people's votes and water down its rent control law.[114]

But does all this spending benefit the landlords whose business models are grounded in renting good-condition properties at a price that ensures a solid return? After all, rent control guarantees those landlords predictable, profitable revenue, pursuant to the US Supreme Court's requirement that regulation of rents guarantee landlords a "fair return."[115] All of the current rent control proposals are designed to allow for regular increases, and a study analyzing two decades of New York City rent control showed that the allowed rent increases outpaced landlord costs.[116]

Yet, for one growing sector of the landlord industry, a "fair return" is not enough. The anti–rent control lobbying is funded predominately by corporate landlords who are in the business of housing speculation, destabilizing neighborhoods and spiking rents with the help of the shared algorithm pricing program that has led to antitrust allegations.[117] We know that these mega-landlords are more likely than local, smaller landlords to poorly maintain properties and evict their tenants. And we know from chapter 4 that they transform their top executives into multibillionaires who are notorious for avoiding paying taxes.[118]

For those types of toxic landlords, rent control is likely to clip their wings. But smaller, local, responsible landlords will enjoy under rent control stability of renters and a guaranteed return on their investments. These landlords should give rent control a closer look. Ashley and the rest of us should insist our lawmakers do the same.

HOW WE FIX THIS—PUBLIC AND SOCIAL HOUSING

At first glance, our clients Margaret and Tina do not seem to have much in common.

Margaret, who lives on a $1,100 per month disability check, is being evicted from her apartment. The $850 monthly rent finally became more than she could scrape together. Once her court-ordered eviction happens, Margaret has no idea where she will sleep.

Tina has affordable rent. She too only has a disability check income, one that is even lower than Margaret's. But Tina has a public housing apartment that caps her rent at 30 percent of her income.

Yet Tina's living environment is abysmal. It is so bad that we were forced to file a lawsuit against the local public housing agency on Tina's behalf and on behalf of other residents of her building. The elevators are often broken, leaving persons with disabilities stranded on high floors. The building has a mice infestation, and bedbugs are rampant. The stairwells are littered with human feces and urine and drug paraphernalia, presumably from the nonresidents who come into the building during the hours when there is no security present.

Tina's apartment has been broken into twice. A few months ago, she witnessed a shooting as she walked down the hallway to the laundry room. The shooter, a nonresident, turned and saw that Tina had watched the whole thing. There was a long, terrifying pause before the shooter's companion took his arm and said, "Leave her alone."

Margaret is on a long waiting list for public housing. Tina has public housing, but the conditions are deplorable. So they do have something in common after all, something they share with millions of Americans: they need public housing to be much better, and for there to be much more of it.

"When people drive past public housing or see it on the news, they too often just see the stigma of crime-ridden projects in bad condition," says Ramona Ferreyra. "But behind those walls they drive past are people with life stories and accomplishments that were able to happen thanks to public housing."[1]

In my interview with her, Ferreyra shared two of those stories.[2] Her grandmother has lived in their Bronx public housing apartment for thirty years. The affordable rent allowed her to retire at sixty-five from a lifetime working as a seamstress, and then enjoy living in a community that included a senior center with recreation and regular programs. As for Ferreyra, the low housing cost and the security of longtime tenancy helped her finish both college and graduate school, while many of her fellow students and friends faced eviction from their private-market homes when money got tight.

So Ferreyra and fellow tenants formed Save Section 9, named after the 1937 Housing Act provision that created US public housing.[3] They promote the Green New Deal for Public Housing Act, which would direct $234 billion to fund desperately needed repairs and retrofits in existing public housing and establish new resident councils to boost democratic management of these communities.[4] Save Section 9 also organizes against efforts to privatize New York City public housing and lifts up the many artists and other successful people who have roots in public housing. "Public housing allowed my family and many others to pursue what people call the American Dream," Ferreyra says.

Yet condemnation of US public housing has been both enduring and bipartisan. Richard Nixon called public housing "depressing" and "crime-ridden."[5] Conservative think tanks label the homes "noxious environments."[6] Republican US representative Richard Baker from Louisiana said after Hurricane Katrina, "We finally cleaned up public housing in New Orleans. We couldn't do it, but God did."[7] Recall from chapter 2 that President Jimmy Carter's HUD secretary, Patricia Harris, in 1976 called public housing units "monstrosities." "We should make it clear that we are abandoning the whole notion of public housing," Harris said.[8]

Yet US public housing is still the home to nearly two million people, many of them members of groups that have struggled in the for-profit housing market.[9] Public housing is particularly important for Black and brown families still impacted by generations of housing racism: 43 percent of heads of housing in public housing are Black, and 26 percent are Latinx. More than a third of public housing households are headed by someone age sixty-two or older, and over half of public housing households rely on disability or retirement checks.[10]

Contrary to a common impression, public housing is not limited to large urban structures. A good deal of public housing is operated by small local housing authorities. And most public housing is now located in single-family homes, duplexes, or low-rise buildings without many units.[11] In many cities, like Austin, Texas; Cambridge, Massachusetts; Portland, Oregon; Pittsburgh; the Bronx; and St. Paul, Minnesota, there are examples of public housing that are attractive, thriving communities.[12] Jackson Gandour, author of a comprehensive 2022 Human Rights Watch report on public housing, agrees with Ferreyra that public housing has been victimized by an overbroad stigma.[13] "The impression is that public housing is a total failure, and that misses a lot of the picture," Gandour told me in an interview.[14]

The most compelling part of the public housing picture is its affordability, which shines through during a time of rapidly rising rents and widespread evictions.[15] Public housing rents are capped at 30 percent of the tenants' income, meaning that the average public housing tenant pays $392 a month in rent, compared to an average of over $2,000 per month for market-rate rentals.[16]

Public housing tenants also enjoy a far more secure tenure than most renters, as they are entitled by law to protections from arbitrary evictions and rent increases.[17] Our lawsuit on behalf of Tina and her neighbors is bolstered by federal law that requires their lease to include a promise by the public housing agency to provide good conditions, a promise that we never see in private rental leases.

So it is no wonder that millions of people apply for subsidized housing.[18] For example, in 2021, Cherry Hill, New Jersey, opened applications for twenty-nine affordable apartments. Over nine thousand people applied.[19] Nationally, the public housing demand is so great that applications are often not even accepted: waiting lists are only opened up every few years. When these waiting lists do open up, people have been physically trampled in the rush to put in applications.[20] As Michael Stegman, the top housing policy adviser in the Obama administration, has said, "Public housing is unpopular with everybody except those who live in it and those who are waiting to get in."[21]

The Sabotage of Public Housing

Yet Tina and other US public housing residents too often face real challenges. Residents of the Bronx building where Ferreyra and her grandmother live could once count on fast-responding management. But now the elevator goes out regularly, a significant hardship for residents living with disabilities, especially on higher floors. Also like Tina's building, Ferreyra's building has leaks and infestation problems, too.

In fact, far too many public housing apartments and buildings are in bad shape. The National Association of Housing and Redevelopment Officials estimated in 2020 that there was a whopping $70 billion in repairs and replacement needed for US public housing.[22] Gandour of Human Rights Watch says we should not be surprised: "If you don't provide for needed maintenance, eventually any home will start falling apart."

The blame for this maintenance crisis lies squarely at the feet of public housing's biggest critics. Since public housing's creation with the Housing Act of 1937, the private real estate lobby undermined it by ensuring public housing was segregated by race and income, built with inferior materials, and blocked from funding for necessary maintenance.[23] "America's public housing was designed to fail, to be unappealing to anyone who could afford to rent," Francesca Mari writes in the *New York Times*.[24] It was this ongoing legacy that motivated Human Rights Watch to add US public housing to its advocacy agenda that is better known for exposing political repression and war crimes. "Purposefully driving people's homes into disrepair is an obvious human rights problem," Gandour says.

As we saw in chapter 2, our massive divestment from public housing began in the early 1980s, when President Ronald Reagan and Congress cut annual funding from $83 billion all the way down to $18 billion.[25] Then the 1998 Quality Housing and Work Responsibility Act, as part of its fulfillment of President Bill Clinton's promised "end welfare as we know it" cuts to federal antipoverty programs, enabled public housing agencies to use capital funding to tear down developments without replacing the demolished units.

The same legislation also featured the odious Faircloth Amendment, which capped the number of public housing units. Cash-strapped agencies' inability to maintain existing units has ensured that the no-growth goal of the Faircloth Amendment has been easily achieved: there are more than 400,000 fewer public housing units today than there were in 1996.[26] In our Indianapolis community alone, hundreds of desperately needed public housing homes and apartments are left vacant because of poor conditions.

This massive loss of housing was no accident. HUD's HOPE VI program funded the demolition of public housing, significantly reducing the number of affordable homes available.[27] Under HOPE VI, Atlanta lost a stunning 86 percent of its public housing; Chicago lost 62 percent. HOPE VI has now expired, but neglect and decay still cause the loss of more than ten thousand public housing units each year.[28]

While HOPE VI has been abandoned, the Rental Assistance Demonstration (RAD) program is now in place. RAD furthers the narrative of failed public housing, privatizing much of it by converting the housing from Section 9 public housing to Section 8, with private ownership.[29] The conversion to private ownership is not supposed to reduce available affordable units the way HOPE VI did, but RAD has led to spikes in evictions and widespread lack of accommodation for residents with disabilities.[30]

As we saw in chapter 4, at the same time our government starves public housing of needed funds, it spends lavishly on subsidized housing for wealthy homeowners and corporate landlords. Depending on the calculations, the US government spends anywhere from two to thirteen times more on wealthier homeowners than on renters in need.[31] Subsidies like the mortgage interest and property taxes deduction, which in the US typically benefit only the wealthiest homeowners, do not exist in comparable nations like the United Kingdom, Canada, and Australia.[32]

Nor do other nations match the US's array of generous tax expenditures for landlords we discussed in chapter 4, including deductions for depreciation and access to tax-avoidance schemes such as like-kind exchanges and pass-through exemptions. For example, New York provided a tax break for real estate developers of new multifamily construction—including luxury apartments—that cost $1.7 billion in fiscal year 2021, more than the city or federal government spent on the area's public housing and subsidized housing development.[33]

Redirecting toward public housing some of the tax expenditures that now reward wealthy homeowners and corporations would dramatically reorient our economy toward greater equity. We could provide subsidized housing to every eligible US renter—an entitlement that is already the law in the UK and Australia. The government money now spent on wealthy homeowners in one year alone could instead fund in full the tens of billions in accumulated capital costs for public housing across the nation.

Public Housing Is Great, Actually

How do we know that investments in public housing can bear fruit? Because, in addition to the benefits public housing has historically provided US families like Ferreyra's, multiple other countries offer shining examples of success. As we will see in more detail in chapter 9, Austria, Finland, and Singapore are among the many nations with vibrant public housing programs.[34] Germany flips the policy script from the homeowner-centric US approach, providing renters with subsidies and rights including rent control and strong protections against arbitrary evictions. Germany is now a renter-majority nation where the average tenancy lasts eleven years.[35]

Here in the US, the efforts of the real estate lobby have limited public housing to low-income people. But a wide range of income groups benefit from public housing in these other nations, increasing the programs' base of political support.

As we discussed in chapter 2, the US is also a global outlier in the extent that we divert our affordable housing dollars to for-profit entities. Since the 1970s, the US has switched our affordable housing investment away from public housing to instead subsidizing for-profit landlords via direct payments and tax breaks, in return for their housing low-income tenants.[36] The Section 8 voucher program (also known as housing choice vouchers), the Project-Based Section 8 program, the Low-Income Housing Tax Credit program, and the Emergency Rental Assistance program all directly fund private landlords, often large, for-profit corporations.[37] In fact, this profit-soaked combination of vouchers, project-based subsidies, and tax credit housing accounts for six times more housing units than public housing does. If our goal is to provide truly affordable, enduring housing, that ratio should be reversed.

Common sense tells us that public housing is far more cost-effective than these privatized versions, since it saves taxpayers the cost of paying for the profits of developers and landlords. Further, public housing can be developed and enhanced even in market downturns, a time when for-profit housing construction stalls. And public housing endures longer than other types of subsidized housing like LIHTC and project-based Section 8 developments, which can be converted to market-rate rentals after their subsidized housing commitments expire.

Back in 1949, the American Housing Act set out the goal of ensuring a "decent home in a suitable living environment for every American family," echoing the language of the Universal Declaration of Human Rights, signed by the US the year before. There is no better way to fulfill that goal than public housing.

So it is heartening to see that Representative Alexandria Ocasio-Cortez, Senator Bernie Sanders, and other members of Congress are sponsoring the Green New Deal for Public Housing. This legislation would not only devote the necessary funds to renovate public housing but also repeal the Faircloth Amendment.[38] It is also exciting to see state and local governments across the country embracing a new commitment to public housing.[39] "For me this is primarily about the state stepping up to solve a housing problem that is affecting huge numbers of people," Meghan Kallman, a Rhode Island state senator who sponsors legislation to create a state-level agency to build and operate public housing, told *Vox*.[40]

"It's not rocket science," Jackson Gandour says. "Fundamentally, public housing in the US needs money to achieve its potential. It can be done. Other governments are doing it well every day, and even the US experience shows it is well within our capacity."

Ramona Ferreyra can attest to that. As she moved her way through graduate school and into her professional career, Ferreyra sometimes encountered bosses or peers who marveled at her upbringing in the Bronx. "People used to say to me,

'Look at all you did despite living in public housing!'" she says. "And I have to correct them: No, I accomplished what I did *because* of public housing."

The Market Will Not Save Us

When my students and I represent struggling tenants like Margaret as they face eviction and homelessness, we get a clear view of our communities' most urgent housing need: secure housing that is affordable for all. Just as clearly, we can see that private, for-profit housing cannot meet that need.

We should not be surprised by this, Professor Keeanga-Yamahtta Taylor writes in *Race for Profit: How Banks and the Real Estate Industry Undermined Black Homeownership*. "Satisfying basic human needs, like the provision of shelter, medical treatment, water or even education run counter to business's objective of maximizing return on investment or simply making money," she says. "One of the most pressing questions has been how to secure the provision of safe, sound, affordable and decent housing for everyone. The obstacles to that goal have always been business's bottom line."[41]

Samuel Stein, housing policy expert and author of the highly regarded book *Capital City: Gentrification and the Real Estate State*, agrees. "Building expensive housing is just far more profitable than building affordable housing. As long as our system depends on for-profit actors to build, own, manage, and maintain our homes, good quality affordable housing will always be out of reach," Stein says. "We need nonmarket actors to produce social housing."[42]

We should keep these admonitions in mind when prominent voices claim that the answer to our housing crisis is simple: we just need to build more market-rate housing. For example, in early 2023, in an editorial titled "The U.S. Can Solve Its Housing Crisis, It Just Needs to Start Building," *Bloomberg* news editors wrote, "For all its complexities, America's nationwide housing crisis boils down to a problem of supply and demand: The country needs a lot more homes than it has."[43]

Sometimes labeled the YIMBY (yes in my backyard) perspective, the argument here is that more construction dollars accompanied by "upzoning"—allowing denser development by way of multiunit buildings—will fix our housing ills. "Filtering," a kind of trickle-down concept for housing, envisions that building even luxury housing will ultimately result in more of the remaining housing stock becoming more affordable.

There is some evidence that zoning changes that allow for more housing to be built can have a modest overall impact in lowering prices.[44] But the evidence also shows that high-end housing, often the focus of private developers, can gentrify the communities where it is built. That means the new housing is raising—not lowering—the price of the housing all around it.[45] When the public invests in transit and other services to support the new housing, private developers and wealthier landowners disproportionately benefit from those investments.[46]

The "build more" elementary supply-and-demand analysis has another flaw. It does not account for the millions of property owners opting for financial reasons to keep units vacant rather than renting them for lower prices. As we learned in chapter 4, empty condominiums in cities are sometimes known as "safe deposit boxes in the sky." (Sometimes those safe deposit boxes hold ill-gotten gains: the purchase of US residential housing is one of the world's most favored forms of money laundering.)[47] In some US cities, there are more vacant units than there are homeless persons.[48] Nor does the YIMBY approach factor in the effect of wealthy people owning second and third homes. Those extra buildings do not add to the number of people being housed.[49]

Even more fundamentally, the just-build-more solution fails to account for the fact that even the least expensive market-rate housing is still too pricey for our client Margaret and millions of others like her. As two of our most respected US housing scholars, Alex Schwartz and Kirk McClure, have written,

> As experts on housing policy, we agree that increasing the supply of homes is necessary in areas with rapidly rising housing costs. But this won't, by itself, make a significant dent in the country's afford-ability problems—especially for those with the most severe needs. In part that's because in much of the country, there is actually no short-age of rental housing. The problem is that millions of people lack the income to afford what's on the market. . . . In other words, even if land-lords set rents at the bare minimum needed to cover costs—with no profit—housing would remain unaffordable to most very-low-income households—unless they also receive rental subsidies.[50]

Urban development scholar Max Holleran also has Margaret and our other very low-income clients on his mind. "Building market-rate housing is not going to solve the major problems because many people cannot afford the market rate," Holleran insists. "We need to stop thinking that the market can provide for everyone—it's just not going to happen anytime soon."[51]

A Call for Social Housing

In my view, public housing is the most direct and scalable answer to our clients' affordable housing crisis. But it is not the only one. Public housing is one of several proven approaches that can be grouped under the broader umbrella of "social housing."

Social housing is owned by the government, or by nonprofit organizations that respond to democratic control by residents.[52] Social housing is decommodified—protected from the profiteering of the private market. It is affordable for the life of the building or unit—no expiration date.[53]

In this way, social housing is like public education, fire and emergency services, infrastructure like roads, sewers, and water, our justice system, and other public goods. It acts on the principle that access to a safe, secure home is too important to be dependent on whether a family has enough money to ensure a profit to a private landlord.[54] Simply put, social housing sees housing as a human right, not a commodity or wealth-building tool.

Too often, the US subsidizes only the final stage of housing—the actual renter occupancy—after relying on the for-profit market to finance the earlier stages. The Section 8 / housing choice voucher program and project-based housing subsidies are examples of this flawed approach.[55] Social housing can go further upstream, and we have active, successful examples showing us how.[56] For instance, governments at all levels already use land banks and other mechanisms to acquire land from the for-profit market, sometimes by taking over distressed properties or seizing tax-delinquent ones.[57] We should dedicate that land's use for affordable housing, not simply resell it to for-profit developers as land banks too often do.[58]

Another way to decommodify our current housing stock is through the Tenant and Community Opportunity to Purchase Acts. TOPA and COPA provide first rights of purchase—and sometimes government funding to support that purchase—to entities that will convert the property into permanently affordable social housing.[59] Even more impactful versions of this legislation impose a right of first refusal for tenants or the community, meaning the landowners must accept the bid if it matches the best offer.[60] Public financing can then support the construction or rehabilitation of the property, along with the necessary maintenance.[61] There is obvious financial benefit to be gained when government housing dollars are solely dedicated to affordable housing, not diverted in substantial amounts to the rich via tax credits or surpluses for the benefit of for-profit landlords or developers.

As we see in court, tenants in privately rented housing are often powerless. Their landlords' attorneys have drafted the terms of their take-it-or-leave-it leases, then those landlords are often unresponsive to maintenance needs. Social housing can hand control back to the renters by embracing a democratic approach to operation of the housing. That can be accomplished through cooperative resident ownership or with nonprofit or government owners constrained by a rent board, along with direct accountability to tenants.[62] Those tenants would preferably be organized into a tenant union with legal rights akin to workplace collective-bargaining units.[63]

Again, there are many successful models we can emulate, both in the US and internationally. When residents are the owners, the landlord-tenant conflicts over rent and maintenance tend to fade away, and all involved are dedicated to the prosperity of the housing.[64] The value of this structure was proven during the housing crisis of 2007–2009, when social housing entities saw far fewer foreclosures and delinquencies compared to private market housing.[65]

Social housing has a positive effect on the overall housing market as well, driving costs down by forcing for-profit housing to reduce its prices to compete with social housing.[66] Social housing at large scale in other nations amplifies the price-dampening effect, an impact that is not felt in the US because only 4 percent of our housing is subsidized. And by removing the profit percentages, social housing provides cost savings for the government in construction, management, and maintenance costs.[67]

Of course, the people doing that construction, management, and maintenance work will be members of the community. So the public, nonprofit nature of the enterprise can ensure that these are well-paying jobs with good benefits and security rather than positions that are as temporary and low-paid as a for-profit entity can get away with.[68] People's Action's Homes Guarantee program calls for a school-to-union pipeline created by union-designed apprenticeships in social housing projects.[69] Those social housing jobs can endure through economic downturns, avoiding the workforce shrinkage the for-profit construction industry inevitably suffers through during those periods.[70]

As we discussed in chapter 3, social housing is a logical and appropriate reparation for the generations of well-documented racist US housing practices.[71] Social housing investments should be disproportionately targeted, especially initially, to benefit the Black and brown communities whose resources have been extracted under the racist US housing approach we have followed for multiple generations.[72]

More broadly, housing's core role in family health and stability means that the improvements generated by social housing will have dramatically positive effects throughout our communities. Research shows that children who live in subsidized housing are healthier and have better educational outcomes than comparable children living in for-profit rental housing.[73] Low-income households with money left over after paying rent will spend that money in their communities.[74]

None of these benefits can be realized by making small tweaks to the current system. We can see in eviction court each week that private for-profit developers and landlords, even when heavily subsidized, are unable to create and provide affordable housing for the millions of Americans in need. By contrast, there is abundant evidence that public land acquisition, financing, construction, and operation will make massive improvements in housing affordability.[75] We will review some of those examples here.

Social Housing Momentum Is Growing

The US is far behind other wealthy nations in providing social housing. But the foundation for a massive increase in US social housing is already in place. Hundreds of US communities have land banks and/or housing trust funds.[76] Some, like Minneapolis and Indianapolis, are following the European example of directing public real estate and public funding to social housing.[77] North Dakota has had a public bank for over a century, Philadelphia has a city-owned public bank, and California now allows public banking statewide. Advocates are calling for nationwide support for public banking.[78]

In Minnesota, New York, and California, corporate-owned properties have been converted to community ownership. San Francisco is raising public dollars for affordable housing by assessing taxes on high-end real estate.[79] Community Opportunity to Purchase Act (COPA) legislation has passed or is pending in multiple states and communities including Washington, DC, and Portland, Oregon. Baltimore community advocacy successfully forced the creation of a housing trust fund, and San Francisco requires landlords to recognize and meet with tenant associations or face a mandated rent reduction.[80]

Increasingly, state and city governments have realized that the private housing market will not meet the needs of their communities.[81] States like Rhode Island, Hawaii, and Colorado are investing in building social housing, as are communities like Montgomery County, Maryland.[82] "What I like about what we're doing is all we have effectively done is commandeer the private American real estate model," Zachary Marks, the chief real estate officer for Montgomery County's housing authority, told *Vox* in 2022. "We're replacing the investor dudes from Wall Street, the big money from Dallas. . . . Both because we don't have to meet the private sector return requirements, and because it's much easier to set policy on things that you own, all of that [revenue] just gets poured back into overall housing production and operation."[83]

One social housing approach that is attracting widespread support is community land trusts, known as CLTs.[84] In a community land trust, the nonprofit trust retains ownership of the land while the resident purchases the house on it.[85] The purchase cost is lowered because of the discount for not buying the land, and is often supported with subsidies.[86] In exchange for the reduced price and the subsidy, the resident agrees to limit their resale price to make sure the home is permanently affordable.[87]

CLTs have a legacy that traces back to Black-owned projects like the New Communities that grew out of the southern US civil rights movement.[88] There are now over 225 CLTs in the US, with cities like Indianapolis supporting them by acquiring land and buildings from private ownership and transferring title to CLTs to develop and manage.[89] Government funding and land grants have played an important role in the success of CLTs, including the US's largest program, the Champlain (Vermont) Land Trust.[90]

Yet even all this activity only scratches the surface of the potential for transforming our housing systems.[91] Governments at all levels hold the power to raise revenue for social housing by taxing high-end housing and housing speculation, to tightly regulate for-profit housing activity, and to exercise eminent domain, especially on vacant or distressed corporate properties.[92] These governments can prioritize and fund adaptive reuse, turning existing vacant or for-profit buildings into affordable housing.[93] The federal government can repeal the 2017 legislation that gifted capital gains tax breaks to wealthy developers through so-called opportunity zones, a program that we saw in chapter 4 too often fuels gentrification.[94]

That's not all. Governments can significantly increase the resources and power of public land banks, institute the first rights of purchase to tenants and the community via TOPA and COPA legislation, and then subsidize those organizations' development and maintenance efforts via public housing finance agencies. Housing researchers Gianpaolo Baiocchi and H. Jacob Carlson have proposed a Social Housing Development Authority to coordinate the acquisition of real estate and its transfer to social housing.[95] "It would intervene in the troubled parts of the housing market and, rather than let those units go to corporate speculators and house-flippers, finance their transfer to tenant cooperatives, land trusts, and non-profits," they write. "This would crowd out speculators and expand the share of housing shielded from the private market."[96]

At the federal level, perhaps the most ambitious and straightforward current US social housing proposal is Representative Ilhan Omar's Homes for All Act. The legislation would devote $1 trillion to building twelve million new, permanently affordable public and social housing units, among other social housing investments. Like the Green New Deal for Public Housing Act, the Homes for All legislation would repeal the Faircloth Amendment.[97] So would the Homes Act, a proposal that Senator Tina Smith (D-Minnesota) and Representative Alexandria Ocasio-Cortez introduced in September of 2024. The Homes Act aims to create a federal development authority to finance and build homes where rent is capped at 25 percent of a household's income. The Homes Act program would create 1.25 million new social housing units from an investment of $30 billion per year, the equivalent of the annual cost of the mortgage interest deduction provided to homeowners.[98]

Another proposal, led by the National Low-Income Housing Coalition, is the "HoUSed" campaign to expand rental assistance to every eligible household and create a national housing stabilization fund to provide emergency help.[99]

As our clients like Margaret can painfully attest, all these proposals are much needed. The view from eviction court—not to mention a homeless shelter or a subsidized housing waiting line—shows that the US's dominant approach to housing is irretrievably broken. It is time to finally reject the failed model of relying on the private, for-profit market to ensure housing for all. It is time to embrace and fully fund public housing and other robust social housing options.

LESSONS FROM OTHER COUNTRIES AND OUR OWN HISTORY

My visit to Vienna was inspiring . . . and embarrassing.

The inspiration came from witnessing firsthand what the *New York Times* has called a "renter's utopia."[1] I toured the legendary Karl-Marx-Hof, a municipal housing complex that spans more than a kilometer and includes more than twelve hundred apartments. The residents of those apartments pay a maximum of 25 percent of their income to live in flats that can be as large as four bedrooms. Many feature expansive balconies with colorful geraniums cascading down their front, looking out over courtyards graced with towering chestnut trees and modern playgrounds.

At Karl-Marx-Hof's official opening on October 12, 1930, Vienna mayor Karl Seitz said, "When we are no longer here, these stones will speak for us." And they do, along with the 380 other municipal "estates" built in Vienna during the 1920s and 1930s that ultimately housed a quarter million people.[2]

I visited some of the other complexes built during the era, including the Suditroler Hof in the city center and the Goethe Hof, where some of the apartment balconies overlook the Danube. Most are built around spacious courtyards, where I saw older residents sitting on benches, chatting or reading while children played soccer on the grass. The buildings are scattered throughout the city, and the two-hundred-plus architects enlisted to design them assured there is variety in both structures and layout.

This Viennese municipal housing was built and managed by the government, making it akin to what we call public housing in the US. The early twentieth-century municipal housing boom has not been repeated at that scale, but there is still decommodified housing being built in Vienna. Today, that housing is created mostly by limited-profit associations, organizations that often receive subsidies in return for tight government restrictions on rent charged and a requirement that any profits be returned to social housing.[3]

These regulations pull Vienna's municipal housing, limited-profit housing, and rent-restricted cooperatives all into the category of social housing. A hallmark is the range of household incomes of people living in these communities. Persons with incomes as high as US $77,000 annually, well above the city's average, can qualify for subsidized housing.[4] And even if their household income increases substantially after they move in, residents are allowed to stay. One member of Parliament who lives in municipal housing makes more than $105,000 per year.[5]

Social housing communities in Vienna are not only diverse, but they are also quite stable. Tenants' long-term tenure in their apartments is guaranteed under the law. The amount of rent charged is calculated at a percentage of household income, which means that renters in Vienna are also protected from losing their home when illness or job loss occurs.[6]

These protections and the housing's high quality make renting so attractive that half the city's 1.8 million residents live in subsidized housing.[7] A US Department of Housing and Urban Development publication marvels that Vienna has avoided the common pitfalls of housing in our country: "[Viennese] housing developments do not devolve into middle-class enclaves nor do they become stigmatized concentrations of poverty."[8] The city has virtually no visible homeless population and no "slum" areas of concentrated poverty and low-quality housing.[9]

The sheer volume of Viennese social housing, along with its mixed-income nature, also has a price-dampening effect on for-profit housing, which is forced to compete with high-quality subsidized housing.[10] That competitive pressure combines with vigorous rent control on private housing to make Vienna one of the cheapest renting cities in all of Europe, even on the for-profit market.[11] Because good housing is central to both a household's and a city's well-being, it is no surprise that Vienna is ranked virtually every year as the most livable city in the world.[12]

That was the inspiring part. The problem was that I did not take in these marvels alone. As we walked and talked, my Viennese companions, experts on the local housing situation, were polite enough to ask about the housing situation in my own community and country. That was where the embarrassment came in.

Armin Puller, a Vienna city councilor and political science professor at the University of Vienna, showed me several social housing complexes, explaining that anyone with an urgent housing need can be placed in a municipal housing unit immediately. How was I supposed to tell him that we have an official US homeless population of nearly six hundred thousand—widely acknowledged to be a significant undercount—and three of every four households eligible for a federal housing subsidy don't get it because of underfunding?[13]

Puller told me that tenant protections under Viennese and Austrian law are so strong that "evictions are really not a thing here. . . . After all, people need to live someplace, right?" I could not argue with his rhetorical question, of course. But I felt compelled to admit that in my city alone, hundreds of people are forcibly removed from their rented homes every week.

Puller grew up in the same community that he now represents on the city council. At his recent elementary school reunion, Puller and virtually all his classmates realized they still lived in the same district. Unlimited renting tenure in Vienna social housing means people tend to move into their flats in their twenties or thirties and never leave. If the residents wish, they can pass apartments to their family members on the original terms the parents signed on to.

That is my cue to confess that most of our eviction clients are living with year-to-year leases, and thus are always at risk that their landlord will choose not to renew. By now, I was getting the impression that Puller was becoming grossed out by our treatment of renters and was just too polite to say it. I decided not to mention that many of our clients are even forced to accept month-to-month lease terms.

Puller explains that living in a well-designed, well-maintained, and attractively located municipal or limited-profit housing apartment causes no stigma in Vienna. His mother lived out her final years in a municipal apartment that had been in the family for over six decades. She paid the equivalent of about US $300 per month. I nodded, choosing to keep to myself that the unfunded neglect of public housing here often leaves it so dilapidated and dangerous that my clients dream of leaving if they could just afford to do so.

I did not feel any better about my community and country when I talked with Maria Maltschnig and Sebastian Schublach of the Renner Institute, the political academy of the Austrian Social Democratic Party. Maltschnig and Schublach walked me through Vienna's social housing origin story, which began after World War I.

In the postwar elections, the Social Democratic Workers' Party gained power, ushering in an era known as "Red Vienna."[14] The new government leaders inherited a housing crisis so dire that overcrowding forced 170,000 Vienna residents to become what were called "bed-goers," leasing bed space to sleep in shifts. Dozens of strangers were forced to share a single sink and toilet, while still paying extremely high rents.[15] Tuberculosis spread so readily in these cramped quarters that it was known across Europe as "the Viennese disease."[16]

So the new Viennese government devoted its resources to building municipal housing complexes. These were named after figures like Karl Marx and George

Washington, demonstrating the ruling party's commitment to both its "social" and "democratic" missions.[17] Then Nazi occupation stalled the progress, even though some of the social housing complexes became for a time de facto fortresses resisting fascist takeover.[18] After World War II, the Social Democratic Party regained power, and Vienna renewed its commitment to ensuring housing is a fully realized human right.

The Social Democrats are still the party leading the government, which shines a spotlight on its social housing philosophy and history. "Contrary to other European cities, the treatment of municipal housing estates as an object of profiteering was always out of the question," the City of Vienna's website states. "The fundamental need that is housing and the possibility for all income groups to live in our city are more important than the financial gain achieved by just a few."[19]

That approach predicts the progressive taxation that has always financed Vienna's housing success story. The original municipal housing building boom was funded by "Breitner Taxes," a system created by city finance councilor and former banker Hugo Breitner. Breitner Taxes featured aggressive levies on luxuries like champagne, horse racing, private villas, and domestic servants. The Karl-Marx-Hof onsite museum displays a Breitner Tax poster of the time depicting a frightened tycoon recoiling in horror as a muscular red arm grabbed bottles of the tycoon's chilling champagne.

Apartment-dwellers helped finance the construction, too, but the vast majority of that revenue was collected from the highest-income residents. High tax assessments on unused land either raised a great deal of revenue or motivated private owners to sell to the government, which often repurposed the land for municipal housing.[20]

Although Vienna continues to have a very progressive tax structure, Schublach shows me a comparative analysis of the Austrian state's housing expenditures that place it far below the costs incurred by other European nations like the United Kingdom, France, and Germany.[21] The reason, he and Maltschnig explain, is that limited-profit housing is the top source of new social housing, and it costs the government very little. Sale of land is tightly regulated, including a requirement that at least two-thirds of any large private land plots sold must be diverted to rent-limited housing.[22] "Since the ground that can be built on is a limited resource, we don't see housing as a fit for the private market," Maltschnig says.

Eighty percent of Viennese residents are renters, and it appears most are quite content to stay that way.[23] For someone like me coming from the US homeowner culture, this of course is surprising. The reason for renter contentment, Maltschnig says, is stability, pointing to rent control, unlimited tenure of leases, and the ability to pass apartments down among generations. There are also no

US-style tax incentives for homeownership. "Broad acceptance by people for long-term renting instead of buying only comes with long-term stability," she says. Maintaining excellent condition of social housing is a must, too. "The big thing about social housing here is that it's not just for poor people. It is for the broad, middle class."

As a final demonstration, Schublach takes me on a tour of the Sonnwendviertel neighborhood where he and his wife and two daughters live. This city-center area, developed over the past ten years on the site of a former massive rail yard, is now the home to more than fourteen thousand people, almost half of them living in subsidized apartments.[24] A true "fifteen-minute city" where all necessary goods and services can be reached within a few minutes' walk, there are four separate grocery stores that Schublach and his family can easily access. Last year, when he helped host a US delegation, Schublach was stunned to learn that this feature was uncommon in many US cities. "The idea of a food desert is inconceivable here," he says.

Walking-distance access is a must, since the Sonnwendviertel is a car-free area. Buildings are flanked on one side by a fifteen-acre park and on the other by the Bloch-Bauer Promenade, where children ride scooters and bikes and adults sit at cafés or walk through ground-level retail stores, topped by upper floors dedicated to apartments.

Schublach's family lives in one of those buildings, Gleis 21—Gleis translates to "track," commemorating the area's former use. The larchwood Gleis 21 is so attractive that a photograph of it was featured in a *New York Times Magazine* feature article on Vienna housing. It is owned and operated by a resident cooperative that houses thirty-eight apartments above a ground-floor coffee shop, music school, and an event space used for multiple performances each week. The top floor is dedicated to a rooftop garden, a large kitchen and dining area for entertaining and meetings, a library, and a sauna.

From that rooftop, looking west, we can see a gleaming black-and-silver building, eight stories stacked on top of a ground-floor commercial area featuring floor-to-ceiling mirrored windows. This is limited-profit housing, Vienna style. Since most residents of limited-profit housing are required to submit a down payment, it is often less accessible to the poor than pure municipal housing like the Karl-Marx-Hof. But I could not help but reflect on the fact that the monthly rent paid by this beautiful building's residents is cheaper than the rent paid by our clients living in for-profit housing that is often roach-infested, leaky, and crumbling.

I decided not to spoil our tour by voicing that depressing observation. For the moment, I wanted to hold on instead to the hope that the US could someday follow Vienna's lead and start building a renter's utopia of our own.

Other Success Stories

Other cities and nations share Vienna's commitment to ensuring that high-quality housing is available to all. Finland's goal to fully end homelessness by 2027 may seem outlandish by US standards, but it is actually a realistic target for the Finns: unlike virtually every other nation, they have been steadily reducing homelessness since 1987.[25] They rely on a model social housing program that fulfills the right to housing in Finland's constitution with a Housing First approach that immediately places unhoused people into homes.[26]

Unlike in the US, the Finnish pipeline to social housing has no gaps where profiteering can interfere with either affordability or quality. Most of the land in the capital city, Helsinki, is owned by the municipal government, which also operates its own public construction company with funding provided by a public bank and the national housing agency.[27] The result is that one of every six housing units in Finland is public housing.[28] With this stellar housing system, it is no coincidence that Finland can lay claim to some of the same good vibes as Vienna: Finns have been ranked as the world's happiest people six years running.[29]

In Singapore, three of every four residents live in government-developed housing, much of it on land cleared via eminent domain in the 1960s.[30] The government proudly points to its public housing program as "a Singapore icon."[31] That is no idle boast. A World Bank publication in 2018 declared Singapore's "the best public housing in the world"—and insisted that its success is quite replicable.[32]

That success is made all the more remarkable by how quickly it came about. At the time of Singapore's independence in 1959, less than 10 percent of the population lived in public housing. Like the Viennese model, rapid build-up of public housing in Singapore was accomplished with careful attention to connecting the housing to nearby schools and public transportation. From the beginning, a mix of household incomes was included in the buildings, each of which also featured easy access to socializing and commercial spaces.

Hawaii state senator Stanley Chang, who has visited Singapore's housing program multiple times and has sponsored legislation to replicate it in his home state, told me in an interview that Singapore's success provides a definitive response to any social housing resistance in the US. "A big hill that we have to climb is that the neoliberals have won the argument in both parties that the government is always late, always over budget, and can't do anything right," Chang says. "So that is why it is mind-blowing for people to see in Singapore that 80 percent of the population lives in public housing, where it is not stigmatized, it is well-maintained, and it is constantly upgraded. When you see a program that works so incredibly well, it completely changes your view of the housing problem.

"A lot of the other housing solutions that we talk about might be 5 percent or 10 percent solutions," Chang says. "But social housing in Singapore is a complete solution. It is a silver bullet. It is not one of many actions that need to be taken. It is *the* answer."[33]

Social housing programs do not have to be one-size-fits-all. For example, Uruguay boasts a successful public housing program built on a federation of five hundred self-managed housing cooperatives.[34] Spain, Chile, and Belgium all have built striking examples of architecturally beautiful social housing.[35] Before the Margaret Thatcher government began underfunding and privatizing "council" housing in the 1980s, 42 percent of Brits lived in their version of public housing.[36] In Sweden, workers unions have come together to form a cooperative that builds and manages housing, while a National Tenants Union bargains for tenant rights and lower rents, along with creating its own banking and housing cooperative.[37]

As with Vienna and Singapore, Sweden responded to its housing crisis by thoughtfully but urgently creating a large amount of high-quality subsidized housing. During the 1960s and 1970s, Sweden built a full one million affordable units, increasing Sweden's net housing stock by 20 percent.[38]

The US should take note, housing researchers Peter Gowan and Ryan Cooper point out, since the "Million Homes Program" would equate in the US today to building 18.5 million homes over the course of a decade. Coincidentally enough, you may recall from chapter 6, eighteen million people in the US endure so-called "deep poverty," trying to survive on incomes below $13,000 for a family of four.[39] "The lesson which should be drawn from the Million Homes Program is that state financing of municipal housing can eliminate a major housing shortage over a short period of time," Gowan and Cooper write.[40] As we learned in chapter 8, Representative Ilhan Omar's Homes for All Act calls for the US to build twelve million new social housing units.[41]

Given the huge amount of US vacant homes and apartments owned for tax or investment purposes, new construction is not the only option for quickly increasing the supply of subsidized housing. Since 2016, the Catalonia region of Spain has allowed the seizure of vacant corporate-owned apartments, which are then rented to low-income tenants.[42] In 2021, Berlin residents passed a referendum to seize the property of large corporate landlords and convert the apartments to social housing.[43] That is an attractive option in Germany, a renter-majority nation that shuns the many homeowner tax benefits the US provides. As we saw in chapter 8, rent control and eviction protections provide so much stability to German renters that the average tenancy lasts eleven years.[44]

There are many more international examples of effective housing policies. For example, there are persons in nations like Denmark, Greece, and the United Kingdom who are technically homeless, but almost all are provided access to provisional housing and a path to permanent housing.[45] The US can and should follow the lead of these nations that have avoided the tragedies of our nation's housing crisis, says California Assembly member Alex Lee, who has sponsored social housing legislation in his state. "When the Red Vienna period started, 25 percent of the people were homeless, people were starving and poor and defeated in the war. When Singapore began its program, it had just been decolonized," he told me in an interview. "Compare that to the United States now, the most powerful and wealthy country in the world. Our state of California is the wealthiest state in the union. If Vienna and Singapore could do it, we certainly can do it."[46]

I agree. And beyond these shining international examples, we can even look to our own history for social housing inspiration. The US has taken dramatic, positive action on affordable housing before.

As we saw in chapter 8, the US proved in the second half of the twentieth century that we are capable of building a great deal of public housing. And we proved in that same era that we can use housing investments—through the FHA and VA, for example—to pull millions of families into middle-class stability. We even have precedent for fixing the current problem of needed housing being kept vacant as tax shelters and "safe deposit boxes in the sky" investment vehicles—by seizing the property.[47] (As mentioned in chapter 5, residential housing in the US is also a notoriously common vehicle for global money-laundering.)[48] The US's reputation for being a fierce protector of private property can obscure our surprisingly robust history of government seizures of that private property, particularly in times of economic crisis.[49]

All the same, there is one important element that many other nations possess that the US does lack: a clear legal commitment to recognizing and enforcing a human right to housing. But this too is a model we can and should follow.

Housing as a Human Right—Internationally

The email I received from a local lawyer was not a surprise. Mostly, it repeated many of the same themes I often see in response to articles I publish about housing. The lawyer talked about trusting the wonders of the capitalist real estate market to do right by all. He complained about how difficult it is for landlords nowadays, and that tenants facing eviction usually richly deserve their fate. He shared a story about alleged horrors inflicted by tenants in one of his legal cases.

But the lawyer's email had an added twist: "I am an alum of the school where you teach, so I was appalled to read you refer to housing as a human right. As you well know, not only is housing not a human right, it never can be one."

Franklin D. Roosevelt disagreed. When the concept of treating housing as a human right began to gain traction in the mid-twentieth century, it looked like the US would be a leader in the movement. In Roosevelt's 1944 State of the Union address, he proposed a "Second Bill of Rights," which featured a right to a decent home.[50] Then Eleanor Roosevelt served as chair of the United Nations Commission on Human Rights that drafted the Universal Declaration of Human Rights (UDHR), modeled in many respects on President Roosevelt's blueprint. Mrs. Roosevelt played a key role in both drafting the document and securing its passage in 1948.[51]

The UDHR rejects the idea that housing is merely a privilege or a commodity. Instead, it considers housing to be a right possessed by every human being.[52] Article 25 of the UDHR states, "Everyone has the right to a standard of living adequate for the health and well-being of himself and his family, including food, clothing, *housing* [emphasis added]."[53] Unfortunately, the UDHR is not something our clients can carry into court and use to demand housing: it is not a treaty. But it is considered to be an indicator of "customary international law," which suggests that it may be on the path to being enforceable one day.[54]

Fortunately for most people in the world, there is an enforceable global treaty on housing. In 1966, the aspirations of the UDHR were made concrete by the binding treaty language of the International Covenant on Economic, Social and Cultural Rights. Article 11 of the ICESCR states, "The States Parties to the present Covenant recognize the right of everyone to an adequate standard of living for himself and his family, including adequate food, clothing and housing."[55] Nations that are party to the ICESCR commit to "take appropriate steps to ensure the realization of this right."[56]

This tracked with Roosevelt's call for global governments to look forward and aim for a better future. "Too many who prate about saving democracy are really only interested in saving things as they were," he said years before proposing his Second Bill of Rights. "Democracy should concern itself also with things as they ought to be."[57]

Unfortunately, in the years after Roosevelt's death, the US abandoned our leadership role on international economic rights. We are one of a handful of nations not to ratify the ICESCR, and the only one in the Americas or Europe not to do so.[58] While President Jimmy Carter did sign the treaty in 1977, ratification requires that his signature be accompanied by the approval of two-thirds of senators, which has not occurred. Yet that presidential signature at least commits our government to refraining from actions that undermine its purpose, per the Vienna Convention on the Law of Treaties.[59]

So the local landlord lawyer was partially correct, at least in the US. My guess, though, is that he was not thinking much about international law. More likely, he was referring to the US Bill of Rights, which has usually been interpreted by our courts as only protecting so-called "negative rights." That means we prioritize civil and political rights that prevent government from doing things: interfering with free speech, integrity of home and person, etc. Think "Don't Tread on Me" flags and bumper stickers. Other nations, and the ICESCR, also embrace "positive rights" that require affirmative government action on human needs like housing, food, and medical care.

But there is not yet any right to housing enshrined in US constitutional law. The Supreme Court in the 1972 case of *Lindsey v. Normet* said it found no right to housing arising out of the due process or equal protection clauses of the Constitution. "We are unable to perceive in that document any constitutional guarantee of access to dwellings of a particular quality, or any recognition of the right of a tenant to occupy the real property of his landlord beyond the term of his lease without the payment of rent or otherwise contrary to the terms of the relevant agreement," Justice Byron White wrote. "Absent constitutional mandate, the assurance of adequate housing and the definition of landlord-tenant relationships are legislative, not judicial, functions."[60]

While the US was shrinking at the notion of a human right to housing, other nations embraced it. The ICESCR commitments do not compel the government to provide a free home to each and every individual, but they do assign to the government the ultimate responsibility for ensuring a fully housed populace. If you or I can meet our housing needs through the for-profit market—as most Americans can—all well and good. But when the market fails to meet a person's housing needs, the ICESCR says the government must step in, whether by subsidizing access to the private market or directly providing government-managed housing.[61]

The Committee on Economic, Social, and Cultural Rights, which interprets the ICESCR and monitors compliance with it, says this: "The human right to housing cannot be viewed in a narrow or restrictive sense which . . . views shelter as exclusively a commodity." Instead, housing must be "ensured to all, regardless of income." The committee understood that this assurance will likely cost money and made it clear that cost will not be an excuse for noncompliance. "Discharging such duties may require the mobilization of resources by the State, including by enforcing progressive taxation schemes," the committee insisted.[62]

ICESCR compliance among its ratifiers is a mixed bag, but many nations take their ICESCR commitments very seriously. They have followed up on their ICESCR promises with guarantees of housing contained in their constitutions and/or statutes.[63] Finland, Germany, South Africa, France, the Netherlands, and multiple other countries have created legal rights to housing in their national law and followed up with well-funded programs to ensure their enforcement.[64]

For example, the Homelessness Act of 2003 in Scotland ensures that anyone assessed as unintentionally homeless has a right to "settled accommodations in a local authority or housing association tenancy or a private rental."[65] Section 19 of the Constitution of Finland states, "Those who cannot obtain the means necessary for a life of dignity have the right to receive indispensable subsistence and care. . . . The public authorities shall promote the right of everyone to housing and the opportunity to arrange their own housing."[66]

These laws do not magically create full housing, but they do set the stage for it. As mentioned, Finland is a global leader in reducing homelessness.[67] Athens adopted a Homeless Bill of Rights that includes a right to housing, and the law included expanded temporary housing and street outreach and services.[68] The City of Vienna's official description of its legendary social housing program cites the human right to housing provisions in the European Social Charter.[69] In Scotland, application of its law has made homelessness a "brief, rare, and a non-recurring phenomenon," writes Eric Tars of the National Law Center on Homelessness and Poverty.[70]

Housing as a Human Right—the US

Despite the US so far ducking the ICESCR or constitutional commitments to housing, there is still a strong national legacy of acknowledging housing as a human right, in both word and deed. We saw in chapter 2 that federal housing support was robust in the middle of the twentieth century. Remember the words of Western Regional Advocacy Project director Paul Boden describing the US before we slashed $50 billion in affordable housing investments in the early 1980s: "Racism, poverty, and addiction all existed before 1982. What did not exist was a homeless shelter."[71] This previous deep well of funding reflected a tangible commitment to the goal of the US Housing Act of 1949: "a decent home and suitable living arrangements for every American family."[72]

Eric Tars and others point out that, even without signing on to the ICESCR, the US has several times supported international human rights recommendations and reports that endorsed a right to housing.[73] States including Rhode Island, Connecticut, and Illinois, the US territory of Puerto Rico, and municipalities like my hometown of Indianapolis have all adopted homeless bills of rights.[74] Advocates in California and Connecticut are pushing to add the human right to housing in their state constitutions.[75] Proposed legislation in Congress includes the "Housing Is a Human Right Act," which would prohibit criminalization of homelessness and devote funds to affordable housing.[76]

More broadly, while the political philosophy of the US has traditionally been dominated by the view that individuals' circumstances result mainly from their own choices, that attitude may be changing. In recent years, public understanding about the effects of structural racism and class discrimination appears to be increasing.[77] So it should not be surprising that public opinion polling has shown both a great deal of contemporary concern about housing and a commitment to remedying the problem. A 2021 poll showed that two-thirds of Americans in growing metropolitical areas are "extremely/very concerned" about homelessness and the high cost of housing, ranking it as their number-one priority.[78] Earlier surveys showed that three-quarters of Americans consider safe, secure housing to be a human right.[79]

Those Americans are not content for that right to be an abstraction: most of the people expressing support of housing as a human right also support expanded government programs to make that right a reality.[80] As we will see in chapters 11 and 12, ballot initiatives and tenant organizing for increased housing investment and renter protections have been winning victories from coast to coast. Polling numbers suggest those victories may keep coming. In a 2020 survey, 63 percent of likely voters support federal investment in social housing, including 56 percent of Republicans and 53 percent of independent and third-party voters.[81]

These views are held at the very highest level of leadership in the nation. President Joe Biden is on record saying housing is a right, not a privilege.[82] Marcia Fudge, Biden's first secretary of the US Department of Housing and Urban Development, has stated, "If we are to fully achieve justice in housing, we must fully accept what that means: justice in housing is everyone realizing the fundamental truth—housing is a human right."[83] The American Bar Association, the American Public Health Association, and the association of state and local human rights commissions have all officially endorsed an enforceable US human right to housing.[84]

In fact, the discussion of housing as a human right has become so commonplace that it inspired the scorn of liberal *New York Times* columnist Nicholas Kristof in mid-2023. "Slogans can't replace evidence-based policymaking that understands trade-offs and embraces nuances," Kristof wrote. "It's easy to say housing is a human right, but that doesn't get anyone into a home."[85]

I'm not so sure. I side with Eric Tars and the centuries of human rights history showing it is sometimes possible to speak a right into existence. "The human right to housing is a holistic and powerful frame, carrying the weight of international law and tapping into our deep cultural understanding of the importance of upholding human and civil rights," Tars writes.

I agree. But that same human rights history shows that it takes a movement to turn a frame into a reality. Lucky for us, a vibrant, growing tenants' rights movement is taking the stage in the US. We will learn more about that movement in chapters 11 and 12. But first, we'll review what religious communities can contribute to the effort to make housing a fully realized human right.

RELIGIOUS TRADITIONS AND THE HUMAN RIGHT TO HOUSING

One cold December morning in the Indianapolis eviction court where we work, I waited at the entrance to the building. I was scanning the parking lot, looking for a client whose case was set to be heard at the start of the day's busy docket. Instead, I spotted a half-dozen well-dressed older white folks, climbing out of Priuses and mini-SUVs, looking at each other and pointing with hesitation to the building entrance. Then they walked together toward me. "We are with the Housing Justice Task Force at Meridian Street United Methodist Church," one woman said. "We are here to watch court."

They and other churchgoers had read disturbing media reports about our community's housing crisis, then convened a book study of Matthew Desmond's prize-winning book, *Evicted*. Now they were determined to see for themselves. After several court visits, they developed a court-watching survey checklist for other volunteers, and began training people from various congregations to follow their lead. They use their experiences to inform state lawmakers, demanding that they push reform of Indiana's landlord-tenant laws.

Rabbi Aaron Spiegel directs the Greater Indianapolis Multifaith Alliance, which supports the now-thriving multi-congregation eviction court-watching program and the advocacy that has grown out of it. "All religious traditions teach that we must take care of the 'least among us,' and as such, housing is a human right," Rabbi Spiegel told me in an interview. "Religious communities have historically functioned as support networks to people in crisis. Now we are learning that they need to be proactive and part of the solution by preempting housing insecurity."[1]

As of 2021, three in four Americans said they identify with a specific religious faith.[2] Of those, a large majority—69 percent—identify with a Christian religion, with 2 percent identifying with Judaism, 1 percent identifying as Muslim, and another 1 percent as Buddhist.[3] This chapter will explore how those four religious traditions subscribe to the idea that housing is a human right, and how they can make a major contribution to the movement to ensure all people are safely housed, a movement we will describe in this book's final two chapters.[4]

The major religious traditions have many areas of disagreement, of course. But on the question of housing they are in lockstep.[5] As Richard Kearney and James Taylor write in their introduction to the anthology they edited, *Hosting the Stranger: Between Religions*, "Hospitality is a central and inaugural event in the world's great wisdom traditions. . . . Most major wisdom traditions, as this volume hopes to show, share a sacred commitment to hosting the stranger."[6]

But does this consensus have any impact? After all, many Americans today are alienated from religious traditions, often for very understandable reasons. And active engagement in religious communities has lessened in recent years.[7] In 2023, the *Wall Street Journal* and the National Opinion Research Center (NORC) at the University of Chicago surveyed around one thousand American adults about the importance of religion, and only 39 percent of respondents said religion was very important to them.[8]

But that number can be misleading, since the total climbed to 60 percent when "somewhat important" responses were included. And the United States is still a more religiously observant country than similar nations in Western Europe. Religious leaders and themes still play key roles in our political elections and debates, especially on issues of poverty.[9]

I am convinced that religious communities have an important role to play in housing advocacy. In this chapter, I offer four reasons why.

1. Religious Communities Are Already Engaged in the Housing Struggle

By directly providing housing for people in need, religious communities and religion-motivated individuals are already "walking the walk" on housing. In my own community of Indianapolis alone, the Episcopal diocese, the Roman Catholic diocese, and evangelical churches all operate their own homeless shelters and housing programs. So does another organization that relies deeply on an interfaith network of Jewish, Christian, Muslim, and Hindi congregations and organizations. As described in chapter 6, just up the road from us in South Bend, a Catholic Worker community, in partnership with other local churches, renovated a former Knights Inn motel to create Housing First–inspired low-barrier housing for the community's homeless.[10] At a national level, religious housing efforts include the programs of Catholic Charities USA, whose affiliates provide homeless services to more than four hundred thousand people a year and operate more than thirty-seven thousand affordable housing units.[11] Multiple Black-led churches across the country are both developing affordable housing on church property and advocating for more affordable housing investments by local and state governments.[12]

That kind of direct service and expertise provides a platform for meaningful advocacy. The federal HoUSed campaign led by the National Low Income Housing Coalition, which features a call for universal housing assistance and strong renter protections, is joined by multiple religious groups, including Catholic Charities chapters, the Union for Reform Judaism, and the national leadership of the Episcopal and Methodist Churches.[13]

Similarly, there are many examples at the local levels of religious communities combining service and advocacy. One of these is happening in downtown Charlotte, North Carolina, where several homeless people live on the grounds of St. Martin's Episcopal Church.[14] The congregation welcomes and supports them. At the same time, St. Martin's works with the advocacy organization Action NC in its campaign to bring accountability to corporate landlords.

St. Martin's efforts are coordinated by its mission board president Kay Miller, who has seen housing struggles before.[15] When she was a teacher and administrator at Central Piedmont College, a community college in Charlotte, Miller taught students who were living out of their cars, sometimes with their families. But the mission board she leads at St. Martin's has not always focused on housing. For many years, the parish had a wide array of ministries that supported multiple community needs. Then its rector, Rev. Josh Bowron, challenged the congregation to do something different, to dive deeper into a few focused projects. Mostly, he challenged the congregation to reconsider its overall approach to responding to community needs.

"We have always sort of punched above our weight class when it comes to mission," Bowron told an Episcopal Diocese publication.[16] He and Miller say the parish has long been guided by the iconic story of St. Martin cutting his cloak in half to share with the poor, along with the Matthew 25 Gospel admonition of "whatsoever you do for the least of these my brothers and sisters, you did it for me."

These guideposts demand something different than just charity, Bowron told his congregation. "He challenged us to truly be *with* the people in our community who are struggling, not just deciding for ourselves what kind of handout or service we wanted to give," Miller told me in an interview. "And that is harder to do. It is a lot easier to just give money or food and get some immediate gratification from it."

So, Miller, the mission board, and the broader St. Martin's congregation spent months talking to different community groups and studying service options. After a group visit to the local eviction court and conversations with several of the Action NC leaders, they decided to focus on housing justice. "We wanted to see how we could be of help before a family becomes evicted, before someone becomes homeless," Miller says.

Now St. Martin's has a team of volunteers following the lead of Action NC tenants and organizers. Parishioners have staffed a tenant crisis hotline, recruited pro bono attorneys to help families facing eviction, and are pulling together a team to do phone canvassing of tenants living in some of the worst corporate-owned housing in Charlotte. They are discussing the possibility of following other churches' leads in helping low-income homeowners pay off the property tax bills and fines that often causes a family to lose a home, and even exploring how to help create more affordable housing units.

"I give credit to the people of St. Martin's for showing us how community and faith-based groups can really help the movement," Action NC organizer Apryl Lewis says. "I try to push faith groups into action, not just praying. And St. Martin's is definitely taking action."[17]

When religious communities and individuals like the congregants at St. Martin's "walk the walk" with direct services and also speak out with calls for broader solutions, their voices carry far and wide. Andrea Palumbo provides an example from the Catholic tradition. Palumbo, an attorney, spends her days giving legal advice to Minnesota tenants who are facing eviction, and working with her colleagues at the nonprofit advocacy group Homeline to push for more affordable housing and improved tenant rights.[18] "We are trying to level the playing field, because there is usually a short timeline to eviction, tenants don't have counsel, and it is often a very high bar for them to pull together the rent they owe," she told me in an interview. "We are working on the side of the underdog."

That is the side of the struggle Palumbo has always been most comfortable with, a trait she traces back to her Catholic childhood in New Jersey. One of her earliest memories is her church hosting a dinner to benefit the striking United Farm Workers fighting for living wages and safer working conditions.

Like many other cradle Catholics, Palumbo drifted away from the church in her young adulthood. Then, in the mid-1990s, she learned that St. Joan of Arc parish in south Minneapolis had responded to the AIDS crisis by converting its rectory into a care and hospice home. First, Palumbo volunteered at Grace House, cooking meals and providing personal care to patients. Then she joined the St. Joan congregation.

Even when Palumbo was separated from the church, she insists she never lost her belief in the mandates of Romans 13:10—love is the law—and James 2:14's call for all to show their faith through deeds. ("What good is it, my brothers and sisters, if someone claims to have faith but has no deeds? Faith by itself, if it is not accompanied by action, is dead.") The works of mercy pulled Palumbo back to Catholicism. Then, after seeing Grace House patients struggle with legal issues, they pushed her to law school.

While volunteering for a law school clinic representing women reentering the community after prison, she discovered how the struggle to afford housing interacts with so many other challenges of poverty. "Housing is so key. If it falls apart, so many other pieces of your life fall apart with it," Palumbo says. "It goes the other direction, too. When I talk to people who are behind on their rent, you hear about the medical and transportation and child care challenges that siphoned off the limited resources they had. And then there's nothing left."

In God's eyes, Palumbo insists, this is an unacceptable state of affairs. She cites Catholic social teaching, papal encyclicals, and Gustavo Gutiérrez, Leonard Boffo, and Oscar Romero, heroes of the liberation theology movement that emphasizes the Gospel mandate to prioritize the rights and needs of the poor. From them, Palumbo finds support for both her direct service and her demands for systemic reform like rent control.

"The Gospels give us very clear instructions for what we are supposed to do, and that includes resisting greed," says Palumbo, who is active in the Religion and Socialism Working Group of the Democratic Socialists of America. "Christ showed us when he cleared the temple that he was here to shake things up. People being homeless is not God's way, and he wants us to put a stop to it."

2. Religious Communities Have Been Pushing for Justice for Generations

The activism of Andrea Palumbo, St. Martin's Episcopal Church, and Rabbi Aaron Spiegel are current additions to the long and storied history of religious community advocacy for human rights. In perhaps the best US example, the movement to abolish slavery was in significant part grounded in Black and white religious communities. Groups like the American Anti-Slavery Society and leaders like Frederick Douglass, Sojourner Truth, and William Lloyd Garrison built the movement with Christian-themed messages, often delivered in religious venues and/or to overtly religious gatherings.[19]

After abolition was achieved, Protestant clergy and congregations fueled the Social Gospel movement of the late nineteenth and early twentieth centuries.

Social Gospel activists saw universal guarantees of adequate food, shelter, and living wages as the tangible manifestation of God's "Kingdom, on earth as in heaven."[20] At the turn of the twentieth century and beyond, the Women's Christian Temperance Union and other religious organizations helped lead the successful fight for women's suffrage.[21]

Several US religious groups, especially the Catholic Church, provided theological and logistical support to the workers' rights movement of the early twentieth century.[22] As Andrea Palumbo learned in her childhood, churches did the same for the Latino farmworkers movement a half century later.[23] The US civil rights movement, one of history's best-chronicled and impactful social movements, drew much of its strength from religious communities. Its most iconic leaders, including Rev. Dr. Martin Luther King Jr., and most significant organization—the Southern Christian Leadership Conference—arose from the Black Social Gospel tradition.[24]

These Black leaders and organizations received key support from white religious counterparts in the Protestant, Catholic, and Jewish traditions. "The movement's rhetoric abounded with biblical references. Churches often served as sites of communication, training, and solace for movement participants," the *Encyclopedia of Religion in America* states. "Religion energized black and white protesters, gave them confidence they were fighting for the right thing, and made them feel confident that they would eventually win."[25] That template for a religious community bolstering a US human rights movement was copied in the peace movement of the Vietnam War era of the 1960s and 1970s and the resistance to South African apartheid in the 1980s and early 1990s.[26]

A recent example of impactful advocacy by religious communities presents several parallels to the current housing challenge: activism for health care as a human right. Multifaith coalitions played a key role in mobilizing support for the 2010 Affordable Care Act, which expanded health care to tens of millions of Americans.[27] When efforts to repeal the Affordable Care Act seemed close to victory in 2017, dozens of religious denominations and organizations responded by issuing joint statements, mobilizing their congregations, and conducting a Capitol Hill vigil.[28] They also published a March 2017 letter signed by leaders of forty faith organizations, stating, "The scriptures of the Abrahamic traditions of Christians, Jews, and Muslims, as well as the sacred teachings of other faiths, understand that addressing the general welfare of the nation includes giving particular attention to people experiencing poverty or sickness."[29]

With this health care effort, US religious communities followed in the footsteps of their counterparts in Canada, where Baptist-minister-turned-provincial-governor Tommy Douglas mobilized religious community support to create Canada's universal health care system.[30] One Canadian religious community advocate calls that system "the Good Samaritan writ large."[31] Douglas explained the connection between religious beliefs and political action for human rights: "You're never going to step out of the front door into the kingdom of God. What you're going to do is slowly and painfully change society until it has more of the values that emanate from the teaching of Jesus or from the other great religious leaders."[32]

"Government Has a Social Responsibility"

Tommy Douglas's reference to a multiplicity of great religious leaders was on target, because religious human rights activism has always been a multifaith effort. For example, Jewish leaders like Rabbi Abraham Joshua Heschel joined with Christian clergy to play important roles in the US civil rights movement. Heschel famously responded to a question about whether he found time to pray during the historic march from Selma to Montgomery in 1965 by saying, "I prayed with my feet."[33]

Muslims have been at the forefront of global human rights activism, with women's rights activists like Malala Yousafzai, Jawakkil Karman, and Shirin Ebadi all recognized with Nobel Peace Prizes for their efforts.[34] During the middle to late twentieth century, a series of Buddhist leaders of Burma, Cambodia, Laos, and other Asian countries cited the dharma as the foundation for reforms that included guarantees of housing and other subsistence needs for all.[35]

In US history, this multifaith commitment to taking action for human rights was perhaps most dramatically demonstrated in the iconic 1963 March on Washington. The march was organized by labor and civil rights leader A. Philip Randolph, the son of an African Methodist Episcopal (AME) minister, and Bayard Rustin, a Quaker who had gone to prison rather than violate his faith's antiwar beliefs by fighting in World War II.[36]

Randolph and Rustin turned to church communities to recruit participants and build momentum for the march, which was widely credited with tipping the scales toward passage of the landmark Civil Rights Act of 1964.[37] Among the featured speakers were a Catholic archbishop, the leader of the Presbyterian Church USA, and two rabbis.[38] The speaker immediately preceding Dr. King and his iconic "I Have a Dream" speech was Holocaust survivor Rabbi Joachim Prinz, president of the American Jewish Congress, who said, "The most urgent, the most disgraceful, the most shameful, and the most tragic problem is silence."[39]

Access to good housing was one of the ten demands of the march. Those demands were formally pressed by Rustin in his speech on the steps of the Lincoln Memorial to the crowd of 250,000 and a live television audience, including

President John F. Kennedy.[40] In the final months of his life, King followed up on that demand via the Poor People's Campaign, which called for a massive increase in government-subsidized housing.[41]

King died before that campaign reached fruition, but its themes helped inspire the St. Louis Rent Strike of 1969, the year after King's death. It was the first and largest US public housing rent strike, and it helped shape the Brooke Amendment of 1969, which capped public housing tenants' rent at 25 percent of their income (later increased to 30 percent by Congress in 1981) and increased federal subsidies for housing.[42] The strike was led in part by United Church of Christ minister Buck Jones, and buttressed by broad support from the local religious community.[43]

This is an extraordinarily rich legacy, and it can serve as the foundation for a twenty-first-century US religious movement for housing as a human right. Already, there is meaningful religious community advocacy for housing, blooming in part from the exposure and credibility of religious communities and individuals involved in the direct provision of housing to those in need. A prominent example is Catholic Charities USA, which points out that the tens of thousands of affordable housing units it provides still leave an unmet need that demands a government, rights-based response. "Housing is a human right. Each person must have safe, affordable housing," Curtis Johnson, vice president of housing strategy at Catholic Charities USA, told me in an interview. "For the common good, we believe that government at all levels has a social responsibility to ensure that persons are adequately housed."[44]

"As Long as There Are Homeless People, Our Work Is Incomplete"

One of the most visible religious responses to US housing needs has been the Catholic Worker movement, founded by Dorothy Day during the Great Depression with a guiding principle of hospitality, especially for the homeless poor. It is from this tradition that the Motels4Now Housing First program described in chapter 6 performs its housing justice work. The same is true for Mark Colville.[45] In the early 1980s, after Colville moved to New York City to complete college, his parish in the South Bronx, St. Luke's, responded to that period's alarming spike in homelessness by creating an emergency shelter at the school gym. Colville ended up running it.[46]

He now lives at the Amistad Catholic Worker community in New Haven, Connecticut. Colville and his wife Luz Caterineau Colville helped found the community, and they raised six children there. Amistad's daily schedule is built around common table meals shared with New Haven residents who are living on the streets. Whenever the house has room, unsheltered people are taken in to stay.

"The scripture passages that really influence and motivate me in this work have to do with hospitality," Colville told me in an interview, echoing the theme of Richard Kearney's and James Taylor's *Hosting the Stranger* anthology. "Looking back on the encounters with God in both the Old and New Testament, so often they are related to people giving hospitality to one another. Beginning with the prophets and going through the Good Samaritan story, sheltering those who need it is a primary concern."

Colville's and the Amistad community's response to that concern has been a combination of the works of mercy and pushing for a better government response to the need. "Our work comes out of our Catholic faith and trying to be as close as possible to the experiences of low-income people," he says. "For them, housing is a crisis. And the emergency is tonight."

One of the unhoused people Colville and Amistad are in community with is sixty-nine-year-old Kathleen McKenzie, who goes by the name Gypsy. One January morning in 2023, McKenzie woke up on the steps of a New Haven church, her sleeping bag completely covered in snow. She considers herself lucky that she survived the night.

That same winter, Christina Del Santo spent most of her nights in New Haven drop-in shelters, perpetually wary of the often-intoxicated men surrounding her. Del Santo had been attacked in shelter settings before, so she tried to get some sleep with her shoes and coat on and the proverbial one eye open. Each morning at 6:15, she and the others were ushered back out into the cold.[47]

McKenzie and Del Santo are among the millions of Americans whose incomes are too low to afford market-rate rent, yet also among the three of every four who are eligible for federal housing subsidies but don't receive them.[48] Over thirty thousand people sit on New Haven's subsidized housing waiting list.[49] For many of these people, there seem to be only two options: exposure to the elements by sleeping outdoors, or risking the danger and indignities that often come with congregate shelters.

Then, during the early months of the COVID pandemic in 2020, a third option emerged. In New Haven and in dozens of other US cities, the shuttering of shelters contributed to the growth of large encampments, often established on public land. The largest New Haven encampment, called "Tent City" by its residents, was located at a park alongside the West River.

Conditions in Tent City were far from ideal, but the residents looked after one another's needs and helped keep everyone safe. Colville and other Catholic Worker community members provided support. For a few years, local officials left the residents alone. But in March of 2023, the city sent in a backhoe, trucks, and dozens of police officers to destroy the encampments and force all the residents out.[50] Colville was one of the people arrested for refusing to leave the area.

New Haven mayor Justin Elicker justified the evictions and destruction on health and safety grounds.[51] The residents found the rationale ironic, given that a study published last year in the *Journal of the American Medical Association* showed that displacement of unhoused people from encampments actually exacerbates health crises.[52] The night after the New Haven tent city was bulldozed, one of the evicted residents died after a car in which he was sleeping caught fire.

With the city providing bulldozers but not housing, the Colvilles felt their longtime practices of hospitality were no longer enough. So they tacked up a sign in the Amistad backyard declaring the area a "Human Rights Zone." The pronouncement cites the Universal Declaration of Human Rights commitment to housing for all, along with the multiple human rights documents that prohibit the criminalization of homelessness. Then the Colvilles invited people who had been evicted from the encampments to set up their tents in the backyard and offered daily food and support.

"We realized that we don't have quote-unquote homeless people in New Haven: we have economic refugees," Colville says. "These are people who have been excluded from the economy because of jobs that don't pay living wages, and excluded from the housing market that has become a capitalist venture focused on favoring the rich and the wealthy developers that serve them."

Among those who came to stay behind the Amistad House were McKenzie and Del Santo. "When I first arrived, I slept almost constantly for three days. I was exhausted, and it was the most safe and most stable I had felt in years," Del Santo told me in an interview. "This place saved my life, definitely."

When she references safety and stability, Del Santo makes it clear that she is referring to something more than the limited protection from the elements provided by her backyard tent. Government officials may look at encampments and see only health code violations and shelter needs they believe are better met in institutional settings. But those officials are missing a lot, Del Santo and McKenzie and others insist.

"Encampments can offer community, safety, security, companionship, autonomy, and pooled resources to meet other practical needs," says the National Health Care for the Homeless Council. "Encampments prevent the need to carry around one's belongings all day and can offer a stability that overnight shelters cannot. Encampments also allow families to stay together and will accommodate pets. Hence, there are many practical, rational reasons why people would prefer to live in an encampment than stay at a shelter."[53]

Of all these factors, the residents of what they have named the Rosette Neighborhood Village (Amistad House is located on Rosette Street) emphasize the value of community. They established a self-governing structure with shared responsibilities, including with the pay-it-forward practice of preparing and serving meals to other unhoused individuals. During their first summer together, Rosette residents revived a long-dormant community garden on their street.

They also worked with the Colvilles and other supporters to launch a fundraising and friends-raising campaign, culminating on a late October Saturday when nearly a hundred volunteers helped install six tiny homes in the backyard. Now, eight people are living in the tiny homes, and about a dozen more are in adjacent tents. Portions of the Amistad House are being renovated to include community kitchen and shower areas for the Rosette Village residents.

Del Santo, Colville, and others point out that there is a great deal of unused or rarely used public space in New Haven and beyond, much of which could be used to house unsheltered people. And they align with housing experts like Jenny Schuetz of the Brookings Institution, who have long advocated for the relaxation of regulations that block shared housing and temporary structures.[54]

Rosette Village is showing how it can be done. "This is successful, and we are changing the way people think about the unhoused," Del Santo says. "This can happen anywhere, and we are showing an example of how things can be different."

Gypsy McKenzie agrees. The pushback against Rosette Village from city officials continues, but McKenzie decided during a local radio show interview to respond by singing her own adaptation of a Tom Petty classic:

> We need housing now
> And it ain't no lie
> You can keep on trying to push us around
> But we won't back down.[55]

Reflecting on all this activity, Colville traces it to biblical teachings. "At the common table in the Catholic Worker, we form our own individual and collective conscience about what the times are demanding of us. What is God doing in the world, and how are we being called to respond?" he says. "The conclusion is clear: In terms of a New Testament understanding, as long as there are homeless people existing in our community, our work is incomplete."

3. Religious Communities Can Build on Deep Scriptural and Historical Foundations to Advocate for Housing Justice

It is no accident that religious housing activists like Mark Colville, Rabbi Aaron Spiegel, and Andrea Palumbo say that both scripture and their traditions' histories provide a mandate to take action for housing rights. Christians, Jews, Muslims, and Buddhists alike can cite chapter and verse to support their housing advocacy.

Christianity and the Human Right to Housing

Christianity launches with the origin story of Jesus Christ being born into homelessness. No room at the inn was Jesus's first earthly struggle, one that millions of Americans share every day.[56] The infant Jesus's state of homelessness was renewed in his itinerant adulthood. Jesus told a would-be follower in Luke 9:58 that the life was one of struggle: "Foxes have dens and birds have nests, but the Son of Man has no place to lay his head."[57] (When the city government here in Indianapolis bulldozed an encampment a few years ago, one of its residents held up a sign, "How can you worship a homeless man on Sunday and persecute one on Monday?")[58]

Beyond his own personal unhoused condition, Jesus made it clear in Matthew 25:38 that he embodied all others who are left without a roof over their head: "I was a stranger, and you invited me in."[59] These messages should come as no surprise, since Jesus framed his agenda in his very first public address in the synagogue in Nazareth: "The Spirit of the Lord is on me, because he has anointed me to preach good news to the poor," he said, citing the prophet Isaiah.[60]

So how are Christians to respond to the needs of those who are unhoused? As Mark Colville says, the parable of the Good Samaritan provides an unequivocal answer: stop what we are otherwise doing and prioritize an immediate and full response that provides shelter and other basic needs, even to those people we find undeserving or even objectionable. "Go and do likewise," was the action item Jesus delivered in the conclusion of the parable.[61]

Helpfully, Jesus also provided a what-not-to-do illustration in another parable, the story of Dives and Lazarus. Dives was a rich man who ignored the poor Lazarus at the gate of his home, leading to Dives being condemned to eternal torment in Hades.[62] Simply put, it is unforgivable to enjoy abundance while others are unhoused. "Again, I tell you," Jesus said in Matthew 19:24, "it is easier for a camel to go through the eye of a needle than for a rich man to enter the Kingdom of God."[63]

The earliest Christians took Jesus's admonitions to heart, ensuring that housing and all other essential needs were met for all: "All who believed were together and had all things in common; they would sell their possessions and goods and distribute the proceeds to all, as any had need," was the community described in the Acts of the Apostles.[64] Further along in Acts: "There was not a needy person among them, for as many as owned lands or houses sold them and brought the proceeds of what was sold. They laid it at the apostles' feet, and it was distributed to each as any had need."[65]

The early church leader James—who some believe was Jesus's brother—said that the practice of ensuring that essential needs are met far exceeds the value of worship: "If a brother or sister is naked and lacks daily food, and one of you says to them, 'Go in peace; keep warm and eat your fill,' and yet you do not supply their bodily needs, what is the good of that?"[66]

This was not a throwaway line. Theologian David Bentley Hart insists that these maxims and the practices that followed them were the core of the early church. "The church was a kind of polity, and the form of life it assumed was not merely a practical strategy for survival; but rather the embodiment of its highest spiritual ideals."[67] In the era where the small group of Christians came together, community support for the needs of those who cannot otherwise meet them was not a foreign concept: historians estimate that more than three hundred thousand people in the city of Rome were receiving some sort of public assistance during this period.[68]

As Christianity grew, exhortations continued to ensure that housing and other essentials were provided to all. Saint Basil of Caesaria famously condemned the possession of any excess when others go without: "The bread in your hoard belongs to the hungry; the cloak in your wardrobe belongs to the naked; the shoes you let rot belong to the barefoot; the money in your vaults belongs to the destitute. All you might help and do not—to all these you are doing wrong."[69] One can only imagine how Basil would react to the 7.5 million American households who own multiple homes—and receive generous tax breaks for doing so—while a half million of their neighbors are homeless.[70]

Basil was not guilty of empty sermonizing. He gave away his inheritance to the poor, created housing for those in need, and provided health care through a hospital.[71]

During the same era, Saint Jerome reminded the faithful that Jesus's condemnation of the wealthy continued to be in force. "All riches come from injustice. Unless one person has lost, another cannot find. . . . The rich person is either an unjust person or the heir of one."[72] Saint Augustine of Hippo would later agree: "Riches are neither real nor are they yours. . . . Assisting the needy is justice."[73]

Christians in the Middle Ages acted in accordance with these admonitions, with the church bearing a primary societal responsibility of aiding the poor, particularly shelter when needed.[74] As social worker and Professor Alan Keith-Lucas writes in *The Poor You Will Have with You Always*, the church of the era was the go-to provider of "hospital, hospice, and sanctuary."[75]

Thomas Aquinas, widely regarded as the most influential theologian in the Roman Catholic tradition, lifted up the early church leaders' message in his thirteenth-century seminal work, *Summa Theologica*: "According to natural law, goods that are held in superabundance by some people should be used for the maintenance of the poor. . . . 'It is the bread of the poor you are holding back; it is the clothes of the naked that you are hoarding.'"[76] When Aquinas recognized that the government plays a critical role in the provision of those necessities like food and clothing, Keith-Lucas says he "came within measurable distance of calling for a welfare state."[77]

That small distance between Christian doctrine and a welfare state was later fully bridged by a series of post-Aquinas Christian clergy, laypeople, and organizations, who spent generations issuing full-throated exhortations for societal guarantees of universal housing and other necessities. Baptist minister George Washington Woodbey, born into slavery in the US and later known as "the Great Negro Socialist Orator," said that the financial struggle to afford a house and other needs should be in the past: "You will not have to worry about how you live any more than you need to worry now about whether you can walk on the street from this meeting."[78]

Later in the twentieth century, Roman Catholic John Cort helped found the Religion and Socialism working group of the organization that came to be known as the Democratic Socialists of America (DSA)—the same organization Andrea Palumbo belongs to today. Cort delighted in delivering speeches at Catholic parishes where he would read from the many papal encyclicals that called for ambitious welfare guarantees and restrictions on wealth accumulation. When he completed reading the excerpts, Cort would ask his audience to guess the author. Their most common response: Karl Marx.[79]

Judaism and the Human Right to Housing

For as long as he can remember, Alex Slabosky has felt an obligation to work for justice. His mother Molly chaired the social action committee at Congregation Ohabai Sholom, known as "the Temple," the Reform Judaism congregation in Nashville, Tennessee, where Slabosky grew up. While Molly coordinated projects like the purchase and renovation of homes for low-income families, Slabosky's father David reached out to ailing veterans along with fellow members of the B'nai B'rith service organization.

Molly Slabosky was also active in the National Council of Jewish Women, which cites as the guide for its long legacy of civil rights activism the straightforward admonition of Deuteronomy 16:18: "Justice, justice, shall you pursue."[80] The Temple was so actively involved in the historic movement to desegregate Nashville restaurants and stores that its rabbi was physically attacked by white separatists. The Temple received bomb threats, and dynamite destroyed the front of the Jewish Community Center. The Temple still has a social action fund in the elder Slaboskys' names.

Such were the topics of discussion at both the Slabosky family dinner table and at temple. "Reform Judaism talks about justice, justice, justice—and going out and taking action," Slabosky told me in our interview. He quotes Isaiah's admonition: "Is not this the fast that I have chosen? To loose the bonds of wickedness, to undo the heavy burdens, and to let the oppressed go free, and that ye break every yoke?

"These are the messages we would hear constantly at religious school and services," Slabosky says. So it was natural for him to close out his career as the leader of Indiana nonprofit health organizations by cochairing a statewide push to expand Medicaid under the Affordable Care Act. That campaign succeeded, making Indiana one of the first Republican-led states to expand Medicaid. Then, Slabosky turned his attention to the affordable housing crisis.

Slabosky and his wife Marcella helped lead the Indianapolis Hebrew Congregation's involvement with Family Promise of Greater Indianapolis, a partnership of congregations and community groups providing housing and other services to homeless families. Slabosky served as Family Promise's board president and now is a member of the steering committee of the statewide housing needs coalition. He helped persuade the Greater Indianapolis Multifaith Alliance to dedicate itself to housing, which resulted in the Alliance helping to coordinate the local eviction court watch program—and Slabosky to join the organization's board of directors. Diving deep into advocacy comes naturally, Slabosky says. He is just following the charge he has heard all his life: "The message I've been given is very clear: we as a community have an obligation to support these people who are struggling."

Abraham's radical act of hospitality in Genesis 18:1–15, where he rushed to welcome three strangers and in so doing welcomed God, has a special and enduring impact for Jews. Rabbi Stephen Lewis Fuchs, formerly president of the World Union for Progressive Judaism, says that Abraham's founding example, along with the Jewish experience of spending extended periods in collective exile, inspired the commandment to welcome the stranger. That commandment is stated in the Torah no fewer than thirty-six times, the most-repeated mitzvah in the scripture.[81]

"With this interpretation of the narrative structure of Genesis 18, Jewish tradition expressed one of its own majestic ideas," writes Jonathan Sacks, chief rabbi of the United Hebrew Congregations of the Commonwealth. "Greater is the person who sees God in the face of the stranger than one who sees God as God in a vision of transcendence, for the Jewish task since the days of Abraham is not to ascend to heaven but to bring heaven down to earth in simple deeds of kindness and hospitality."[82]

An annual reminder of the heaven-to-earth task is provided in the Passover celebration, where Jews reflect on their history as a people who have needed some kindness and hospitality themselves. Starting with Adam and Eve's eviction from the Garden of Eden, through the forty years of Israelites wandering after the Exodus, to extended periods of being without a homeland after each destruction of the Temple, the Jewish people have too often struggled to find a home. It is this collective experience that triggers an obligation stated in Leviticus 19: "The stranger who resides with you shall be to you as one of your citizens; you shall love him as yourself, for you were strangers in the land of Egypt."

To that broad obligation the Law of Moses affixed tangible tasks. Jews are instructed to leave for the poor a portion of their harvests from fields, olive trees, and grapevines. Interest-free loans must be provided to those in need, and the Sabbath (*shmita*) and Jubilee (*yovel*) years require debt forgiveness and free access to harvests for the poor. Tithes shall go to widows, orphans, and the homeless.

Multiple passages in the Torah make it clear that practices that redistribute wealth are not just acts of charity by those with excess. Isaiah affirmed that the poor have human rights that must be enshrined in the law. He condemned leaders who "make iniquitous decrees, who write oppressive statutes, to turn aside the needy from justice and to rob the poor of my people of their right." More explicitly related to housing, Isaiah called Jews to "bring the homeless poor into your homes."

Rabbi Jill Jacobs, a Conservative rabbi writing on "Judaism and the Homeless," says that Jewish law, halakah, includes the rights of the poor to housing. "Housing [is] one of the obligatory types of tzedakah. The Bible commands that a poor person be granted 'sufficient for what lacks, according to what is lacking to him,'" she writes. "One Talmudic text understands each phrase in that command as referring to a specific type of assistance one might grant a poor person: 'Sufficient for what he lacks'—this is a house. 'What is lacking'—this is a bed and table."

(Jacobs also addresses the fact that most texts of the era—in multiple religious traditions—focus on the requirement to feed the poor, rather than housing the poor. In these eras, Jacobs notes, housing was quite a bit cheaper and easier to obtain than a consistent food source. Those feed-the-poor mandates translate today to a house-the-poor mandate, she says.)[83]

As Rabbi Jacobs and other Jewish scholars point out, these requirements trigger obligations for Jews today under the concept of tzedakah, a term whose root word *tzedek* literally means justice. "Tzedakah is sometimes translated today as charity, but it's not charity," Rabbi Michael Knopf of Temple Beth-El in Richmond, Virginia, says. "The analogy is to our current tax system. People had obligations to give to tzedakah in a graduated way—people who had more had to give more, people who had less were required to give less. And there were priorities for how it should be used, chief among them providing for the physical well-being of persons in the community who were in need."[84]

"The term 'human rights' does not appear in the Bible or in rabbinic literature," Rabbi Knopf says. "But when you distill down to the essence what a community has an obligation to provide people, and the claim people can make on the community, it boils down to rights by another name."

This is not to say there is no personal Jewish obligation to those who struggle for housing. For example, medieval rabbinic scholars Moses Maimonides and Jacob ben Asher both outlined landlords' obligations to treat their tenants well.[85] But, as Rabbi Knopf points out, there is a collective responsibility as well. The Mishnah—the first major work of rabbinical literature—makes it clear that the obligations to assist the poor can and should be discharged by the collective.

"This is the rabbinic moment: the move from a personal obligation for each and every person, to an obligation upon each and every person, which is mediated by the city," says Professor and Rabbi Aryeh Cohen, writing on "Justice, Wealth, Taxes: A View from the Perspective of Rabbinical Judaism." "Formerly, each person had an individual obligation which was fulfilled by transferring resources to a specific poor person. Now, each person's obligation is fulfilled by transferring resources to the city, which distributes them to the poor in an equitable manner. . . . This is a move from the personal to the political."[86]

Advocacy for that kind of government-provided, society-wide assistance has long been a path for Jews to fulfill their obligations to pursue justice. The early twentieth-century Jewish Labor Bund in Russia and Poland, and their heirs in the US, made improvements in housing a central demand of their movement.[87] The twentieth-century tenant rights movement in New York City, the most consistent and insistent such movement in US history, was led at multiple stages by Jewish communities.[88] Today, the Union for Reform Judaism has formally affirmed in its adopted resolutions that housing for all should be a societal goal.[89]

"Starting with Genesis and all the way through rabbinical literature and more recent response literature, Jewish text and traditions tell such a clear story of commitment to centering the widow, the stranger, the most oppressed, and building a society of norms, laws and values to protect the most vulnerable," Rabbi Jonah Dov Pesner, director of the Religious Action Center of Reform Judaism, which advocates for the right to housing, told me in an interview. "The physical house, along with things like health care and food security, are the tangible, concrete ways we actualize this vision God had for us."[90]

Rabbi Pesner's call, and the scriptures he cites, continue to resonate with Alex Slabosky. Although religious groups in Indiana already provide emergency services and eviction interventions, he is challenging them to do more. "We are not going to solve the homelessness and eviction problems until we create more affordable housing," he says. "And that means pushing for more government investment, at not just the federal level but at the local level," he says.

"The community together has an obligation to see that justice is done."

Islam and the Human Right to Housing

Like Judaism, Islam embraces Abraham as a patriarch, and also as a model for ensuring that all people have a safe and secure place to lay their heads. Both Islamic and Jewish traditions hold that Abraham designed his tent with four entrances, facing north, south, east, and west, just so he could welcome guests coming from all directions of the compass.[91] In Islam, Abraham is known as Abu-l-Dhifan, the father of hosts, the example to be followed by future generations.[92]

The Quran features multiple unequivocal mandates that Muslims must ensure that the needs of all people are met, including the core requirement of safe and secure shelter. "Hast thou seen the one who denied religion? That is the one who drives away the orphan and does not urge feeding the indigent."[93] Also: "In their wealth is an acknowledged right for the needy and destitute."[94]

Multiple hadiths expand on those statements, including, "He is not a Muslim who goes to bed satiated while his neighbor goes hungry."[95] The Prophet's servant, Anas ibn Malik, said, "A house which is not entered by a guest is not entered by angels."[96] And the Prophet himself stated "It will be taken from their rich and given to those in the community in need."[97]

The tangible application of these mandates is evidenced on an individual level by zakat, one of Islam's five pillars. Zakat requires that Muslims contribute a significant share of their wealth to the needs of others who struggle.[98] On a systemic level, the earliest days of Islam, dating back to the Prophet-founded state of Medina, showed a commitment to meeting the shelter needs of all. The first caliphate, Abu Bakr, the Prophet's father-in-law, instituted a guaranteed minimum income.[99] Caliph Umar issued a similar mandate that all in need have their necessities met by the community.[100]

Islam's prohibitions against hoarding are colorful and unequivocal: "Woe to every slanderer backbiter who gathers wealth and counts it over, thinking that his wealth has made him immortal. By no means. He will be thrown into the Crusher."

These antihoarding admonitions have been the inspiration for multiple Islamic societies that functioned as welfare states, guaranteeing that shelter and other needs were met for all.[101] That practice was codified in the Cairo Declaration on Human Rights in Islam in 1990, Article 17(c): "The state shall ensure the rights of the individual to a decent living that may enable him to meet his requirements and those of his dependents, including food, clothing, *housing*, education, medical care, and all other basic needs" (emphasis added).[102] Modern-day Muslims find that same obligation in their scriptures. The organization American Muslim Healthcare Professionals was part of an interfaith advocacy coalition that worked in 2017 to stop the attempted repeal of the Affordable Care Act. "There is a verse in the Holy Qur'an that if you save one life, it is as if you have saved all humanity," AMHP's director, Arshia Wajid, told me in an interview. "All faiths have similar sayings where human beings are prompted to fight for social justice and help their fellow brethren."[103] Specifically targeting housing, the US congresswoman Ilhan Omar, a Muslim, has taken on the role of chief sponsor of the Homes for All Act, which would dramatically expand the public housing stock in the United States and guarantee housing as a human right.[104]

Iman Javed, a medical resident and active member of the Muslim Caucus of the Democratic Socialists of America, says that support for guarantees of all human needs is spurred on by the Muslim faith. "There's so many different statements in the Quran and in the hadith that clearly point to the goal of the society being to provide for the needs of everyone, and discussing how can we create a more just society," he told me in an interview. "The Quran itself says, 'Work toward justice, even if it means justice against yourself.' So, any step we take toward a more socialist society is taking a step toward that goal of being able to provide for everyone's needs. It's just really clear as day."[105]

Buddhism and the Human Right to Housing

Buddhism embraces as a core notion the interdependence of all beings. "Your suffering is my suffering," a saying attributed to the Buddha goes. "Your happiness is my happiness."[106] Buddhists like Kenneth Inada, professor of philosophy and longtime editor of the SUNY Press Buddhist Studies Series, conclude that interdependence is deeply connected to the idea of human rights: "It can be asserted that the Buddhist sees the concept of human rights as a legal extension of human nature. It is a crystallization, indeed a formalization, of the mutual respect and concern of all persons, stemming from human nature."[107]

Since they believe that necessities like housing must be guaranteed at the societal level and that unrestrained wealth-gathering jeopardizes universal welfare, many Buddhists have concluded that the dhamma, the teaching of the Buddha, points toward socialism. They include monks and political leaders in the "Dhammic Socialism" movement, supporters of a tradition called Buddhist Economics, and current-day socialist activists.[108]

Among this group is Tenzin Gyatso, the fourteenth Dalai Lama, spiritual leader of the Tibetan people. The Dalai Lama has said, "Of all the modern economic theories, the economic system of Marxism is founded on moral principles, while capitalism is concerned only with gain and profitability. . . . For those reasons, the system appeals to me, and it seems fair."[109]

More specifically on the question of housing, Inada identifies the struggle of the unhoused as a struggle that is borne by all beings, which in turn must inspire actions to make dramatic change: "Our eyes turn away from homelessness as if it were somebody else's problem," he writes. "But, guided by Buddha's eyes of loving-kindness, our eyes can be opened and transformed into kind and gentle ones, eyes that see the suffering of others, because we know we are part of the cause of that suffering. The actions that naturally flow from this transformation create new causes and conditions that will inevitably change our society and our world."[110]

As the editors of the Buddhist journal *Buddhistdoor Global* have written, citing United Nations declarations and Finland's Housing First model, "No one should accept the lack of safe and stable housing as a natural or inevitable part of human society."[111] Buddhists across the world act on these mandates, including a US collaboration working with Catholics to create green affordable housing projects.[112]

4. Religious Communities Can Still Have a Powerful Effect on Public Policy

As we learned in previous chapters, the US's default approach to housing is to treat it as a commodity. Many are able to afford it, sometimes in opulence and abundance. Others go without. To mitigate these tragic outcomes, people from religious communities often choose charitable responses. Christian, Jewish, and Muslim congregations and organizations provide direct charitable housing support across the country.[113]

That response is fine, as far as it goes. But, as minister and housing advocate Peter W. Peters has written, "In my experience faith communities are far more comfortable with doing works of charity and reluctant to get into the work of advocacy."[114] Peters's observation lines up with survey data showing US religious communities and people lean toward philanthropy rather than pushing for systemic change.[115] Too many religious individuals and communities in the US prefer personal, voluntary, small-scale responses to poverty.

This approach reflects a US attitude that goes back at least as far as the early nineteenth century, when Alexis de Tocqueville observed that Americans were eager to form and support volunteer efforts.[116] Still today, more US households give to charity than households in comparable nations.[117] (Interestingly, the poor in the US are more charitable than the wealthy, when measured by the percentage of income they donate to those in need.)[118] But the US also spends far less on government social programs than comparable countries: only 19 percent of gross domestic product on assistance with essentials like housing, health care, and food, compared with 25–30 percent or more of GDP spent on those programs by Western European nations.[119]

The US being more charitable individually and less so on a societal level would be fine if the balance evened out. But it doesn't. That was demonstrated most disastrously in the 1980s, when President Ronald Reagan colorfully invoked the US soft spot for charity. "The truth is that we've let Government take away many things we once considered were really ours to do voluntarily out of the goodness of our hearts and a sense of community pride," Reagan pronounced. "I believe many of you want to do those things again."[120] Reagan said the housing crisis could be solved if only "every church and synagogue would take in 10 welfare families" each.[121]

Then, as we saw in chapter 2, Reagan and the US Congress used the cover of charity to justify slashing the US funding for subsidized housing by over 80 percent, throwing thousands of families and individuals into homelessness and chaos. The US charity system Reagan praised never came close to compensating for this devastation. As we know, more than a half million people are homeless across the country, and millions more are at the risk of losing their homes.[122]

In her 1998 book *Sweet Charity?*, the sociologist Janet Poppendieck reported on her study of the volunteers and structures of the food pantries and soup kitchens that sprang up in the 1980s as federal housing and other antipoverty programs were being scaled back. That spike in charitable efforts was laudable. But it was not matched by a similar increase in advocacy, which Poppendieck says was not a coincidence. "The growth of kindness and the decline in justice are intimately interrelated," Poppendieck writes. "This massive charitable endeavor serves to relieve pressure for more fundamental solutions."[123]

In other words, charity is not very effective at alleviating poverty, especially the grinding, every-month housing struggle that can't be fixed with a free meal or a winter coat donation. But charity does do a great job of alleviating the guilt over the suffering that is going on every day in our communities.

On a more tangible, fiscal, level, the US policy preference for charity robs the cupboard of what could be resources applied to government programs. Since 1917, US law has allowed individuals, corporations, and estates to deduct as much as half of their annual taxable income in an amount equal to charitable gifts made to qualified nonprofit organizations.[124] The US deduction provides the most generous incentive for charitable giving of any developed nation.[125]

As a result, the US Treasury estimated that the annual cost of those deductions in 2021 would be $56 billion, nearly the amount it would cost to give every eligible household in the US a housing voucher.[126] In addition, the so-called "plutocratic bias" of replacing government programs with tax-deductible donations has been demonstrated to favor charities that either don't target poverty—such as symphony sponsorships or college sports donations—or are inefficient at doing so. Those donations are especially deficient when compared to government programs—like housing assistance—that are proven to be remarkably effective at improving the health and well-being of the Americans that benefit.[127]

Religious Communities and Transcending Charity

Because of their direct service to the poor, religious communities are in an ideal position to persuasively point out that the US charity emperor has no clothes, especially when it comes to housing. From their front-line vantage point, these religious actors can point out that even their sometimes herculean charitable efforts are nowhere close to meeting the need.[128]

Religious people should insist that, as Saint Augustine said, "Charity is no substitute for justice withheld." In so doing, they can point out that this kind of justice comes from large-scale, community-wide efforts that can be accomplished only by governments acting in our name.[129] There is a strong biblical foundation for this position, Professor John D. Mason writes in *Biblical Teachings and the Objectives of Welfare Policy in the U.S.*:

> Assistance from the wider community becomes necessary. This is the consistent message of the entire Bible. It is taught clearly in the Law of Moses in the provisions to be considered immediately below. It is repeated systematically in the wisdom literature and by the prophets in their instructions to the princes of Israel (Job 29:7–12, Ps. 72, Jer. 22:15f, Ezek. 34, Micah 3). It is there in the well-known judgment scene of Matt. 25:31ff, and in Paul's admonitions for wealthier churches to provide economic assistance to their poorer brothers and sisters (II Cor. 8). Indeed, the fundamental message of the New Testament is that each one of us, however self-sufficient we may think we are, is so unable to avoid all the adversities of life, and thereby to resolve our ultimate problems on our own, that we need outside assistance.[130]

The point: it is clearly not enough for religious Americans to settle for the good vibes of individual charity. Vida Dutton Scudder, the early twentieth-century educator, activist, and writer honored with a feast day by the Episcopal Church USA, called philanthropy "a sedative to the public conscience." Fundraising efforts only "squeezed a little more reluctant money from comfortable classes, who groaned and gave but changed not one iota," Scudder said.[131]

Saint Basil in the fourth century cast the same side-eye toward charitable donations that came from the excess of the giver: "Whoever loves his neighbor as himself owns no more than his neighbor does. But you have a great fortune. How can this be, unless you have put your own interests above others?"[132]

So, instead of just writing a check from their surplus, religious people are called to raise their voices loud for justice. Croatian Christian theologian Miroslav Volf calls for a "public faith" of Christians vigorously advocating for the common good: "An authentic religious experience should be a world-shaping force."[133] In agreement with this demand for advocacy are Catholic popes like John Paul II in 1995 ("The Gospel of life [should] be implemented also by means of certain forms of social activity and commitment in the political field") and Francis in 2013 ("We need to participate for the common good. . . . Good Catholics immerse themselves in politics by offering the best of themselves so that the leader can govern.").[134]

In fact, Pope Francis has explicitly called for the human right to housing to be implemented, a call based on the Compendium of the Social Doctrine of the Church, which describes housing as a human right.[135] During his 2015 visit to the US, Francis lunched with several hundred homeless and low-income people at St. Patrick's Church in Washington, DC. "Let me be clear," he said on that visit. "There is no social or moral justification, no justification whatsoever, for lack of housing."[136]

The Evangelical Lutheran Church in America has stated that "housing is a fundamental human right."[137] The Episcopal Church in 2018 adopted a resolution similarly affirming housing as a human right.[138] The Book of Discipline of the United Methodist Church supports equal access to housing for all.[139] The Church of Jesus Christ of Latter Day Saints' Doctrines and Covenants requires church bishops to gather the collective's resources and redistribute them as the Acts of Apostles society did, "according to their wants and needs."[140]

Congresswoman Cori Bush, an ordained minister, slept on the steps of the US Capitol in August 2021 as part of her successful advocacy for an extension of the COVID-era eviction moratorium.[141] Her motivation, as she explained later: "Housing is a human right."[142] Bush's sleep-in was joined by several other members of Congress and faith-motivated activists, including Representative Jimmy Gomez of California. Gomez told the National Catholic Reporter, "Growing up Catholic, but also my parents looking out for the community, just taught me that when somebody's suffering, when someone's hurting, you want to try and go and relieve that suffering and that hurt. . . . Caring for other people is how my parents raised me and how I was raised in the church."[143]

Every week, versions of that same message are delivered in synagogues, mosques, and other houses of worship. Jews are directed to push for a systemic response to the housing crisis, says Rabbi Jonah Dov Pesner. "I would argue that the whole framework of biblical literature is an attempt to set up a system of justice in which the marginalized are centered," says Pesner, who has written on the Jewish history of creating social welfare systems dating back to the Talmudic period.[144] "There are all these regulations behind that such as the gleaning of the fields and not delaying payment to workers. There are systems and legal frameworks that don't hinge on the individual grace of one who has [food, shelter, money, etc.] choosing to share with one who doesn't."

Rabbi Jill Jacobs agrees that Jewish teaching recognizes that full provision of basic needs like housing can be accomplished only by government institutions acting for the collective. "What is the most effective way for us to create the society envisioned by Jewish law? Charitable donations to organizations that help house the homeless are one obvious way," she writes. "But with a problem this large and complex, a more effective means of working to end homelessness might be political action, advocating for governmental policies and programs that provide housing to those in need and/or give people the means to afford housing on their own."[145]

US Christians, Jews, Muslims, and Buddhists are provided with an abundance of opportunities to act on these mandates to elevate housing as a human right. Representative Omar's groundbreaking legislation and the broader call to treat housing as a human right are supported by a wide range of advocacy groups, including the National Low Income Housing Coalition, People's Action, the Center for Popular Democracy, and tenant unions across the country.[146]

The campaigns for universal affordable housing access, rent control, tenants' rights, and decriminalizing homelessness all take important steps in the direction of decommodifying housing. Active religious community support would significantly bolster the cause. Religious communities can persuasively make the case that a market-driven approach is no more sufficient in housing than it is in infrastructure like roads and sewers, or for public safety like fire responses, or with schools, the postal service, parks, and justice systems—all core societal requirements that are considered common goods.

Instead of inadequate, patchwork charity, a public guarantee of housing for all should be the destination all religious communities push us toward. As Saint Gregory said in the sixth century, indelibly framing the struggle of the unhoused in human rights terms, "When we furnish the destitute with any necessity we render them what is theirs, not bestow on them what is ours. We pay the debt of justice rather than perform the works of mercy."[147]

Today, we are blessed with a vibrant, growing movement, led in significant part by tenants themselves, demanding that this debt of justice be paid. That movement is the subject of this book's final two chapters.

BUILDING A MOVEMENT

On a recent weekday morning in Indianapolis, one court docket featured 152 households facing eviction in a single half-day session. This is just one of ten courts in our city that issue orders putting people out of our homes. With about five hundred new eviction cases filed here each week, even that many courts struggle to keep up.

As for the tenants, they trudge into court in groups of ones or twos. Some climb out of cars already stuffed with their belongings. Others walk to court from home or remote bus stops, sometimes carrying or leading small children. Many days, there are far more people congregated than there are folding chairs in the rooms outside the courtroom. Most of the time, everyone retains kindness and courtesy. When chairs get scarce, elderly people get precedence, then pregnant moms.

So many people facing eviction, but all doing so alone.

What if that changed?

The history of social movements shows time and again that dramatic, sweeping change is possible. World-changing moments usually happen only after years of effort, but then often occur quite suddenly, with tipping-point timing that can surprise even the movement activists themselves.[1]

Housing movements are no exception. As we saw in chapter 9, nations like Finland and Singapore have far more affordable housing and far less homelessness than the US. The impressive social housing track record in those and other nations did not emerge out of a vacuum: reforms happened because of advocacy. Their origins can be traced to tenant and labor union campaigns in Sweden, grassroots organizing in Germany for expropriating corporate landlord property, activists occupying banks and homes in Spain, and a postwar socialist movement in Austria.[2]

Arguably the most consistent and insistent housing movement in the US was the twentieth-century tenant rights movement in New York City. Tenants used tactics ranging from rent strikes to lobbying politicians to win multiple struggles with individual landlords on issues of rent increases and poor conditions, as well as the enactment of broader rent regulation and tenant control of housing.[3] After the 1963 March on Washington and Martin Luther King Jr.'s final Poor People's Campaign both featured demands for housing rights, the St. Louis Rent Strike of 1969 helped create changes in federal housing law that reduced public housing rents.[4] As we mentioned in chapter 10, the St. Louis strike and other US tenant activism had deep connections to faith communities.[5] The St. Louis action was followed in the 1970s by successful rent strikes and other actions across the country that led to the forming of the National Tenants' Union.[6]

Now, a current wave of campaigns is winning rent control measures, affordable housing funding, and tenants' bills of rights.[7] Activists are canvassing door to door, occupying vacant buildings, and pushing ballot initiatives to win social housing commitments in cities like Minneapolis, Philadelphia, San Francisco, Baltimore, and Los Angeles.[8] In Oakland, a two-and-a-half-year rent strike by a building's renters forced the for-profit owner to sell to a community land trust.[9] Community activists are engaged in current social housing campaigns in Las Vegas, Philadelphia, California, Rhode Island, Kansas City, Seattle, New York, and beyond.[10]

The National Low-Income Housing Coalition is leading a "HoUSed" campaign to expand rental assistance to every eligible household and create a national housing stabilization fund to provide emergency help.[11] Chicago activists erected a tent city in the lobby of City Hall during the mayor's 2022 budget address, to dramatize the need for an increase in the real estate transfer tax on properties over $1 million.[12] Tenants took over the yearly conference of the National Multifamily Housing Council in September 2022, chanting "Down with corporate greed!" and "Housing is a human right!" and then seizing the stage to talk about their struggles to afford rental housing.[13]

Rent control advocacy is robust in California, Florida, and Michigan, while North Carolina community groups and Philadelphia tenants are targeting corporate landlords.[14] The campaigns share a common theme: we must reclaim our housing system from those whose sole mission is to extract as much money as possible from people who need a roof over their heads to survive. As Professor Keeanga-Yamahtta Taylor, author of *Race for Profit: How Banks and the Real Estate Industry Undermined Black Homeownership*, says, "Solving the perpetual

US housing crisis is complex, but it begins by disconnecting the power of government from the private sector's insatiable profit motive."[15]

Across the US, tenants are starting to come together to make that happen. I had the chance to spend time with tenants in Louisville, Kentucky, who are helping lead the way.[16]

"We Need Housing in This Spot, Not a Rich Kid Parking Lot!"

Private police officers guide a line of late-model SUVs through the January morning's cold rain, waving them into a lane of Louisville's Grinstead Avenue specially cleared all the way to the entrance of Collegiate School. As brake lights flash through the gloom, children in plaid uniforms climb out of the vehicles and head inside. Collegiate, founded by a plantation-owning Kentucky family and led by a board president who is the heir to the Brown-Forman liquor dynasty, has a tuition of $26,000 per year.

Just to the west of a new, modern Collegiate playground is the Yorktown Apartments, separated from the school grounds by a chain-link fence topped with barbed wire. Outside one of the Yorktown buildings, where the monthly rent averages $845, two dozen people stand in the rain. Jasmine Harris, her winter coat partially open to show a crimson red Louisville Tenants Union T-shirt, steps to a microphone facing television news cameras.

"Everyone deserves a home that is safe, but too many of us are choosing between medicines and food and paying the rent," she said. "And that ain't right!"[17]

"That ain't right!" repeat the people assembled behind Harris. Most are wearing the same red shirts.

"Landlords think they can treat us however," Harris continued. "They keep us living in terrible conditions and evict us if we speak up!"

"That ain't right!"

"Our landlords are nameless, faceless corporations like Collegiate School, and they want to demolish our homes to build parking lots!"

That, it turns out, is why these people have gathered this morning. A few years ago, Collegiate purchased Yorktown, which has thirty-five low-cost apartments in a community where city officials have agreed there is a need for thirty-one thousand more affordable housing units.[18] But Collegiate has other priorities: it is seeking government permission to tear down the Yorktown Apartments to clear the way for a fifty-six-car parking lot.

This time, the reply chant to Harris includes a young man with a bullhorn. The message is singsong, but quite specific.

"We need housing in this spot / Not a rich kid parking lot!"

Harris introduces several of the Yorktown residents. Across the courtyard from the speakers is a ground-level apartment with a two-foot-by-three-foot hole in its front door and broken windows surrounding it. The residents have already shown the gathered media their apartments, pointing out mold, rodent tracks, and water and fire damage. They describe futile efforts to get maintenance responses from Collegiate. "Since we got the notice in October that they want to tear the buildings down, they just quit taking care of the place," Yorktown resident Patrick McCarthy says.

Harris returns to the microphone and changes the tone from grievance to power. This press conference was scheduled to be a prelude to a local architectural review commission meeting set later that day, where Collegiate's demolition application was on the agenda. The tenants intended to show up at the meeting and make these same points, loudly. But Collegiate pulled its demolition request the day before, the second time it has done so when word of a protest was leaked.

Harris lists the demands for Collegiate: help tenants with moving costs and the increased rents for nearby living, and stop demolition plans until all tenants are safely relocated. These demands will be met, Harris insists. Six weeks later, at a meeting attended by Yorktown residents and other Louisville Tenants Union members, the local architectural review committee voted 3–2 to deny Collegiate's request to demolish the Yorktown buildings.[19]

"We are poor, we are working class, we are old, young, Black, brown, white, and everything in between. We are organizing across lines others use to divide us," Harris said. "We know the people who run Collegiate are the descendants of wealthy plantation owners, and they are used to pushing people like us out of the way."

"Tenants Will No Longer Be Silent"

The March 2020 killing of medical worker Breonna Taylor in her apartment by Louisville police officers led to months of demonstrations. One of the protest themes centered on the area's police violence and the raid on Taylor's apartment being fueled in part by government-funded gentrification and displacement in Louisville's historically Black neighborhoods.[20] In response to Taylor's killing, a group of advocates found that they shared deep and personal interests in the rights of tenants.

Harris and her children had been struggling to get their landlord to respond to unsafe conditions. Shemaeka Shaw had been assaulted by law enforcement during an eviction. Josh Poe from rural Kentucky and Jessica Bellamy from Louisville's urban Smoketown neighborhood had endured their own housing insecurity and were already organizing Black and white tenants. In early 2022, they and other renters came together to form the Louisville Tenants Union, or LTU.

The original LTU plan was to do a policy-focused effort, likely around a tenants' bill of rights with a right to counsel in eviction proceedings. But as they talked through these ideas, several of the LTU members reported problems they faced with the CT Group, a Maryland-based private corporation. CT Group had a contract with the Louisville Metro Housing Authority, or LMHA, to manage two of the city's largest public housing sites. LTU members and others in CT Group–managed housing were dealing with flooding, mold, rodents, and broken lights in parking areas, with little to no response to their outreach to management.

So, the tenants' bill of rights plans were put on hold, and the fight to improve public housing conditions began. "We organize through struggle," Josh Poe said. "Our vision as part of the national tenants' movement is a homes guarantee, but when we get a group of tenants together we have to deal with their immediate issues. That is how we build a powerful base—which ties into the larger goals."

So LTU shared tenant complaints on social media, used public records requests to document the pattern of neglect at CT Group–managed housing, and staged a "walk in" to present demands at an LMHA board meeting.[21] At a demonstration and press conference outside CT Group's local offices, Shemaeka Shaw said, "As an impacted resident, my mission is to create housing for every tenant in Louisville that is safe, decent and permanently affordable. We believe that housing is a human right, not a commodity."[22]

Shaw's self-description as an impacted tenant was an understatement. After growing up in Louisville, and never having been evicted or arrested before 2016, she endured a nightmarish sequence of events. First, she alleges that she was sexually assaulted by her landlord, who had a Section 8 housing contract with the LMHA. When Shaw reported the assault, the landlord retaliated by filing a court action for eviction, despite Shaw being current on her rent.

A mediation agreement with the landlord gave Shaw and her two-year-old son thirty days to move. But just ten days later, the landlord and two deputy sheriffs showed up at the home to put her out. When Shaw tried to explain the thirty-day agreement, one of the deputy sheriffs knocked her to the ground, carried her out of her home—in her nightgown and without underwear—and charged her with criminal trespassing and resisting arrest.

A jury eventually exonerated Shaw on all charges, and the sheriff deputy was later convicted of perjury and tampering with evidence on multiple cases.[23] But, by that time, Shaw had spent time in jail after her arrest and then had been hospitalized for the injuries she sustained. She lost most of her possessions in the process. Shaw and her son were homeless for eight months. "We were pillar to post, just living with what family would take us in," she said.

Shaw's next rental home failed four inspections for exposed wiring before catching fire in April 2018.[24] Again, she lost all her belongings. Remarkably, her renting troubles were still not over. Shaw and her son, along with a teenage niece, moved into yet another Section 8–subsidized home. She had neither the time nor resources to be choosy. So she did not know that her new landlord, who owned hundreds of properties, had been branded Louisville's worst landlord by a local television station investigation a few years earlier.[25] Shaw filed complaints with the city about serious mold and mildew problems, the windows being nailed shut, and some of the electricity not functioning. Her landlord responded by filing a court action to evict her.

So, in mid-May 2019, Shaw was again forcibly removed from her home and the locks changed. When she and some family and friends returned shortly after to pack up some of her items that the landlord and deputies had thrown into the yard, Shaw was again arrested, this time charged with felony burglary. She spent six days in jail.

Clearly, Shaw endured an exceptionally horrible set of harms and abuses. But she and other LTU members point out a larger theme: these were acts of state-sponsored violence, visited on Shaw when she challenged real estate capital. It is a response they say is part and parcel of the structural violence routinely visited on Black people in US communities.

Shaw and her son now live on Louisville's west side. She is convinced that tenants coming together is the best way to prevent others from enduring what she has experienced. "I've learned to redirect my trauma into fire," she said. "I would have had different outcomes if I had the tenant union behind me. The powers that be told me I was crazy, but that's harder to say when I am standing next to one hundred other people who have gone through the same thing."

So Shaw and other LTU members kept up the pressure on CT Group and the LMHA. When they made a presentation to the Louisville Metro Council about the crisis, they gained the attention of Metro councilor Jecorey Arthur. Arthur ended up joining LTU members at a press conference to announce he was filing a resolution calling for the LMHA to terminate its contract with the CT Group.

"The LTU is showing tenants they have power," Arthur said. "I've seen tenants who were hopeless about change get motivated by the union. Even if they haven't joined it yet, they are seeing a group of people who live where they live and go through what they go through get wins."

After weeks of tenants advocating to council members, the Metro Council unanimously passed Arthur's resolution. Less than a week later, the CT Group announced it was walking away from its contract with the LMHA. The city's top newspaper, the *Louisville Courier-Journal*, made it clear why that happened: the decision was due to "consistent pressure from members of the Louisville Tenants Union."[26]

Councilor Arthur agrees. "The LTU made an example out of the CT Group," he said. "The example was that tenants will no longer be silent about housing injustice. They believed in a better future, organized for it, and won."

Demanding a "Fair Lease"

Jasmine Harris's path to a microphone in front of Yorktown Apartments traveled through her own housing struggles. She and her children have endured homelessness, including a period of several nights where the only spot they could find was in the lobby of a family shelter where every bed was already full. Harris, who was eight months pregnant, huddled in a chair with her infant daughter, with Harris's coat serving as their blanket. Finally, Harris persuaded a relative to let them sleep on her couch, then she eventually got an apartment owned by an organization called New Directions.

The apartment was better than being homeless. But, from day one, when her daughter crawled on the carpet and came up with her leggings stained black from dirt, Harris experienced problems with the home. She and other residents called for maintenance help with mold, discolored tap water, and infestations of roaches, mice, and bedbugs. The responses were slow, when they happened at all. Harris received the same reaction when she notified management about her ceiling caving in because of water leaks above. "At one point, the manager told me, 'Ms. Harris, if you don't like it here, you can just turn in your keys.'"

Harris had a better idea. She already had experience as a community activist in campaigns against police brutality and for healthy food options in the neighborhood. "I knew that the more people who speak up, the better," she said. "I knew there was power in numbers." She began reading about the history of tenant organizing, and then pulled her neighbors together to form the New Directions Tenant Union.

They began by putting together a list of demands, mostly focusing on maintenance response. Harris had learned that the landlord-tenant transaction is at its core a contractual relationship, so they decided to start changing the terms of that contract. "The landlords have tons of lawyers who write up the leases in a way that gives them all the power and nothing to the residents," Harris said. So the tenants began organizing over the demand that the landlord sign a new, "Fair Lease."

Variations of the Fair Lease have been included in demands in other national tenant campaigns. They take most of the tenants' bill of rights terms, including rent control and good-cause eviction protections, and put them into the individual rental contract. The model Fair Lease limits rent increases to no more than 2 percent each year and requires fast and full response to maintenance requests. It provides tenants with automatic renewal to prevent against eviction by lease termination.

After drafting their Fair Lease, the tenant union gathered together other tenants and community supporters and held a rally. They marched to the New Directions complex office to present the Fair Lease, waving signs like "No more bugs / No more mold / Bring our buildings up to code."[27] (I reached out to a New Directions spokesperson, who denied Harris's claims that it did not respond to tenants' complaints, and pointed out that its properties pass regular federal housing inspections.)

The Fair Lease has not yet been accepted, but the New Directions union has had other victories. It fought off the landlord's plans to allow police unrestricted access to enter the residents' apartments, and it helped one union member resist three separate attempts to evict her. "I have never had anyone to support me like this," the resident told a local television station as the union members occupied the complex office until her new lease was signed. "If things aren't right, speak up," she said to the TV cameras. "There are people out here who have your back."[28]

Government-Funded Gentrification

Jessica Bellamy grew up on Lampton Street in Smoketown, a neighborhood southeast of downtown Louisville. After the Civil War, thousands of formerly enslaved Black people moved to Smoketown from rural areas. Bellamy's mother owns Shirley Mae's Café, a soul food restaurant on the corner of Clay and Lampton Streets, where Bellamy has worked on and off since she was twelve years old. The restaurant founded by Shirley Mae Beard, Bellamy's grandmother, is well known for hosting during Kentucky Derby week the Salute to Black Jockeys festival, which has attracted the likes of B. B. King, Morgan Freeman, and Whoopi Goldberg. "I grew up seeing what is possible when people come together in community," Bellamy said.

But when the notorious HUD HOPE VI program triggered the 2012 demolition of more than three hundred units of public housing in Smoketown, gentrification forces emerged.[29] When Bellamy began organizing community members to resist, she was surprised to learn who was bankrolling the opposition. "It turned out that the main gentrifiers are developers funded by the city," she said. Bellamy points to multimillion-dollar projects in historically Black neighborhoods where city dollars were going to developers aiming to create market-rate housing, despite that housing being unaffordable for current residents. She cites Census figures showing that one historically Black neighborhood in Louisville, Russell, lost almost twenty-five hundred Black residents from 2010 to 2020, with a corresponding influx of white, likely wealthier, residents.[30]

This story is not unique to Louisville. When Robert came to the Indianapolis eviction court where my students and I represent tenants, his case initially made no sense. His landlord had filed for eviction against Robert, alleging he had paid his rent late. But Robert had receipts to show differently. Lots of receipts. Robert, now in his eighties, had been living in his apartment for more than two decades.

When we confronted the landlord's attorney with this, he shrugged. "OK, we'll dismiss this case," he said. "But his lease is up in three months anyway, and the new property owner is not going to renew."

It turns out the attempt to evict Robert was one of a stack of cases filed by the investor-owned real estate company that recently purchased his building. The plan was to clear out the current tenants, most of whom were, like Robert, Black and longtime residents of the neighborhood. The next steps were to make a few cosmetic changes in the building, rename it, and start renting to the wealthier, predominately white people who had begun moving into Robert's neighborhood.

As we saw in chapter 3, Black households in our community have been displaced for generations. When Robert was younger, the era of "urban renewal" saw the bulldozing of entire blocks of Black communities near downtown to make way for interstate highways, an urban university campus, and a medical complex.

In the surviving neighborhoods close to urban cores, a new wave of Black and working-class displacement is now occurring.[31] There are no government-contracted bulldozers clearing out Black-owned housing, so the current displacement is often portrayed as less connected to government policies than the urban renewal era of the mid-twentieth century. But today's gentrification is not simply the effects of shifting preferences for urban living or the so-called invisible hand of capitalism. Governments are making zoning decisions, investing in infrastructure, and handing over government land and federal development funds controlled by local governments to private capital. The displacement of Robert in Indianapolis, Jessica Bellamy's neighbors in Louisville, and hundreds of thousands of others in urban centers across the country is the intentional, predictable result of choices made by government policymakers.[32]

"Gentrification is not about a Starbucks suddenly appearing in a community," John Washington, an organizer with the Tenant Union Federation, says. "Displacement and homelessness are actually the goals of the architects of our housing market, and they are backed by government dollars and policy." The driving force of government handing over land, cash, and enormous tax subsidies to private developers—as we saw in chapter 4—is so undeniable that even the corporate-sponsored Center for American Progress admits that "displacement today is the result of policy choices."[33]

But not everywhere.

"Using Our Tax Dollars to Displace People Is No Longer Acceptable"

Bellamy and others' research showed that the Louisville local government had been repurposing US Department of Housing and Urban Development funds to distribute millions of dollars to developers. The developers used those funds on projects that spiked up the cost of housing for everyone in the community.[34]

So Bellamy and other residents worked with Councilor Arthur to draft a new antidisplacement ordinance. The terms were straightforward: if a project will result in housing costs that were unaffordable for a neighborhood's current residents, no local government money, land, or staff support will be provided. Like Bellamy, Arthur also grew up in Louisville's historically Black neighborhoods and had long fought against displacement—a musician and teacher, he recorded the song "Gentrification" in 2019. But he makes it clear that residents drove the ordinance campaign from day one.

"It is important for other cities that are trying to address displacement to realize that a remedy is not going to come just from electoral politics," Arthur says. "You need to have grassroots organizing at the center of the effort. That is what gets reform passed."

When Arthur introduced the legislation, most of the council refused to endorse it. Louisville mayor Craig Greenberg, a former developer himself, aggressively opposed it. But the Louisville Tenants Union and others canvassed door to door in support of the ordinance and held phone and text banks and public events in councilors' districts. They collected fifteen hundred signatures on a petition and recruited fifty organizations to endorse the ordinance.

"No one can articulate the struggle better than the people going through the struggle," Arthur says. So the residents spoke at community events and held one-on-one meetings with councilors. On the day of the November 2023 vote, the mayor sensed the momentum shifting and reached out to every councilor to lobby against the ordinance. But it was too late. The antidisplacement ordinance passed 25–0 and became law, even though the mayor refused to sign it. "The end result is that using our tax dollars to displace people is no longer acceptable to the people of Louisville," Arthur says.

Louisville joins Boston, which in 2020 adopted a similar requirement that developers seeking zoning approvals first meet antidisplacement guidelines.[35]

Housing researchers at the RVA Eviction Lab say the Louisville ordinance is changing the narrative and stopping government complicity in Black displacement. The Lawyers Committee for Civil Rights says the Louisville example will inspire other communities to follow suit.

John Washington agrees, saying the national tenant union movement is looking to build on the Louisville victory. "This ordinance is so valuable because governments have for too long been deflecting their responsibility for gentrification," he says. "People living in these neighborhoods have pointed the finger right back at government, demanding it stop displacing entire communities."

Jessica Bellamy has advice for other communities struggling with displacement. "You got to be all the way done with waiting for someone else to do something," she says. "Anyone can do this—and should do this, all over the damn country."

"Shared Self-Interest" from Appalachia to Louisville

Josh Poe's mother was just fifteen years old when he was born. Raised mostly by his grandparents, Poe grew up in the Appalachian region of northeastern Kentucky in a home without an indoor bathroom. He started working in the tobacco fields at age seven. None of that prevented his family and community from providing him a model of advocacy and solidarity. Tobacco farming, Poe points out, was essentially a socialist enterprise, with price supports and quotas that benefited smaller farmers. "That did not come from any big farmer's benevolence, it came about because farmers organized. And that shaped my understanding of political power," he said.

Like many people in his rural community, Poe became addicted to opioids as a young man. After his addiction spread to heroin, Poe was homeless for a time. He was incarcerated for a while, too. Others in his family died as a result of addiction, but Poe eventually made it into recovery.[36] After organizing housing and labor campaigns in Seattle, he returned to Kentucky. There he met Bellamy, and they bonded over how their seemingly dissimilar backgrounds were actually not so different. "I learned the geography of Smoketown and Appalachia have a lot of material commonalities," Poe said. "It just showed how much shared self-interest poor white people have with Black people."

Although many of LTU's current campaigns revolve around historically Black communities, it has several white members and has helped organize mostly white trailer park residents on Louisville's south side and elsewhere in Kentucky. Like Poe, LTU member Steph Smith grew up poor in Appalachian eastern Kentucky.

Her family was often forced to move from dilapidated trailers when lot rental fees spiked, or mold or other conditions got too bad. They slept in other family members' living rooms or in an old church.

"I come from 'Trump country,' and I know some people hear my accent and wonder if I am racist," she said. "But it became clear to me that poor white people in Appalachia being taught to hate Black people was a way to make it easier for the capitalist ruling class to exploit all of us generation after generation."

The LTU meetings feature testimonials where Black and white tenants get the chance to see their own experiences reflected in other people's stories, including people they have been taught to see as their enemy. LTU members say their experiences give lie to any narrative that Black people and whites cannot be organized together in a tenant movement. "That is why the LTU and tenant organizing in general is so dangerous," Smith said. "I've never been a part of something that gives me so much optimism and keeps racking up tangible, material wins."

Under the banner of an organization they call Root Cause Research Center, Bellamy and Poe have gathered a wealth of data and analysis on Kentucky poverty and injustice. But they say this LTU multiracial organizing, not statistics or rhetoric, is the real key to reform. "There is not a report that Josh and I have written that brought material change," Bellamy said. "It is going to take people standing up as their own political class to get these wins."

"We Are the Ones to Keep Us Safe"

In collaboration with the People's Action Homes Guarantee campaign, which mobilizes tenants across the country, LTU members including Shemaeka Shaw traveled to the White House to demand that President Biden issue an executive order on rent control and other tenant relief measures.[37] Biden responded with a "Blueprint for a Renter's Bill of Rights." It was short on tangible guarantees, but it did include a statement of federal commitment to protecting tenants. Organizers decided to use that statement as a foundation for continued pressure.[38]

Tara Raghuveer, the leader of the Tenant Union Federation and of KC Tenants, says that LTU is at the core of the national movement, proving that tenants can have success even in the challenging political geography of a southern city. "The Louisville Tenants Union represents a new edge to the tenant movement, with deepening roots throughout the South and the Midwest," she said in an interview with me. "They are building durable infrastructure that is already transforming political terrain in Louisville and will continue to set the pace for tenants across the country."[39]

So, even as it was winning the CT Group campaign and other interim victories for local tenants, the LTU has kept one eye on its broader goals. Along with its national work, the LTU pushes for statewide laws instituting rent control, good-cause requirements for evictions, and a "clean hands" requirement that would block landlords with pending code violations from evicting tenants.[40] It aims to transform the community's landlord-tenant dynamic so that tenants can start dictating the terms of the relationship, especially through the Fair Lease terms.

Almost every LTU leader has experienced homelessness and retaliation for speaking up for tenant rights. They have too many battle scars to harbor any illusion that the process will be easy. In a conversation among LTU leaders, Shaw swept her hand toward the entire group: "We are all traumatized," she said. The others nod in agreement. But their response is to tangibly embrace the power of a union. "We are the ones to keep us safe," she added.

Back at the Yorktown Apartments, Harris describes to the crowd how LTU members went to Washington multiple times to pressure the Biden administration. "If we can take on the White House, we are not afraid to take on wealthy Louisville elites," Harris said into the microphone. "We are here to promise that if Collegiate does not meet the tenants' demands, the next time we will be back with hundreds of our neighbors from across the city.

"That's right: We are here now, and we will keep coming back until we win!"

AHA: Anger, Hope, Action

The promise to return was not an idle one. Five months later, in the corner of a Dollar General parking lot on the southwest side of Louisville, across the street from the Nottingham Plaza Drive-Thru Liquor Barrel and an abandoned coin laundry—502-933-WASH—the Louisville Tenants Union convenes for Sunday afternoon canvassing.

It is nearly ninety degrees, with no clouds to block the sun beating down from the midday sky. Poe invites the red-shirted union members to gather beneath the spotty shade provided by a small tree at the corner of the parking lot. Most have canvassed before, but Poe still delivers a pep talk. "The person at the door is trying to assess whether we're a Jehovah's Witness. a cop, or some kind of a scam," he says. "But we don't apologize for bothering someone at their home because we aren't sorry that we're doing this. We're confident, and we're bold."

Poe distributes the flyers they will be using, and the canvassers pair off and mock out a doorway conversation. "Remember, we are looking for the 'AHA' moment: Anger, Hope, Action," Poe says. After twenty minutes of practice and then the distribution of sign-up clipboards, the pairs head off to the six different buildings of the Newberry Parc Apartments.

Newberry Parc has been in the local news lately after a massive water leak in one building led to a total shutdown of water to residents for more than three days.[41] But LTU is here because of a less-publicized fact about the complex: its owners have benefited greatly from US government assistance, with seemingly none of those benefits being felt by the tenants.

In 2019, those owners, Durham Hill Properties LLC, received an $8.2 million loan backed by government-sponsored entity Fannie Mae—backing that typically leads to lower financing costs.[42] The Federal Housing Finance Agency manages both Fannie Mae and Freddie Mac, which play a big role in the multifamily housing market. The Newberry Parc arrangement is quite common. In 2022, Fannie Mae and Freddie Mac purchased a combined $142 billion in multifamily housing loans.[43]

The problem, LTU members and a nationwide network of tenant organizations say, is that our tax dollars provide these huge benefits to landlords without requiring those landlords to protect the rights of tenants. So LTU and other tenant unions insist that the federal government should require these federally backed landlords to limit their rent hikes, keep the housing in good condition, and agree not to evict or not renew tenant leases except for good cause. If they are successful, it could make a seismic impact: greater tenant protection in federally backed housing could apply to over twelve million rental units, nearly one in three renting households in the country.[44]

Biden's January 2023 creation of a new public process by the Federal Housing Finance Agency (FHFA) to "examine proposed actions promoting renter protections and limits on egregious rent increases" was far less than the immediate rent control and eviction protections that tenants are demanding. But, as they did with the Biden tenants rights' blueprint, they decided to use the new process as an opportunity to ratchet up the pressure on the Biden-Harris administration, and to organize and grow stronger. "The rent is too damn high, and the government is in business with our landlords," Tenant Union Federation director Raghuveer says. "We need the Federal Housing Finance Agency, the chief regulator of their industry, to take tenants' expertise seriously, to weigh it against these profiteering lobbyists, and to enact the tenant protections we need."

I walk with Poe into Building Five. We start with the basement apartments. At the second door we knock on, Serena (I will not use tenants' real names here) answers, head cocked to the side and eyes squinted a bit at the site of two strangers. But when Poe explains the purpose of his visit, Serena is eager to talk. A few months ago, a pipe in the apartment above her burst (it is becoming clear that plumbing issues are a recurring theme at Newberry Parc), unleashing a torrent of water that caved in her ceiling and flooded the family living room.

It took the landlord more than a week to clean up the mess. Two of Serena's daughters have asthma, and they struggled to breathe through the whole ordeal. Serena says she did not expect better: the property has had four or five different managers in the past three years—she has lost count—yet her monthly payments have increased by $200.

Poe walks Serena through the process of submitting an online comment to FHFA via her phone. Like most tenants, in her comments she highlights rent hikes and poor maintenance. She writes down her contact information on Poe's clipboard. "We'd love to have you join us at the next meeting of the tenants' union," he says. "We got child care, we got good food. You can come meet your neighbors and share what is going on."

One floor up, Jemani responds to Poe's question about whether her rent has increased, too. "Hell, yes it has!" she replies. While a dog growls behind the apartment door across the hall, Poe explains the reason for the visit. "Did you know your landlord used government money to buy this building? This is your chance to say that tenants should have rights in buildings we taxpayers helped pay for."

Two weeks later, many of these same LTU members join hundreds of other tenant leaders at the national People's Action convention in Washington, DC. Among the speakers at the opening rally was LTU member Jasmine Brown, who told the crowd about the time they had spent living out of their car, dealing with raw sewage pouring into their rented apartment, and pest infestation (Brown uses they/them pronouns). "But now we are actively building power with tenants from public housing complexes to trailer parks!" Brown said, then paused for the applause and yells of support. "It is our vision that one day we will have rent control and quality maintenance. Housing security belongs to everyone!"

The convention closes with nine hundred activists flooding the street and sidewalks outside the Washington offices of the National Multifamily Housing Council. The council is the lobbyist for the biggest corporate landlords and a die-hard opponent of rent control and other renter protections. It and other housing industry powerhouses pushed hard against Biden taking more significant action regulating government-backed rental properties.[45]

Wearing "The Rent Is Too Damn High!" T-shirts and chanting, "Do you see us?" to the eleventh-floor NMHC office windows, a series of tenants told their stories and called for action. "The government is in business with our landlords!" Katie Talbot from the Neighbor to Neighbor organization in Massachusetts yells into a megaphone. Talbot lists some of the biggest corporate landlords that are NMHC members—Greystar, Related, Starwood Capital. "They got richer, and we got priced out," she says. "And that ain't right!" The crowd repeats, "That ain't right!"

Talbot, a formerly unhoused woman, continues. "There are $150 billion in loans backed by public money that go to these landlords every year—no strings attached. And that ain't right!"

"That ain't right!" the crowd responds.

The next tenant to speak is Jer Zonio from LTU. "I live in a property funded by a loan from Fannie Mae," he says. "I wait tables and work hard, but it isn't enough. My landlord raised my rent, and I go to bed and wake up stressed the f— out. If I get sick or injured, I won't be able to go to work, and I will lose my home."

"That ain't right!"

"I'm tired of paying half my wages just to have a place to live. Especially when I hear about this sweet deal my landlord got from my government!

"But I am organizing along with my neighbors like our lives depend on it. Because they do!"

Back in Louisville, while Poe is making his way through Building Five, Zonio knocks on Building Three doors with LTU activist Elizabeth Reid. Adrian Silbernagel and Scott Pittman knock on Kenneth's door in the basement of Building One. Kenneth immediately pulls his neighbor Manuel out into the hallway for an animated conversation. They explain how the landlord shadow-raised their rent by pulling gas and water into their monthly bill, only to hide what that monthly amount was until the last minute. Then, if the tenants are a day late, the landlord fines them $200 extra, with an additional $100 for every day after.

Kenneth, a Lyft driver, introduces his wife and two small sons, then shows the LTU members a big hole in his kitchen wall where yet another leak had to be repaired. The maintenance office has ignored his calls and texts about fixing the hole. Like Serena and her family, Kenneth plans to move at his first opportunity.

But he knows he risks the same problems at the next home, so he is happy to join the union. So is Daniel, walking outside on his way to his Building Three apartment. His rent has increased nearly 30 percent in four years, while his salary has barely budged. "We are all just living paycheck to paycheck," he says. He is excited to see the union walking his neighborhood. "I've been waiting a long time for someone to come out here to talk about all this."

The goal for the door-knocking is to have conversations at three of every ten homes visited. LTU canvassers are doing better than that today, maybe because families are staying close to their air conditioning on the hot afternoon. But there is no air flow to the hallways, so Poe wipes sweat off his forehead. It is Father's Day. Poe he says his daughter understands why he is working today. Perhaps not surprising for the child of an organizer, she led the negotiations with her dad to trade their original Father's Day plans for a later, bigger event.

Poe is glad it all worked out, because he did not want to skip this canvass when so many union members were eager to go. "There are ten people here today, and I am the only one getting paid," he marvels.

Why do all these LTU members come out on a hot Sunday afternoon—this is the fifth LTU canvass this week—to knock on strangers' doors? Why pursue such an analog form of organizing in a digital age? "The most powerful interactions are in person," LTU's Erika Sommer says. "When you think about it, people online often don't really recognize that the person on the other end is a real human being—but that is not a problem when we are standing outside your door."

Brenda Vazquez points out that unknown callers usually are diverted to voicemail. Reid says older folks often shun social media. Zonio says that showing up at someone's doorstep proves the movement's authenticity. The others nod at these responses, then head back to the doors.

Poe puts the rest of the paperwork in his truck, grabs his own clipboard, and follows. "I wish we could just do a text blast or social media post and organize a tenants' movement," he says. "But it doesn't work that way."

"NO HOUSING, NO PEACE"

Louisville tenants are not alone. The organization Action NC coordinated "Cancel Rent" protests at the Charlotte, North Carolina, courthouse in the early days of the COVID pandemic, led tenants in chants of "Housing is a human right!" at various government meetings, and organized canvassing and phone banks to pull together tenants to advocate for their rights.[1] A focus is calling out corporate landlords, like one in Charlotte who was repeatedly cited by government inspectors for refusing to address rampant mold, vermin, and dangerous wiring.[2] A similar campaign is targeting a corporate landlord in Philadelphia that receives generous government subsidies but has tenants living with roach infestation, leaks and mold, and buildings that are inaccessible to renters in wheelchairs.[3]

A few summers ago, Action NC organizer Apryl Lewis and other tenants joined with other organizations affiliated with the Center for Popular Democracy to make an uninvited appearance at the Washington, DC, meeting of the National Multifamily Housing Council, the trade association of corporate landlords. Dozens of tenants took over a conference room, poured themselves glasses of the fancy lemon- and orange-infused water, and chanted, "Corporate landlords you can't hide, we can see your greedy side!"

"We go everywhere," Lewis said in her interview with me. "We not only go door to door, we do banner drops and disrupt official meetings—just be there and be loud so they can't ignore what is happening to these tenants."[4]

Lewis has fought for her own housing, too, juggling multiple jobs as a single mom and barely avoiding eviction multiple times. "The rent kept going up, so I had to be pretty crafty just so I could keep my daughter housed," she said. When

Lewis later began working with youth and families as a counselor, the challenges shared with her kept coming back to housing, by far the top expense in most US households.[5]

Apryl Lewis and her fellow activists have the public's attention. Polls show both a great deal of contemporary concern about housing and a commitment to remedying the problem. Two-thirds of Americans in growing metropolitan areas are "extremely/very concerned" about homelessness and the high cost of housing, ranking it as their top priority.[6] "Housing is the most critical component for a successful community," Lewis said. "A lot of issues we are struggling with, like crime, are connected to people not being able to stay housed."

At a more individual level, as we discussed back in chapter 1, housing insecurity is associated with all manner of health crises, from asthma and heart disease to violence and suicide. "If you are not secure in your housing, your mental health is in jeopardy. You are always stressing, you are always at level 10 because you are fighting for housing," Lewis said. "I can tell you myself that me sitting here in a comfortable position in my housing, my thought patterns are way better than when I was struggling to stay housed."

So it should be no surprise that polls also show that three-quarters of Americans agree with the tenants' chants in Charlotte, Louisville, Philadelphia, and around the nation: safe, secure housing should be considered a human right. Those Americans are not content for that right to be an abstraction: Nearly all the people expressing support of housing as a human right also support expanded government programs to make that right a reality.[7]

That support is beginning to show at the ballot box, too. Across the country, the biggest winner of the 2022 midterm elections was not the Republicans who regained the US House, nor the Democrats who held on to the Senate. The biggest winner was affordable housing. From Kansas City to Portland, Maine, to the entire state of Colorado, ballot measures mandating and funding more affordable housing won, often by comfortable margins.[8]

Kansas City voters voted to invest $50 million in affordable housing for low-income residents. Boosted by the grassroots campaigning of KC Tenants, the largest affordable housing investment in Kansas City history was approved by an overwhelming 71 percent–29 percent margin.[9] A Columbus, Ohio, proposal to spend $200 million for housing and support for homeless persons was pushed by a broad advocacy coalition and won nearly 70 percent of the vote.[10]

"Housing is a winning campaign issue. It's one that voters show up for and it's one that should cause policymakers at all levels to act," Diane Yentel, president and CEO of the National Low Income Housing Coalition, told the Associated Press after the 2022 midterms.[11] If those policymakers don't act fast enough, voters are willing to force their hands. In Colorado, a statewide ballot measure approved a sixfold increase in the income tax dedicated to housing and home-lessness initiatives.[12] Long Island voters enacted a real estate transfer tax to fund affordable housing, and 70 percent of Austin, Texas, voters approved a $350 mil-lion affordable housing bond.[13]

Palm Beach voters endorsed an additional $200 million for new affordable housing. Action NC's push helped lead to $50 million being approved for hous-ing, while down the road the people of Asheville, North Carolina, said yes to $40 million.[14] Portland, Maine, Richmond, California, and Orlando, Florida, voters all provided majorities to rent control proposals to cap rent increases.[15]

A new vacancy tax in San Francisco was approved to address the problem of corporations and wealthy individuals owning multiple vacant homes while thousands are without shelter. Despite supporters of the new law being outspent 3-to-1, the tax passed and will require owners of empty homes to be assessed as much as $20,000 per year.[16] Corporate landlords' expensive campaign ads were similarly unsuccessful in convincing Los Angeles voters to oppose the "mansion tax" levy of at least 4 percent on property sales of $5 million-plus.[17] This success followed on the 2020 approval by South Side Chicago voters of a housing pres-ervation ordinance for the Woodlawn neighborhood, which requires 25 percent of city-owned vacant land to be set aside for affordable housing, dedicates funds for helping homeowners repair their buildings, and gives renters the right of first refusal if a landlord seeks to sell their building. The Chicago campaign was led by a coalition featuring the tenant unions Not Me We and STOP, Southside Together Organizing for Power.[18]

And the efforts of the Louisville Tenant Union and other tenant unions to pressure President Biden and Vice President Harris to use the power of federal housing dollars to control rents led to some success. In early 2024, the Biden-Harris administration announced it would impose a cap on rent increases on Low-Income Housing Tax Credit (LIHTC) housing. The 10 percent annual increase limit is far higher than the 3 percent cap that tenant unions have been pushing for, and the limitation to the LIHTC program leaves out a great deal of other federally financed and subsidized housing. But the rule could apply to over a million households.

"It's a huge win, and it wouldn't have happened if not for tenant unions beat-ing the drum for the past several years demanding that every dollar of federal financing and subsidies be conditioned on tenant protections," Tara Raghuveer of KC Tenants and the national Tenant Union Federation told me in an inter-view. "The federal government is finally recognizing its responsibility to pro-tect tenants from price gouging." Later in 2024, after becoming the Democratic Party's presidential candidate, Vice President Harris echoed President Biden's earlier call for a 5 percent rent cap on all rental housing that relies on federal tax breaks, a reform that would require congressional approval. Harris also proposed a $25,000 first-time homebuyer subsidy, announced plans to build more than three million housing units, and said she wanted to withdraw some of the tax breaks enjoyed by corporate landlords.[19]

The landlord lobby seems to agree with tenant advocates that these plans are significant. The same organizations that cheered the words-only Biden tenant rights' blueprint of 2023 came together to bitterly criticize the new LIHTC rent cap. "You're discouraging the creation of supply," the CEO of the National Housing Conference complained to the *Washington Post*, repeating the discredited argument (see chapter 7) that rent limits decrease the supply of affordable housing.[20] The National Multifamily Housing Council pronounced the Biden-Harris 5 percent rent cap proposal "misguided"; the National Apartment Association called it part of "failed policies that don't work."[21]

Raghuveer is not having it. "For many of these landlords, rent-gouging, evictions, and poor conditions are part of the business model, and what makes their business model work is the favorable terms they receive from our federal government," she says.

The tenant movement aims to change all that. And it is finding a powerful ally in the labor movement.

Low Wages and Housing

DeJuan comes to the eviction court where we work wearing the royal-blue short-sleeve button-down shirt uniform of a fast-casual restaurant chain. His plastic assistant manager name tag is pinned above his left pocket. Another client, Regina, is anxious about how long court will take, since she had to clock out from the call center job she performs from her kitchen table.

Jorge is still limping from the fall he took through the unfinished ceiling of the construction site where he worked. His employer says Jorge is an independent contractor, so he is not eligible for workers compensation for his injuries. Aaron is off work too. His security guard job dissolved without notice when the company lost its contract for the building where he worked.

Keyanna drives for a couple of different ride-hailing apps, picking up riders whenever she can get child care. April is a home health care worker. So are two other people we represent the same day as April. There are so many home health care workers in eviction court.

I have represented DeJuan, Regina, Jorge, Aaron, Keyanna, and April for years. Well, not them personally. But I have represented hundreds of others who are in the same situation. They work hard at physically and emotionally demanding jobs, but they don't make enough in wages to keep themselves and their families safely housed.

In fact, a decade ago I wrote a book about these workers called *If We Can Win Here: The New Front Lines of the Labor Movement*.[22] The book told the stories of home care workers, food servers and dishwashers, janitors, and security guards who were trying to raise our state's minimum wage and bargain for better wages and benefits at their workplaces.

That struggle continues. Nearly one in every three US workers makes less than $15 per hour, far below the amount necessary to pay for rent and other necessities in our city and virtually every other community across the country.[23] Those wages are the lowest in the industrialized world, and in real dollars are lower than they were a half-century ago—despite massive gains in worker productivity.[24]

For our clients, it is rare that even these low wages are paid to them for a full forty-hour work week. Many are among the one in five US hourly workers who are not informed of their schedules until less than a week in advance.[25] That means their lives are yanked around by scheduling practices that ensure their hours are far less than they need to pay rent, while also too unpredictable to secure reliable child care arrangements or add on a second job. Most of our clients, especially Jorge and Keyanna and others who are classified as independent contractors—often a self-serving misclassification by employers looking to dodge payroll taxes—get no paid time off, no sick days, and no health insurance.

The well-documented far higher eviction rates for Black-led and women-led households that we discussed in chapter 3 mirror the shameful wage gap those workers endure. The average Black worker makes 21 percent less than the average white worker; women earn an average of 28 percent less than male workers.[26] Many immigrant workers like Jorge take home less than minimum wage, yet they pay on average more in taxes than they ever receive in government benefits.[27]

The workers profiled in *If We Can Win Here* did not win an increased minimum wage: in our state, it is still only $7.25 per hour. Their unionization efforts had mixed results. The limited protections for workplace organizing under US law meant that many were fired or bullied into abandoning their union campaigns. In 1960, one of every three workers belonged to a union. Only one in ten do today.[28] For the workers we see lined up in eviction court, the drop in union membership tracks with the drop in their real wages.[29]

The Labor Movement and Housing

Yet even a diminished US labor movement carries significant influence on US politics and the economy. In the early and mid-2020s, United Auto Workers,

Teamsters, Hollywood writers and actors, Amazon workers, Starbucks workers, and others won high-profile labor victories, while in 2022 unions received their highest public approval rating in Gallup polls since 1965.[30] So it is good news for tenants that US unions are increasingly making housing rights a priority.[31]

The Chicago Teachers Union's 2024 bargaining proposal called for the city and the Board of Education to create ten thousand affordable housing units with the priority to Chicago Public Schools students and families. The teachers also demanded that unused city and board property be identified and transformed into public housing. The contract of the Boston Teachers Union includes a similar pilot program to house homeless families of one thousand students, and Los Angeles and Oakland teachers' unions have won commitments to identify publicly owned locations that could be developed into affordable housing.[32]

Multiple unions played core roles in supporting Los Angeles's winning mansion tax ballot measure in 2022, which is expected to yield $600 million a year for affordable housing and eviction prevention.[33] UAW and SEIU locals were involved in the successful 2022 campaign to win collective bargaining rights for tenants in San Francisco.[34] Minnesota rent control legislation was passed with active SEIU support.[35] UNITE HERE is pushing forward in the Los Angeles City Council an ordinance that would require developers to replace any housing lost to hotel development and solidify a program to provide temporary housing for unhoused people.[36]

United Food and Commercial Workers' canvassing, phone-banking, and funding helped push through the winning November 2023 Tacoma, Washington, bans on cold-weather evictions and school-year evictions of households with students or teachers, a campaign that also had support from a half-dozen other unions.[37] Along with the ongoing housing campaigns labor is supporting, multiple teachers' unions are pressing their school districts to create affordable housing for teachers near the schools where they teach.[38] The AFL-CIO's Housing Investment Trust has used a union workforce to develop affordable housing across the country.[39]

This labor attention to housing is on the upswing, but it also has plenty of precedent. The landmark National Housing Act of 1937 was pushed by the AFL's Labor Housing Conference.[40] During the twentieth century, unions like the International Brotherhood of Electrical Workers and the Amalgamated Clothing Workers built cooperative housing for workers.[41]

"There is an obvious reason why housing is part of the labor agenda," Stephen Lerner, senior fellow at Bargaining for the Common Good, a partnership between unions and community organizations and architect of the SEIU Justice for Janitors campaign, told me in an interview. "Even if we negotiate a great wage increase for our members, they are losing ground if rent goes up by twice that amount."

This is not an idle concern. Since 1985, rent hikes have outpaced wage increases by a whopping 325 percent.[42] So it is no wonder that when unions ask their members about their priorities, housing dominates the answers. "Regardless of if you're a janitor or a nurse or a health care worker or a home care worker, everyone overwhelmingly said the number one issue was housing affordability," David Huerta, president of the California SEIU State Council, told *Vox* in 2023. "We have members sleeping in their cars, who have big families sleeping in one-bedrooms, who are traveling hours and hours to get to work because they can't afford to live near their jobs."[43]

When unions turn their attention to housing, they often find familiar names and faces on the other side of the struggle. "Increasingly, the same people who own the housing are the ones who are screwing over workers," Lerner says. "When you look to see who is the ruling class with political and legislative influence, especially in urban cities, it is real estate."

Lerner and others cite the example of Blackstone, the private equity firm that is the nation's largest landlord, employs well over a half million workers, and is notorious for hiking rents and opposing rent control.[44] "One lesson we have learned in the union movement is that you have to go up the financial tree to find not just the building owners, but who is funding them," Lerner says.

Today, unions actively push to reform the tax policies we reviewed in chapter 4 that give huge breaks to the passive income that landlords collect while vigorously taxing the wages workers and renters earn by their labor.[45] "The richest people in the world use real estate to avoid taxes, to hide their assets, and to add to their wealth," Sara Myklebust, research director at Bargaining for the Common Good, told me in our interview. "A lot of those same people own companies and are large employers, too."

It follows that unions are increasingly committed to fighting the use of workers' pension dollars to fund the investment firms and corporations that price workers out of housing. Public employee pension funds alone hold nearly $6 trillion in assets, some of which are invested in rent-gouging companies.[46] Myklebust calls this practice "assisted suicide," and she and Bargaining for the Common Good urge that the pension funds instead be investing in affordable housing. "That is workers' money," she says. "Blackstone even used the money from California workers' pensions to fund their opposition to rent control."

Unions can demand that their employers follow their lead and divest from these bad actors as well. Public-sector workers can call for the governments they work for to stop selling off government-owned property to gentrifying private developers. Private-sector workers can bargain for their employers to stop funding anti–rent control campaigns.[47] AFSCME Local 3299 has demanded that the University of California divest from the rent-gouging Blackstone. In early 2024, AFSCME members who worked for the university marched to the chancellor's office chanting "Break up with Blackstone!" and "No housing, no peace!"[48]

Labor and Tenants Join Forces

Hope Vaughn was a tenant union organizer before she knew there was a tenant union.

When her New Haven, Connecticut, landlord Ocean Management refused to address the rodents and mold in her apartment, and ignored the standing, rancid water in the building basement, Vaughn's response was obvious to her. After more than a dozen years as a long-term-care Certified Nursing Assistant member of SEIU Local 1199 NE, she knew the value of fighting back but had no intention of doing so alone. She began knocking on her neighbors' doors and gathering signatures on a petition that demanded repairs and a cleanup.[49]

"My union experience taught me that it may be easy for a landlord to ignore one tenant's complaints. But even powerful people in high places are forced to listen when a lot of us come together," Vaughn says. "There is strength in numbers."

One day, Vaughn overheard someone outside a neighbor's door, asking the same questions she had been posing about the bad conditions in the building. A tenant union organizer was making the rounds. Vaughn joined on the spot, and soon became vice president of the Quinnipiac Avenue Tenant Union. She was part of the team elected by fellow tenants that in 2023 negotiated an agreement with Ocean Management to rescind eviction notices to sixteen residents and enter into Connecticut's first-ever agreement to collectively bargain with tenants.

The public rallies in support of those tenants were bolstered by a big union presence, and every member of the tenant negotiating team had labor union experience. "Tenants and workers have one thing in common: they have a rich person who is oppressing them," says Dave Richardson, a longtime Carpenters Union member who joined Vaughn on the tenants' negotiating team. "The contractor and the landlord are both committed to giving as little as possible."

Vaughn says that her labor union experience was helpful when she needed to reassure her fellow tenants. "Especially at the beginning, we got some pushback from some neighbors who were scared to make management mad," she says. "We were able to tell them that we all have rights, and a union is how we can stand up for ourselves."

Richardson explains it to fellow tenants this way: "Being union teaches you that you can't win a fight that you don't fight."

The success won by Vaughn and Richardson and their fellow members of the Connecticut Tenants Union is one of the most promising examples of labor-tenant partnership. Rob Baril, president of SEIU Local 1199 NE, points out that the union's long-term-care workers in Connecticut often struggle to make ends meet in a state where it can cost $90,000 a year to cover the high cost of living. "We won 33 percent raises in 2020, but that can quickly get eroded by inflation, especially the cost of housing," he says.

So Local 1199 began collaborating with the tenants' union, not just with organizing help and rally turnout but also with financial support. "Our members were very ready to have some of their dues money going to support tenant organizing," Baril says. "They get it, because they are living it. Even if they individually are not getting crushed by housing costs, they know many coworkers who are."

Hannah Srajer, president of the Connecticut Tenants Union, says the collaboration with Local 1199 has helped the tenants create a labor-inspired organizing methodology that prioritizes democratically elected committees, majority-based membership, and strike readiness. "A lot of people in labor know how to fight, they know how to win material gains for their members, and they know how to build lasting organizations," Srajer says. "We are starting to do all that in tenant unions."

Tara Raghuveer of KC Tenants and the Tenant Union Federation agrees. "Labor has figured out not only how to build power but to exercise power, in a way that the tenant movement is still learning how to do," she says. "For example, the strike power is a profound one. A labor strike and a rent strike are not identical, but there are a lot of lessons to be learned from organizers who have taken shops out on strike."

Beyond alliances with tenant unions, there is deep labor support for the groundbreaking Green New Deal for Public Housing Act, which would dramatically increase the stock of social housing. This support makes sense for labor on multiple levels. A massive investment in social housing would help workers meet their housing needs while at the same time creating union jobs in the building of those homes. Those social housing construction jobs can endure during the economic downturns when jobs in the for-profit construction industry traditionally dry up.

For anyone familiar with other nations' housing success, a growing labor-tenant alliance in the US is exciting stuff. Organized labor played a big role in the creation of social housing in places like Sweden, where workers have come together to form a cooperative that builds and manages housing, while a National Tenants Union bargains for tenant rights and lower rents.[50] The labor movement helped spur Vienna's historic commitment to building and maintaining social housing.[51]

Labor and tenants coming together will help both movements grow, Connecticut Tenants Union's Srajer says. "A lot of our members are working low-wage jobs where they need a workplace union," she says. "We are all fighting against corporate greed in the end. The same guys who are buying up whole neighborhoods, jacking up rents, and no-cause evicting folks are the ones bankrolling the nursing homes that underpay and mistreat their workers."

SEIU Local 1199NE's Baril agrees. "We have to construct a twenty-first century, integrated movement for working-class rights. That obviously has to include the ability to have shelter fit for human beings to live in," he says. "Tenant unions are going to be the tip of the spear for that effort, but some of the resources needed are going to have to come from labor unions.

"Us doing that is not charity. That is self-interest."

CONCLUSION

For many years, when a student or colleague would ask me what has to be done to fix our US housing crisis, my answer was fast and unequivocal: more government-subsidized housing.

My answer was wrong.

I came to that realization over the course of hundreds of hours spent in eviction court. Looking out over the packed courtrooms, I recognized that I was witnessing an abundance of government-subsidized housing.

First, I saw the landlords and their representatives, coming to court to evict dozens of families from their homes. In our city, as is the case across the country, it is increasingly rare for those landlords to be locally owned companies, much less the iconic mom-and-pop landlords renting out a single house or two. Eviction record analysis of our community shows that nearly nine of every ten cases are filed by corporate landlords, many of them national or multinational investor-owned firms.[1]

For these landlords, government subsidies flow their way like a river after a week of rainstorms. We saw in chapter 4 that this river includes deductions for pass-through income, depreciation of real estate, and deferred and often never-paid capital gains taxes, along with a plethora of estate tax exemptions and avoidance schemes. "If you're looking to get richer while telling the tax man you're getting poorer, it's hard to beat real estate development," concluded one analysis of landlords' tax avoidance.[2]

Next, I looked around the room and saw the lawyers there. Most represent landlords, but there are a few employed by nonprofit legal agencies who work alongside my students and me advocating for tenants. None of us lawyers in eviction court have real estate developer–level money, of course. But we too are usually blessed with a generous package of government housing subsidies—because most of us own our homes.

Consider my own situation. After renting for several years, my spouse and I managed to purchase a home for ourselves and our three children. We did so thanks to family help with the down payment. That help was available because our white relatives had benefited from the historic mid-twentieth-century government home-purchasing subsidies. The Home Owners Loan Corporation, the Federal Housing Administration, and the Veterans Administration made it possible for our parents and grandparents and millions like them to buy homes.

Moreover, the government boost allowed my relatives to create wealth through their homes increasing in value—still the top source of wealth in most US households. As we learned in chapter 3, these housing subsidies and the wealth-creation opportunities that came with them were almost fully denied to Black families.

For my spouse and me, the mortgage we signed was affordable in part because of favorable terms created by the federal government insuring our mortgage through the Federal Housing Administration. Then, we benefited from the mortgage interest tax deduction. Our mortgage allows us a whopping thirty years to pay off our debt on fixed terms, borrower-friendly standards that were also created by federal backing of mortgages. That meant that our monthly housing cost as homeowners was both more affordable and more stable than it was when we rented. When we sell, we likely will not be required to pay any taxes at all on the profit we make, up to a half-million dollars.

The bottom line: eviction court lawyers like me—and virtually everyone else who has a mortgage—live in government-subsidized housing.

But what about the families lined up in court, waiting to see what day a constable will show up at their door to change the locks and put their belongings on the curb? One of them, Angela, has a family that is a lot like mine: two parents, three kids, started out as renters. But Angela's former husband is ill and out of the picture. Her family has no generational wealth—they are Black and never had access to the home-buying subsidies my ancestors did.

For a long time, Angela managed a difficult juggling act, devoting as much as 70 percent of her home health care wages to pay the monthly rent. Then the balls fell to the floor.

Angela's longtime patient died, so Angela went weeks without a new patient or a paycheck. The "as is" used car she bought—because she could not afford a down payment on a car with a warranty—broke down. She still owed a substantial debt on the car, and it was her only transportation to her job and to child care. So Angela had to pay to get it repaired. She fell behind on rent, triggering first late fees and then court filing fees.

Alone among the major players in eviction court, Angela and her fellow renters have no government-subsidized housing.

As we saw in chapter 4, Angela and virtually all our other eviction court clients are losers in the cruel musical chairs game we play with low-income housing in the US: three of every four households that qualify for housing vouchers or public housing do not receive it. But once we widen our lens and look beyond the unlucky households like Angela's, we see that their struggles are not because of a lack of government-subsidized housing.

They go without while we generously subsidize those who need it the least.

Informed by the experiences of eviction court, this book aims to lay out the path to remedying this injustice. Immediately, we must take the following steps:

- Enact a Tenants' Bill of Rights, both in state and local laws and tied to every landlord who receives federal financing or tax breaks. That Bill of Rights must include rent control (chapter 7) and a good-cause requirement before refusing to renew leases (chapter 5). These rights would finally provide Angela and other renters with the stability that I and other lucky homeowners have long enjoyed. The Tenants' Bill of Rights also must include enforceable guarantees of good housing conditions. When an eviction case is filed, we should ensure a careful, deliberate legal process with a right to counsel for all tenants. We can and must immediately slow down our government-funded fast-track eviction machine.
- Distribute universal vouchers that bring housing assistance into the same "entitlement" category as SNAP / Food Stamps and Medicaid. Simply put, Angela's and every other household that qualifies for housing assistance should receive it. As we saw in chapter 6, since vouchers rely on the private housing market, this system must include source-of-income antidiscrimination laws that prohibit landlords from refusing to rent to voucher holders. (The US Department of Housing and Urban Development is experimenting with substituting vouchers with cash stipends paid directly to the recipients, an approach that could help alleviate some of the challenge of finding landlords who accept vouchers.)[3]
- Eliminate the billionaire/millionaire landlord subsidies outlined in chapter 4. Instead, create revenue for affordable housing by taxing housing speculators and luxury transactions that meet thresholds like Los Angeles's voter-approved "mansion tax" on home sales over $5 million.[4]
- Mandate that cities and communities that want highly coveted federal funds for highways and mass transit must first remove the zoning restrictions that operate as "covert redlining" preventing the building of dense and affordable housing.

That is just the start. We also need to immediately begin building more enduring solutions. The core long-term remedy is this: We need much better public housing, and much more of it. As we saw in chapter 8, US public housing has been starved of the resources it needs to maintain current units and blocked from funding to create desperately needed new ones. This must change.

As we saw in chapter 9, there are many examples internationally and in the US proving that public housing can be attractive, affordable, abundant, and the foundation of thriving communities. Universal vouchers are a necessary interim step. But vouchers rely on the for-profit market to provide affordable housing, and the US experience over the past half century proves that cannot be a long-term solution. There is no alternative to a plentiful supply of high-quality public housing.

Can we get there? In this book's introduction, I mentioned that seeing our housing crisis from the perspective of eviction court can make it tempting to despair. It is hard to find optimism when standing alongside Felicia explaining how her children have been sickened by mold, rodent droppings, and sewage backups in their home, Ashley facing homelessness when her landlord increased her rent by 40 percent, and Robert, whose disability check is no longer enough to keep him housed in his apartment of two decades.

But, as we saw in chapters 11 and 12, a social movement is building that aims to change all this. The history of such movements should give us hope, because that history shows that momentous changes can occur when dedicated organizers build a strong foundation for change.

For example, we remember the seismic Montgomery, Alabama, bus boycott of 1955 and 1956 and the dynamic leadership of the young Rev. Martin Luther King Jr. that helped launch the most impactful stage of the US civil rights movement. Less well known is that the boycott ignited only after years of organizing by E. D. Nixon, president of the Montgomery, Alabama, NAACP, and Jo Ann Robinson of the local Women's Political Council.[5]

Every American knows about Abraham Lincoln and the Civil War's end-game role in abolishing US slavery. Less appreciated are the years that abolitionists like Frederick Douglass, Angelina Grimké, and William Lloyd Garrison traveled the countryside gathering signatures on petitions and speaking to often near-empty halls. Eventually, those halls began to fill, the petitions swelled with names, and pressure for change mounted.[6]

For housing justice, this sometimes frustrating, two-steps-forward, one-step-back organizing is being done right now by tenants and tenant organizers across the country. The process can be a grind and often is not successful in the short term. But it is how change happens. That is why this book concludes with the story of the burgeoning tenant union movement.

I hope—and I believe—that the tenants in Louisville and Kansas City and Connecticut and North Carolina and beyond are building the foundation for a better future. One day, the US will join the many other nations where housing is a fully realized and enforceable human right for all. I have learned a great deal from my time in eviction court, but I look forward to a day when that courtroom is empty.

Notes

INTRODUCTION

1. Kathryn A. Sabbeth, "Erasing the 'Scarlet E' of Eviction Records," *Appeal*, April 12, 2021, https://theappeal.org/thelab/report/erasing-the-scarlet-e-of-eviction-records/.

2. "Social Determinants of Health," US Department of Health and Human Services, https://health.gov/healthypeople/priority-areas/social-determinants-health.

3. Matthew Desmond and Rachel Tolbert Kimbro, "Eviction's Fallout: Housing, Hardship, and Health," *Social Forces* 94, no. 1 (2015), https://doi.org/10.1093/sf/sov044.

4. Matthew Desmond, "Poor Black Women Are Evicted at Alarming Rates, Setting Off a Chain of Hardship," MacArthur Foundation, How Housing Matters, March 2014, https://www.macfound.org/media/files/hhm_research_brief_-_poor_black_women_are_evicted_at_alarming_rates.pdf.

5. "Eviction Tracking," Eviction Lab, https://evictionlab.org/eviction-tracking; Michael Casey and R. J. Rico, "Eviction Filings Soar over 50% above Pre-pandemic Levels in Some Cities as Rents Increase," *PBS NewsHour*, June 17, 2023, https://www.pbs.org/newshour/nation/eviction-filings-soar-over-50-above-pre-pandemic-levels-in-some-cities-as-rents-increase.

6. "Household Pulse Survey," United States Census Bureau, May 16, 2024, https://www.census.gov/data/tables/2024/demo/hhp/cycle04.html.

7. National Low Income Housing Coalition, "Out of Reach: The High Cost of Housing," https://nlihc.org/oor. (Some 22.4 million households are housing cost–burdened; the average US household consists of 2.51 people.)

8. Portions of this account of eviction court were originally published in Fran Quigley, "Lessons from Eviction Court," *Common Dreams*, December 12, 2021, https://www.commondreams.org/views/2021/12/02/lessons-eviction-court.

9. Henry Gomory, Douglas S. Massey, James R. Hendrickson, and Matthew Desmond, "When It's Cheap to File an Eviction Case, Tenants Pay the Price," Eviction Lab, June 6, 2023, https://evictionlab.org/tenants-pay-for-cheap-evictions/.

10. Julieta Cuellar, "Effect of 'Just Cause' Eviction Ordinances on Eviction in Four California Cities," *Princeton Journal of Public and International Affairs*, May 21, 2019, https://jpia.princeton.edu/news/effect-just-cause-eviction-ordinances-eviction-four-california-cities.

11. US Bureau of Labor Statistics, "Consumer Expenditures—2021," September 8, 2022, https://www.bls.gov/news.release/cesan.nr0.htm; Peter J. Mateyka and Jayne Yoo, "Share of Income Needed to Pay Rent Increased the Most for Low-Income Households from 2019 to 2021," US Census, March 2, 2023, https://www.census.gov/library/stories/2023/03/low-income-renters-spent-larger-share-of-income-on-rent.html.

12. "Robust COVID Relief Achieved Historic Gains against Poverty and Hardship, Bolstered Economy," Center on Budget and Policy Priorities, February 24, 2022, https://www.cbpp.org/research/poverty-and-inequality/robust-covid-relief-achieved-historic-gains-against-poverty-and.

13. Henry Grabar, "New York Needs to Learn a Housing Lesson from . . . New Jersey?," *Slate*, February 8, 2022, https://slate.com/business/2022/02/new-york-good-cause-eviction-new-jersey-housing.html.

1. THE VIEW FROM EVICTION COURT

1. 'How Much You Could Get from SSI," Social Security Administration, https://www.ssa.gov/ssi/amount (monthly payments due to disability under the Supplemental Security Income program are $943 per individual in 2024); "Annual Statistical Supplement," Social Security Administration, https://www.ssa.gov/policy/docs/statcomps/supplement/ (monthly payments due to disability under the Social Security Disability Income program average about $1,483).

2. Gracie Himmelstein and Matthew Desmond, "Association of Eviction with Adverse Birth Outcomes among Women in Georgia, 2000 to 2016," *JAMA Pediatrics*, March 1, 2021, https://jamanetwork.com/journals/jamapediatrics/fullarticle/2776776; Aayush Khadka, Günther Fink, Ashley Gromis, and Margaret McConnell, "In Utero Exposure to Threat of Evictions and Preterm Birth: Evidence from the United States," *Health Services Research*, September 25, 2020, https://doi.org/10.1111/1475-6773.13551; Matthew Desmond and Rachel Tolbert Kimbro, "Eviction's Fallout: Housing, Hardship, and Health," *Social Forces* 94, no. 1 (September 2015): 295–324, https://doi.org/10.1093/sf/sov044; Yerko Rojas and Sten-Ake Stenberg, "Evictions and Suicide: A Follow-up Study of Almost 22,000 Swedish Households in the Wake of the Global Financial Crisis," *Journal of Epidemiology and Community Health* 70, no. 4 (November 4, 2015), https://jech.bmj.com/content/70/4/409; Yerko Rojas, "Evictions and Short-Term All-Cause Mortality: A 3-Year Follow-up Study of a Middle-Aged Swedish Population," *International Journal of Public Health* 62, no. 3 (December 2016), https://doi.org/10.1007/s00038-016-0931-8; *The Health Impacts of Eviction: Evidence from the National Longitudinal Study of Adolescent to Adult Health*, Penn Libraries, 2021, https://repository.upenn.edu/cgi/viewcontent.cgi?article=1063&context=psc_publications.

3. Matthew Desmond, Carl Gershenson, and Barbara Kiviat, "Forced Relocation and Residential Instability among Urban Renters," *Social Service Review* 89, no. 2 (June 2015), https://www.journals.uchicago.edu/doi/pdf/10.1086/681091; Matthew Desmond and Carl Gershenson, "Housing and Employment Insecurity among the Working Poor," *Social Problems* 63, no. 1 (February 2016): 46–67, https://doi.org/10.1093/socpro/spv025; Cleo Bluthenthal, *The Disproportionate Burden of Eviction on Black Women*, Center for American Progress, August 14, 2023, https://www.americanprogress.org/article/the-disproportionate-burden-of-eviction-on-black-women/.

4. Tama Leventhal and Sandra Newman, "Housing and Child Development," *Children and Youth Services Review* 32, no. 9 (2010): 1165–74.

5. Fran Quigley, "We Have to Act Now to Stop the Coming US Eviction Crisis," *Jacobin*, June 27, 2021, https://jacobin.com/2021/06/us-eviction-crisis-post-pandemic-cdc-moratorium-housing-courts.

6. Hyojung Lee, "Who Owns Rental Properties, and Is It Changing?," Joint Center for Housing Studies of Harvard University, August 18, 2017, http://www.jchs.harvard.edu/blog/who-owns-rental-properties-and-is-it-changing/; Kevin Schaul and Jonathan O'Connell, "Investors Bought a Record Share of Homes in 2021. See Where," *Washington Post*, February 16, 2022, https://www.washingtonpost.com/business/interactive/2022/housing-market-investors/.

7. Elora L. Raymond, Richard Duckworth, Benjamin Miller, Michael Lucas, and Shiraj Pokharel, "Corporate Landlords, Institutional Investors, and Displacement: Eviction Rates in Singlefamily Rentals," Federal Reserve Bank of Atlanta, SSRN, January 4, 2017, https://ssrn.com/abstract=2893552.

8. Ko Lyn Cheang and Binghui Huang, "Corporate Landlords Filed 88% of All Evictions in Indianapolis through September," *IndyStar*, October 24, 2021, https://www.indystar.com/story/news/realestate/2021/10/24/indianapolis-eviction-moratorium-top-evictors-during-pandemic/6102198001/.

9. Lillian Leung, Peter Hepburn, and Matthew Desmond, "Serial Eviction Filing: Civil Courts, Property Management, and the Threat of Displacement," *Social Forces* 100 (September 2021): 316–44, https://academic.oup.com/sf/article/100/1/316/5903878.

10. Matthew Desmond and Nathan Wilmers, "Do the Poor Pay More for Housing? Exploitation, Profit, and Risk in Rental Markets," *American Journal of Sociology* 124, no. 4 (January, 2019), https://www.journals.uchicago.edu/doi/full/10.1086/701697.

11. Kriston Capps and Sarah Holder, "Wolf of Main Street," *Bloomberg*, March 3, 2022, https://www.bloomberg.com/graphics/2022-evictions-monarch-investment-rental-properties/.

12. "America's Biggest Multifamily and Single-Family Landlords Continue to Reap Huge Profits and Take Advantage of Tenants," Accountable.US, April 10, 2023, https://accountable.us/wp-content/uploads/2023/04/2023-04-10-Updated-Research-On-Housing-Profiteering-FINAL.docx-1.pdf.

13. Adam Travis, "The Organization of Neglect: Limited Liability Companies and Housing Disinvestment," *American Sociological Review* 84, no. 1 (January 25, 2019), https://doi.org/10.1177/0003122418821339; Desiree Fields, "Automated Landlord: Digital Technologies and Post-crisis Financial Accumulation," *Employment and Planning* 54, no. 1 (May 1, 2019), https://doi.org/10.1177/0308518X19846514.

14. Shane Phillips, "We Need Rental Registries Now More Than Ever," *Shelterforce*, December 18, 2020, https://shelterforce.org/2020/12/18/we-need-a-rental-registry-now-more-than-ever/.

15. Ko Lyn Cheang, "Tenants at Lakeside Pointe Suffered Years of Neglect. Then, Their Homes Caught Fire," *IndyStar*, November 24, 2021, https://www.indystar.com/story/news/local/marioncounty/2021/11/24/indianapolis-apartments-lakeside-pointe-tenants-suffered-neglect-beforefire/8725147002/.

16. Ko Lyn Cheang, "After Landlord Fails to Pay $1.3M Water Bill, Nearly 900 Apartments Have Water Turned Off," *IndyStar*, February 25, 2022, https://www.indystar.com/story/news/real-estate/2022/02/25/indianapolis-apartments-indiana-tenant-rights-landlord-fails-pay-1-3-million-bill-jpc-charities/6921971001/.

17. Allan Mallach, "Meeting the Challenge of Distressed Property Investors in America's Neighborhoods," LISC, https://www.lisc.org/our-resources/resource/meeting-challenge-distressed-property-investors-americas-neighborhoods/.

18. Mallach, 10.

19. Claire Rafford and Ko Lyn Cheang, "'Treated Like Animals': How a Mega Investor Turned Affordable Homes into Rental Nightmares," *Indystar*, September 21, 2023, https://www.indystar.com/story/news/local/indianapolis/2023/09/21/indianapolis-housing-violations-vinebrook-slb-investments-firstkey-homes-marion-county-health/70411917007/.

20. Molly Schramm, "Cincinnati Sues VineBrook Homes after 'Repeated Violations,' Breach of Settlement Agreement," *WCPO Cincinnati*, January 18, 2023, https://www.wcpo.com/news/local-news/hamilton-county/cincinnati/cincinnati-sues-vinebrook-homes-after-repeated-violations-breach-of-settlement-agreement.

21. Claire Rafford, "Settlement Reached over Rent-to-Own Contracts in Predominately Black Neighborhoods," *IndyStar*, March 22, 2023, https://www.indystar.com/story/news/local/indianapolis/2023/03/22/750000-settlement-reached-over-rent-to-own-housing-contracts/70038103007/; Matthew Goldstein, "Divvy Wants to Make Rent-to-Own Deals Easy; Many Customers Find Them Hard," *New York Times*, August 1, 2023, https://www.nytimes.com/2023/08/01/business/divvy-homes-housing-rent.html; Rebecca Burns, "Private Equity Sold Them a Dream of Home Ownership; They Got Evicted Instead," *Business Insider*, July 7, 2023, https://www.insider.com/home-partners-rent-to-own-low-success-rate-2023-5.

22. Matthew Desmond, *Poverty, by America* (New York: Crown, 2023), 54.

23. Desmond and Wilmers, "Do the Poor Pay More for Housing?"

24. Marian White, "The Cost of Moving a Mobile Home in 2023—What You Can Expect to Pay," Moving.com, March 9, 2023, https://www.moving.com/tips/moving-mobile-home-expect-pay/.

25. Portions of this discussion of manufactured housing were originally published in Fran Quigley, "Wall Street Is Holding a Gun to Mobile Home Residents' Heads," *Jacobin*, May 4, 2023, https://jacobin.com/2023/05/mobile-home-park-evictions-rent-wall-street-affordable-housing.

26. Manufactured Housing Institute, accessed June 11, 2024, https://www.manu facturedhousing.org/who-we-are/.

27. "Innovations in Manufactured Homes Network: I'm HOME," Lincoln Institute of Land Policy, https://www.lincolninst.edu/our-work/innovations-in-manufactured-homes-network-im-home.

28. Renia Ehrenfeucht, "Moving beyond the Mobile Home Myth: Preserving Manufactured Housing Communities," Grounded Solutions Network, https://grounded solutions.org/sites/default/files/2018-11/Moving%20Beyond%20the%20Mobile%20 Myth.pdf.

29. "Manufactured Housing Landscape 2020," Fannie Mae, https://multifamily. fanniemae.com/news-insights/multifamily-market-commentary/manufactured-housing-landscape-2020.

30. "Manufactured Housing Landscape."

31. George Kamel, "Are Mobile Homes a Bad Investment?," Ramsey Solutions, May 24, 2024, https://www.ramseysolutions.com/real-estate/mobile-homes.

32. Rupert Neate, "America's Trailer Parks: The Residents May Be Poor but the Owners Are Getting Rich," *Guardian*, May 3, 2015, https://www.theguardian.com/lifeandstyle/2015/may/03/owning-trailer-parks-mobile-home-university-investment.

33. Frank Rolfe, "The Truth about My Notorious Waffle House Quote," Mobile Home University, https://www.mobilehomeuniversity.com/articles/the-truth-about-my-notorious-waffle-house-quote.

34. "Learn Mobile Home Park Investing from the Experts," Mobile Home University, https://www.mobilehomeuniversity.com/mobile-home-park-investing-books-and-courses/virtual-mobile-home-park-investors-boot-camp.php.

35. Vishesh Raisinghai, "Corporate Landlords Are Snatching Up Mobile Home Parks and Jacking Up the Rent," *Yahoo Finance*, January 9, 2023, https://www.yahoo.com/now/corporate-landlords-blackstone-gobbling-mobile-174500027.html.

36. Kori Hale, "Warren Buffett's Exploitative Mobile Home Investment," *Forbes*, April 18, 2019, https://www.forbes.com/sites/korihale/2019/04/18/warren-buffets-exploi tative-mobile-home-investment/?sh=428b4c101507.

37. Abraham Tekippe, "Zell's Equity LifeStyle Faces Protest at Annual Meeting," *Crain's Chicago Business*, May 9, 2012, https://www.chicagobusiness.com/article/20120509/CRED03/120509763/sam-zell-s-equity-lifestyle-faces-protest; "MHU Top 100 U.S. Manufactured Home Community Owners," Mobile Home University, https://www.mobile homeuniversity.com/mhu-top-100-community-owners.php?gclid=.

38. Chris Arnold and Robert Benincasa, "From Floods to Slime: Mobile Home Residents Say Landlords Make Millions, Neglect Them," *NPR*, August 21, 2022, https://www.npr.org/2022/08/21/1112299858/from-floods-to-slime-mobile-home-residents-say-landlords-make-millions-neglect-t.

39. Frank Rolfe, "Blackstone Affirms the Brilliance of the Mobile Home Park Business Model," Mobile Home University, https://www.mobilehomeuniversity.com/articles/blackstone-affirms-the-brilliance-of-the-mobile-home-park-business-model?gclid=.

40. Chris Arnold, Robert Benincasa, and Mary Childs, "How the Government Helps Investors Buy Mobile Home Parks, Raise Rent and Evict People," *NPR*, December 18, 2021, https://www.npr.org/2021/12/18/1034784494/how-the-government-helps-investors-buy-mobile-home-parks-raise-rent-and-evict-pe.

41. Michael Casey and Carolyn Thompson, "Rents Spike as Large Corporate Investors Buy Mobile Home Parks," *PBS News Hour* / Associated Press, July 25, 2022, https://www.pbs.org/newshour/economy/rents-spike-as-large-corporate-investors-buy-mobile-home-parks.

2. HOW WE ABANDONED AFFORDABLE HOUSING

1. P. H. Rossi, "The Old Homeless and the New Homeless in Historical Perspective," *American Psychology* 45, no. 8 (1990): 954–59, https://pubmed.ncbi.nlm.nih.gov/2221566/.

2. Amee Chew, "Social Housing for All: A Vision for Thriving Communities, Renter Power, and Racial Justice," Center for Popular Democracy, March 22, 2022, https://www.populardemocracy.org/socialhousingforall.

3. Richard Rothstein, *Color of Law: A Forgotten History of How Our Government Segregated America* (New York: Liveright, 2017), 63–64; "Legislative History of the VA Home Loan Guaranty Program," August 23, 2006, US Department of Veterans Affairs, https://www.benefits.va.gov/homeloans/documents/docs/history.pdf.

4. Alex Schwartz, *Housing Policy in the* United States (New York: Routledge, 2021), 61.

5. "The History of Homelessness in the United States," National Library of Medicine, https://www.ncbi.nlm.nih.gov/books/NBK519584/.

6. *Without Housing*, Western Regional Advocacy Report, https://wraphome.org/what/without-housing/.

7. Arthur Delaney, "Cutting Social Security Disability Benefits Can Backfire Horribly," NOSSCR, January 15, 2020, https://nosscr.org/cutting-social-security-disability-benefits-can-backfire-horribly/; "History of Homelessness in the United States."

8. Joanne Samuel Goldblum and Colleen Shaddox, *Broke in* America: *Seeing, Understanding, and Ending* U.S. *Poverty* (Dallas: Ben Bella, 2021), 55.

9. Chris Roberts, "The Great Eliminator: How Ronald Reagan Made Homelessness Permanent," *SF Weekly*, 2016, https://www.sfweekly.com/news/the-great-eliminator-how-ronald-reagan-made-homelessness-permanent/.

10. Roberts, "Great Eliminator."

11. Chew, "Social Housing for All," 17.

12. Chew, 16; Rothstein, *Color of Law*, 17–37; "We Deserve a Place to Live: How U.S. Underfunding Public Housing Harms Rights in New York, New Mexico, and Beyond," Human Rights Watch, September 27, 2022, https://www.hrw.org/report/2022/09/27/we-deserve-have-place-live/how-us-underfunding-public-housing-harms-rights-new.

13. Fran Quigley, "Social Housing Can Work: An Interview with Alex Lee and Stanley Chang," *Jacobin*, May 13, 2024, https://jacobin.com/2024/05/social-housing-policy-california-hawaii.

14. Human Rights Watch, "We Deserve a Place to Live."

15. Ross Barkan, "Alexandria Ocasio-Cortez Knows How to Fix Housing," *New York Times*, January 4, 202, https://www.nytimes.com/2021/01/04/opinion/public-housing-faircloth-amendment-repeal.html.

16. "Policy Basics: Public Housing," Center on Budget and Policy Priorities, https://www.cbpp.org/research/public-housing.

17. Human Rights Watch, "We Deserve a Place to Live."

18. "Capital Fund Backlog," National Association of Housing and Redevelopment Officials (NAHRO), https://www.nahro.org/wp-content/uploads/2020/04/capital_fund_backlog_One-Pager.pdf.

19. "Priorities for the Build Back Better Act," National Low-Income Housing Coalition, accessed June 12, 2024, https://nlihc.org/sites/default/files/American_Recovery_Plan.pdf.

20. Francesca Mari, "Imagine a Renters' Utopia: It Might Look Like Vienna," *New York Times*, May 23, 2023, https://www.nytimes.com/2023/05/23/magazine/vienna-social-housing.html?smid=.

21. Rothstein, *Color of Law*; Keeanga-Yamahtta Taylor, *Race for Profit: How Banks and the Real Estate Industry Undermined Black Homeownership* (Chapel Hill: University of North Carolina Press, 2019), 36.

22. Daniel Aldana Cohen and Mark Paul, "The Case for Social Housing," Data for Progress and the Justice Collaborative Institute, November 2020, https://www.filesfor progress.org/memos/the-case-for-social-housing.pdf.

23. Gianpaolo Baiocchi and H. Jacob Carlson, "Housing Is a Social Good," *Boston Review*, June 2, 2021, https://bostonreview.net/articles/housing-is-a-social-good/.

24. Samuel Stein, Capital City: *Gentrification and the* Real Estate State (New York: Verso, 2019).

25. "Housing Choice Vouchers Fact Sheet," US Department of Housing and Urban Development, https://www.hud.gov/topics/housing_choice_voucher_program_section_8.

26. "History and Nature of the Federal Procedural Requirements," National Housing Law Project, https://www.nhlp.org/wp-content/uploads/History-of-PH-GP-unedited-for-CW.pdf.

27. "76% of Low-Income Renters Needing Federal Rental Assistance Don't Receive It," Center on Budget and Policy Priorities, https://www.cbpp.org/research/housing/three-out-of-four-low-income-at-risk-renters-do-not-receive-federal-rental-assistance.

28. Sonya Acosta and Erik Gartland, "Families Wait Years for Housing Vouchers Due to Inadequate Funding," Center on Budget and Policy Priorities, July 22, 2021, https://www.cbpp.org/research/housing/families-wait-years-for-housing-vouchers-due-to-inadequate-funding; Aaron Schrank, "It's a Long Wait for Section 8 Housing in U.S. Cities," *Marketplace*, January 3, 2018, https://www.marketplace.org/2018/01/03/its-long-wait-section-8-housing-us-cities/.

29. Sonya Acosta and Brianna Guerrero, "Long Waitlists for Housing Vouchers Show Pressing Unmet Need for Assistance," Center on Budget and Policy Priorities, October 6, 2021, https://www.cbpp.org/research/housing/long-waitlists-for-housing-vouchers-show-pressing-unmet-need-for-assistance.

30. Acosta and Guerrero, "Long Waitlists for Housing Vouchers."

31. Emma Ockerman, "A Chicago Official Applied for a Section 8 Housing Voucher in 1993—but Only Now 'Made It to the Top of the Waiting List,'" *MarketWatch*, June 6, 2022, https://www.marketwatch.com/story/a-chicago-official-applied-for-a-section-8-housing-voucher-in-1993-but-only-now-made-it-to-the-top-of-the-waiting-list-116541 70167.

32. Joseph P. Fried, "Nixon's Housing Policy," *New York Times*, September 29, 1973, https://www.nytimes.com/1973/09/29/archives/nixons-housing-policy-opponents-say-proposal-for-cash-payments-wont.htm; Maggie McCarty, "An Introduction to Public Housing," Congressional Research Service, January 3, 2014, 5–9, https://sgp.fas.org/crs/misc/R41654.pdf.

33. Human Rights Watch, "We Deserve a Place to Live."

34. Human Rights Watch, "We Deserve a Place to Live."

35. Schwartz, *Housing Policy in the United States*, 192. ("Private developers and developers are interested primarily in the income and tax benefits that can be generated through the construction of subsidized housing. The emphasis is almost always on upfront and short-term gains. Investors usually show less interest in subsidized projects over time.")

36. "Housing Choice Vouchers Fact Sheet," US Department of Housing and Urban Development.

37. Douglas Rice, "Agencies Generally Use All Available Voucher Funding to Help Families Afford Housing," Center on Budget and Policy Priorities, March 24, 2019, https://www.cbpp.org/research/housing/agencies-generally-use-all-available-voucher-fun ding-to-help-families-afford; "Discrimination against Housing Choice Voucher Holders," Urban Institute, accessed June 11, 2024, https://www.urban.org/policy-centers/metropolitan-housing-and-communities-policy-center/projects/housingchoice voucherdiscrimination.

38. Deborah Thrope, "Achieving Housing Choice and Mobility in the Voucher Program: Recommendations for the Administration," *Journal of Affordable Housing* 27, no. 1 (2018): 145, 147–48, https://www.nhlp.org/wp-content/uploads/2018/05/AH-27–1_11 Thrope.pdf.

39. Multi-disciplinary Research Team, "Rent Burden in the Housing Choice Voucher Program," table A3, p. 36, US Department of Housing and Urban Development, October 2017, https://www.nahma.org/wp-content/uploads/2014/04/Rent-Burden-in-the-Hous ing-Choice-Voucher-Program.pdf.

40. "Source of Income Laws by State, County, and City," National Multifamily Housing Council, https://www.nmhc.org/research-insight/analysis-and-guidance/source-of-income-laws-by-state-county-and-city/; Alison Bell, Barbara Sard, and Becky Koepnick, "Prohibiting Discrimination against Renters Using Housing Vouchers Improves Results," Center on Budget and Policy Priorities, December 20, 2018, https://www.cbpp.org/research/housing/prohibiting-discrimination-against-renters-using-housing-vouchers-improves-results; "Q: Can Prohibiting Source-of-Income Discrimination Help Voucher Holders?," *Shelterforce*, July 30, 2018, https://shelterforce.org/2018/07/30/q-can-prohi biting-source-of-income-discrimination-help-voucher-holders/.

41. Philip Tegeler, "What Can HUD Do to Expand Public Housing and Community Ownership of Rental Housing?," Poverty & Race Research Action Council, April 2021, 3, http://www.prrac.org/pdf/hud-social-housing-2021.pdf.

42. "Project Based Vouchers," US Department of Housing and Urban Development, https://www.hud.gov/program_offices/public_indian_housing/programs/hcv/project; Anne Ray, Jeongseob Kim, Diep Nguyen, Jongwon Choi, Kelly McElwain, and Keely Jones Stater, "Opting In, Opting Out a Decade Later," *Cityscape* 20, no. 1 (2018): 63, 73, 78; "Preservation of HUD-Assisted Housing," Congressional Research Service, January 6, 2012, https://www.everycrsreport.com/files/20120106_R41182_98b85679ea576bfd75a7794252 7a9c6a12e562e1.pdf, 34; Vincent J. Reina and Ben Winter, "Safety Net? The Use of Vouchers When a Place-Based Rental Subsidy Ends," *Urban Studies* 56, no. 10 (2019): 2097.

43. Claire Rafford, "Lawmakers Urge BHI to Help Crawford Manor Residents Find Homes," *IndyStar*, May 23, 2023, https://www.indystar.com/story/news/local/boone-county/2023/05/23/lawmakers-help-residents-demolished-zionsville-senior-home-craw ford-manor/70244488007/.

44. "Emergency Rental Assistance Program," US Department of the Treasury, https://home.treasury.gov/policy-issues/coronavirus/assistance-for-state-local-and-tribal-governments/emergency-rental-assistance-program.

45. Quigley, "Social Housing Can Work."

46. Ryan Cooper and Peter Gowan, "Social Housing in the United States," People's Policy Project, April 2018, https://www.peoplespolicyproject.org/wp-content/uploads/2018/04/SocialHousing.pdf.

47. Corianne Payton Scally, Amanda Gold, and Nicole DuBois, "The Low-Income Housing Tax Credit," Urban Institute, 2018, 12–15, https://www.urban.org/sites/default/files/publication/98758/lithc_how_it_works_and_who_it_serves_final_0.pdf.

48. Alyssa Katz, "The Harm to Affordable Housing," *American Prospect*, June 28, 2018, https://prospect.org/power/harm-affordable-housing/.

49. Scally, Gold, and DuBois, "Low-Income Housing Tax Credit."

50. Rachel G. Blatt, "Affordable Rental Housing Development in the For-Profit Sector: A Case Study of McCormack Baron Salazar," Harvard Joint Center for Housing Studies, March 2016, 2, https://www.jchs.harvard.edu/sites/default/files/bratt_mbs_feb_2016_final.pdf.

51. Audie Cornish, "Blackstone-Starwood Merger Creates Largest Rental Home Company in U.S.," *NPR*, August 10, 2017, https://www.npr.org/2017/08/10/542663692/blackstone-starwood-merger-creates-largest-rental-home-company-in-u-s.

52. "Why Blackstone Made a \$5bn Bet on Housing Low-Income Americans," *Financial Times*, August 26, 2021, https://www.ft.com/content/3a60c15a-da53-45be-b246-a3f1288d5034; Patrick Butler, "UN Accuses Blackstone Group of Contributing to Global Housing Crisis," *Guardian*, March 26, 2019, https://www.theguardian.com/us-news/2019/mar/26/blackstone-group-accused-global-housing-crisis-un; "States and Real Estate Private Equity Firms Questioned for Compliance with Human Rights," UN Office of the High Commissioner for Human Rights, March 26, 2019, https://www.ohchr.org/en/news/2019/03/states-and-real-estate-private-equity-firms-questioned-compliance-human-rights.

53. Heather Vogell, "When Private Equity Becomes Your Landlord," *ProPublica*, February 7, 2022, https://www.propublica.org/article/when-private-equity-becomes-your-landlord.

54. Scally, Gold, and DuBois, "Low-Income Housing Tax Credit."

55. Scally, Gold, and DuBois, "Low-Income Housing Tax Credit." See also Allan Mallach, "Is the Solution to Homelessness Obvious?," *Shelterforce*, April 5, 2023, https://shelterforce.org/2023/04/05/is-the-solution-to-homelessness-obvious/. ("Even when we build new so-called affordable housing with the Low Income Tax Credit or other programs, most homeless people can't afford those units . . . unless they can get housing vouchers.")

56. Scally, Gold, and DuBois, "Low-Income Housing Tax Credit."

57. "What Happens to Low-Income Housing Tax Credit Properties at Year 15 and Beyond?," US Department of Housing and Urban Development, Office of Policy Development and Research, June 2012, 4, https://www.huduser.gov/portal//publications/pdf/what_happens_lihtc_sum.pdf; "The State of the Nation's Housing," Harvard Joint Center for Housing Studies, 2022, 41, https://www.jchs.harvard.edu/sites/default/files/reports/files/Harvard_JCHS_State_Nations_Housing_2022.pdf.

58. "Estimates of Federal Tax Expenditures for Fiscal Years 2020–2024," Joint Committee on Taxation, November 5, 2020, 29, https://www.jct.gov/CMSPages/GetFile.aspx?guid=ec4fb616-771b-4708-8d16-f774d5158469. In 2020, the program will cost \$10.3 billion. By 2024, this figure is estimated to rise to \$11.6 billion.

59. Carolina Reid, Adrian Napolitano, and Beatriz Stambuk-Torres, "The Costs of Affordable Housing Production: Insights from California's 9% Low-Income Housing Tax Credit Program," UC Berkeley Terner Center for Housing Innovation, 2020, https://ternercenter.berkeley.edu/wp-content/uploads/2020/08/LIHTC_Construction_Costs_2020.pdf.

60. Stephen Malpezzi and Kerry Vandell, "Does the Low-Income Housing Tax Credit Increase the Supply of Housing?," *Journal of Housing Economics* 11, no. 4 (December 2002): 360–80, https://www.researchgate.net/publication/222410344_Does_the_Low-Income_Housing_Tax_Credit_Increase_the_Supply_of_Housing.

61. Chew, "Social Housing for All"; "Why Blackstone Made a \$5bn Bet."

62. Stanley Chang and Alex Lee, "How We Can Bring Vienna's Housing Model to the U.S.," *Shelterforce*, December 19, 2023, https://shelterforce.org/2023/12/19/how-we-can-bring-viennas-housing-model-to-the-u-s/.

63. "Staff Memorandum: The Cost-Effectiveness of the Low-Income Housing Tax Credit Compared with Housing Vouchers," Congressional Budget Office, April 1992, 2, https://www.cbo.gov/sites/default/files/102nd-congress-1991-1992/reports/doc09b.pdf.

3. "WE HAVE TO ADDRESS THE RACISM"

1. "Warren Township, Marion County, IN," Census Reporter, https://censusreporter.org/profiles/06000US1809780144-warren-township-marion-county-in/.

2. Nick Gratez, Carl Gershenson, Peter Hepburn, and Matthew Desmond, "Who Is Evicted in America," Eviction Lab, October 3, 2023, https://evictionlab.org/who-is-evicted-in-america/; Deena Greenberg, Carl Gershenson, and Matthew Desmond, "Discrimination in Evictions: Empirical Evidence and Legal Challenges," *Harvard Civil Rights–Civil Liberties Law Review* 50 (2016): 116–58, https://scholar.harvard.edu/files/mdesmond/files/greenberg_et_al._.pdf?m=1462385261; Cleo Bluthenthal, "The Disproportionate Burden of Eviction on Black Women," Center for American Progress, August 14, 2023, https://www.americanprogress.org/article/the-disproportionate-burden-of-eviction-on-black-women/.

3. Graetz et al., "Who Is Evicted in America."

4. Ian Lundberg and Louis Donnelly, "How Many Children Experience Eviction during Childhood?," Urban Institute, 2018, https://housingmatters.urban.org/research-summary/how-many-children-experience-eviction-during-childhood.

5. Jeffrey Olivet, Marc Dones, Molly Richard, Catriona Wilkey, Svetlana Yampolskaya, Maya Beit-Arie, and Lunise Joseph, "Supporting Partnerships for Anti-racist Communities: Phase One Study Findings," Center for Social Innovation, March 2018, https://ighhub.org/sites/default/files/attachments/SPARC-Phase-1-Findings-March-2018.pdf.

6. Jack Caporal, "Average House Price by State in 2023," *Ascent*, May 11, 2023, https://www.fool.com/the-ascent/research/average-house-price-state/ ($436,800 average price); "What Will Homes Be Worth in 10 Years?," National Association of Realtors, October 27, 2020, https://www.nar.realtor/magazine/real-estate-news/economy/what-will-homes-be-worth-in-10-years (49 percent increase in house prices over ten years).

7. "The State of the Nation's Housing 2023," Joint Center for Housing Studies of Harvard University, 29–30, https://www.jchs.harvard.edu/sites/default/files/reports/files/Harvard_JCHS_The_State_of_the_Nations_Housing_2023.pdf.

8. Anna Bahney, "The Gulf between Black Homeowners and White Is Actually Getting Bigger, Not Smaller," *CNN Business*, March 2, 2023, https://www.cnn.com/2023/03/02/homes/race-and-home-buying-nar/index.html.

9. Jenny Schuetz, *Fixer-Upper: How to Repair America's Broken Housing Systems* (Washington, DC: Brookings Institution, 2022), 1–3; "U.S. Homeownership Rate Experiences Largest Annual Increase on Record, Though Black Homeownership Remains Lower Than a Decade Ago, NAR Analysis Finds," National Association of Realtors, February 23, 2022, https://www.nar.realtor/newsroom/u-s-homeownership-rate-experiences-largest-annual-increase-on-record-though-black-homeownership-remains-lower-than-decade-ago#:~:text=).

10. Scholastica Cororaton, "Single-Family Homeowners Typically Accumulated $225,000 in Housing Wealth over 10 Years," National Association of Realtors, January 7, 2022, https://www.nar.realtor/blogs/economists-outlook/single-family-homeowners-typically-accumulated-225K-in-housing-wealth-over-10-years.

11. "State of the Nation's Housing 2023," 23.

12. Richard Rothstein, *The Color of Law: A Forgotten History of How Our Government Segregated America* (New York: Liveright, 2017).

13. Keeanga-Yamahtta Taylor, *Race for Profit: How Banks and the Real Estate Industry Undermined Black Homeownership* (Chapel Hill: University of North Carolina Press, 2019), xviii.

14. Students for Fair Admissions, Inc. v. President and Fellows of Harvard College, 600 U.S. 181, Jackson, J., dissenting (2023).

15. Roger L. Ransom, "The Economics of the Civil War," Economic History Association, https://eh.net/encyclopedia/the-economics-of-the-civil-war/.

16. R. P. Lockhart, "How Slavery Became America's First Big Business," *Vox*, August 16, 2019, https://www.vox.com/identities/2019/8/16/20806069/slavery-economy-capitalism-violence-cotton-edward-baptist.

17. Robert L. Reece, "Whitewashing Slavery: Legacy of Slavery and White Social Outcomes," *Social Problems* 67 (2020): 304–23, https://academic.oup.com/socpro/article-abstract/67/2/304/5522935?redirectedFrom=fulltext&login=false.

18. Mehrsa Badaran, *The Color of Money: Black Banks and the Racial Wealth Gap* (Cambridge, MA: Harvard University Press, 2017), 9–11.

19. Vann R. Newkirk II, "The Great Land Robbery: The Shameful Story of How 1 Million Black Families Have Been Ripped from Their Farms," *Atlantic*, September 2019, https://www.theatlantic.com/magazine/archive/2019/09/this-land-was-our-land/594742/.

20. "The Southern 'Black Codes' of 1865–66," Constitutional Rights Foundation, https://www.crf-usa.org/brown-v-board-50th-anniversary/southern-black-codes.html; Keri Leigh Merritt, "Land and the Roots of African-American Poverty," *Aeon*, March 11, 2016, https://aeon.co/ideas/land-and-the-roots-of-african-american-poverty.

21. Rothstein, *Color of Law*, 154.

22. Students for Fair Admissions, Inc. v. President and Fellows of Harvard College.

23. Derick Johnson, "Viewing Social Security through the Civil Rights Lens," NAACP, August 14, 2020, https://naacp.org/articles/viewing-social-security-through-civil-rights-lens.

24. Rebecca Dixon, "From Excluded to Essential: Tracing the Racist Exclusion of Farmworkers, Domestic Workers, and Tipped Workers from the Fair Labor Standards Act," National Employment Law Project, May 3, 2021, https://s27147.pcdn.co/wp-content/uploads/NELP-Testimony-FLSA-May-2021.pdf.

25. Camille Lloyd, "One in Four Black Workers Report Discrimination at Work," *Gallup News*, January 12, 2021, https://news.gallup.com/poll/328394/one-four-black-workers-report-discrimination-work.aspx.

26. Valerie Wilson and William Darity Jr., "Understanding Black-White Disparities in Labor Market Models," Economic Policy Institute, March 25, 2022, https://www.epi.org/unequalpower/publications/understanding-black-white-disparities-in-labor-market-outcomes/.

27. "Racial and Ethnic Achievement Gaps," Stanford Center for Education Policy and Analysis, https://cepa.stanford.edu/educational-opportunity-monitoring-project/achievement-gaps/race/.

28. Wilson and Darity, "Understanding Black-White Disparities."

29. Matthew Desmond, *Poverty, by America* (New York: Crown, 2023), 145.

30. Merritt, "Land and the Roots of African-American Poverty."

31. Rothstein, *Color of Law*, 63–64.

32. "Legislative History of the VA Home Loan Guaranty Program," US Department of Veterans Affairs, https://www.benefits.va.gov/homeloans/documents/docs/history.pdf.

33. Mitchell Hartman, "U.S. 30-Year Fixed-Rate Mortgage an 'Outlier,'" *Marketplace*, October 14, 2015, https://www.marketplace.org/2015/10/14/us-30-year-fixed-rate-mortgage-outlier/.

34. Melvin Oliver and Thomas M. Shapiro, *Black Wealth / White Wealth: A New Perspective on Racial Inequality* (New York: Routledge, 1997), 18; Alex Schwartz, *Housing Policy in the United States* (New York: Routledge, 2021). 61.

35. Merritt, "Land and the Roots of African-American Poverty."

36. Rothstein, *Color of Law*, 64–67.

37. Rothstein, 66.

38. Ta-Nehisi Coates, "The Case for Reparations," *Atlantic*, June 15, 2014. https://www.theatlantic.com/magazine/archive/2014/06/the-case-for-reparations/361631/.

39. Rothstein, *Color of Law*, 78–85.

40. La-Brina Almeida, "A History of Racist Federal Housing Policies," Massachusetts Budget and Policy Center, August 6, 2021, https://massbudget.org/2021/08/06/a-history-of-racist-federal-housing-policies/.

41. Ira Katznelson, *When Affirmative Action Was White* (New York: Norton, 2005), 140.

42. Shelley v. Kraemer, 334 U.S. 1 (1948).

43. Desmond, *Poverty, by America*, 166.

44. Taylor, *Race for Profit*.

45. People's Action, *A National Homes Guarantee*, briefing book, 12, https://homes-guarantee.com/wp-content/uploads/Homes-Guarantee-_-Briefing-Book.pdf; Keeanga-Yamahtta Taylor, "How Real Estate Segregated America," *Dissent*, Fall 2018, https://www.dissentmagazine.org/article/how-real-estate-segregated-america-fair-housing-act-race.

46. Jessica Lussenhop and Joey Peters, "How Contracts for Deed Put Families at Financial Risk," *ProPublica*, November 21, 2022, https://www.propublica.org/article/how-contracts-for-deed-put-families-at-financial-risk.

47. Samuel George et al., "The Plunder of Black Wealth in Chicago: New Findings on the Lasting Toll of Predatory Housing Contracts," Samuel DuBois Cook Center on Social Equity, Duke University, May 2019, https://socialequity.duke.edu/wp-content/uploads/2019/10/Plunder-of-Black-Wealth-in-Chicago.pdf.

48. Natalie Moore, "Contract Buying Robbed Black Families in Chicago of Billions," *NPR*, May 30, 2019, https://www.npr.org/local/309/2019/05/30/728122642/contract-buying-robbed-black-families-in-chicago-of-billions.

49. Ryan Reft, "The Foreclosure Crisis and Its Impact on Today's Housing Market," *KCET*, September 20, 2017, https://www.kcet.org/shows/city-rising/the-foreclosure-crisis-and-its-impact-on-todays-housing-market.

50. "Report Shows African Americans Lost Half Their Wealth Due to Housing Crisis and Unemployment," National Low Income Housing Coalition, August 30, 2013, https://nlihc.org/resource/report-shows-african-americans-lost-half-their-wealth-due-housing-crisis-and-unemployment; Taylor, "How Real Estate Segregated America."

51. "Justice Department Reaches Settlement with Wells Fargo Resulting in More Than $175 Million in Relief for Homeowners to Resolve Fair Lending Claims," US Department of Justice, July 12, 2012, https://www.justice.gov/opa/pr/justice-department-reaches-settlement-wells-fargo-resulting-more-175-million-relief.

52. Charlie Savage, "Countrywide Will Settle Bias Suit," *New York Times*, December 21, 2011, https://www.nytimes.com/2011/12/22/business/us-settlement-reported-on-countrywide-lending.html.

53. Joseph E. Stiglitz, "Capitalist Fools," *Vanity Fair*, January 2009, https://www.vanityfair.com/news/2009/01/stiglitz200901-2.

54. "Wall Street and Single Family Rentals," Americans for Financial Reform, January 17, 2018, http://ourfinancialsecurity.org/2018/01/afr-report-wall-street-and-single-family-rentals/, 35–37; "Where Have All the Houses Gone? Private Equity, Single Family Rentals, and America's Neighborhoods," US House Committee on Financial Services, 1, https://financialservices.house.gov/uploadedfiles/hhrg-117-ba09-20220628-sd002.pdf.

55. Jonathan Rockwell and Andre M. Perry, "Biased Appraisals and the Devaluation of Housing in Black Neighborhoods," *Brookings*, November 17, 2021, https://www.brookings.edu/articles/biased-appraisals-and-the-devaluation-of-housing-in-black-neighbor-hoods/.

56. Tess Moore, "Investors Force Black Families out of Homes, New Research Shows," Georgia Tech New Center, August 6, 2023, https://news.gatech.edu/news/2023/08/07/investors-force-black-families-out-home-ownership-new-research-shows.

57. Kevin Schaul and Jonathan O'Connell, "Investors Bought a Record Share of Homes in 2021. See Where," *Washington Post*, February 16, 2022, https://www.washingtonpost.com/business/interactive/2022/housing-market-investors/.

58. Anjeanette Damon, Byard Duncan, and Mollie Simon, "The Ugly Truth behind 'We Buy Ugly Houses,'" *ProPublica*, May 11, 2023, https://www.propublica.org/article/ugly-truth-behind-we-buy-ugly-houses.

59. "The State of the Nation's Housing," Joint Center for Housing Studies of Harvard University, 2022, 18, https://www.jchs.harvard.edu/sites/default/files/reports/files/Harvard_JCHS_State_Nations_Housing_2022.pdf.

60. David E. Jacobs, "Environmental Health Disparities in Housing," *American Journal of Public Health* 101 (December 2011): S115–S122, https://www.ncbi.nlm.nih.gov/pmc/articles/PMC3222490/.

61. "Who Owns Indy's Houses: A Review of the Largest Single-Family Home Investors," Fair Housing Center of Central Indiana, August 9, 2023, https://www.fhcci.org/wp-content/uploads/2023/08/Who-Owns-Indy-Homes-8-9-23-3.pdf. (More than half of the single-family rental homes in the area where our clients live—the far east side of Indianapolis—are owned by out-of-state investors, with those owners most prevalent in areas with fast-growing Black and Hispanic populations. These out-of-state investors file evictions and accumulate code violations at a higher rate than other owners.)

62. For an example of problems alleged by tenants of a company self-identified as the largest single-family rental landlord in housing costing less than $1,400 per month, see Kavahn Mansouri and Daniel Wheaton, "VineBrook Homes Owns Thousands of Midwest Homes. Tenants Are Crying Foul," NPR, May 10, 2023, https://nebraskapublicmedia.org/en/news/news-articles/vinebrook-homes-owns-thousands-of-midwest-homes-tenants-are-crying-foul/.

63. Jason Richardson, Bruce Mitchell, and Jad Edlebi, "Gentrification and Disinvestment 2020," National Community Reinvestment Coalition, June 2020, https://ncrc.org/gentrification20/.

64. Wildstyle Paschall, "Indiana Avenue: The Ethnic Cleansing of Black Indianapolis," *New America Indianapolis*, February 4, 2020, https://www.newamerica.org/indianapolis/blog/indiana-avenue-ethnic-cleansing-black-indianapolis/.

65. "Homelessness in Indianapolis: 2021 Marion County Point-in-Time Count," Indiana University Public Policy Institute, July 2021, https://policyinstitute.iu.edu/doc/pit-count-2021.pdf.

66. "Renewing Inequality: Family Displacement through Urban Renewal, 1950–1966," University of Richmond, https://dsl.richmond.edu/panorama/renewal/#view=0/0/1&viz=cartogram.

67. Brent Cebul, "Tearing Down Black America," *Boston Review*, July 22, 2020, https://www.bostonreview.net/articles/brent-cebul-tearing-down-black-america/.

68. Cebul, "Tearing Down Black America."

69. Cebul, "Tearing Down Black America."

70. Greg Miller, "Maps Show How Tearing Down City Slums Displaced Thousands," *National Geographic*, December 5, 2017, https://www.nationalgeographic.com/history/article/urban-renewal-projects-maps-united-states.

71. Paschall, "Indiana Avenue."

72. William H. Frey, "Neighborhood Segregation Persists for Black, Latino or His-panics, and Asian Americans," *Brookings*, April 6, 2021, https://www.brookings.edu/arti cles/neighborhood-segregation-persists-for-black-latino-or-hispanic-and-asian-ameri cans/.

73. Ken Ward Jr., "How Black Communities Become 'Sacrifice Zones' for Industrial Air Pollution," *ProPublica*, December 21, 2021, https://www.propublica.org/article/ how-black-communities-become-sacrifice-zones-for-industrial-air-pollution.

74. "Racial Segregation Makes Consequences of Lead Exposure Worse," National Insti-tutes of Health, August 30, 2022, https://www.nih.gov/news-events/nih-research-matters/ racial-segregation-makes-consequences-lead-exposure-worse#:~:text=.

75. Amee Chew, "Social Housing for All: A Vision for Thriving Communities, Renter Power, and Racial Justice," Center for Popular Democracy, March 2022, 15–16, https:// www.populardemocracy.org/socialhousingforall; Rothstein, *Color of Law*, 19–37.

76. Chew, "Social Housing for All," and Edward Goetz, *New Deal Ruins: Race, Economic Justice, and Public Housing Policy* (Ithaca, NY: Cornell University Press, 2013), 78–79.

77. Coates, "Case for Reparations."

78. Rothstein, *Color of Law*; Taylor, *Race for Profit*, 34.

79. "We Deserve a Place to Live: How U.S. Underfunding Public Housing Harms Rights in New York, New Mexico, and Beyond," Human Rights Watch, September 27, 2022, https://www.hrw.org/report/2022/09/27/we-deserve-have-place-live/how-us-under funding-public-housing-harms-rights-new.

80. Goetz, *New Deal Ruins*, 110.

81. Goetz, 112.

82. Dan Darrah, "We Need Public Housing, Not Affordable Housing," *Jacobin*, April 17, 2022, https://jacobin.com/2022/04/us-canadian-social-housing-affordability-ownership-speculation; Rick Perlstein, *The Conservative Politics of Homeownership* (Paris: Cairn, 2007), 59.

83. Taylor, *Race for Profit*, xvii.

84. "Single Family Housing Direct Home Loans," US Department of Agriculture, https://www.rd.usda.gov/programs-services/single-family-housing-programs/single-family-housing-direct-home-loans,

85. Desmond, *Poverty, by America*, 145–46.

86. Connor Nakamura, "Affordable Housing as Local Reparations for Black Ameri-cans: Case Studies," Other and Belonging Institute, August 24, 2022, https://belonging. berkeley.edu/affordable-housing-local-reparations-black-americans-case-studies.

87. Channele Chandler, "How Reparations Pioneer Evanston, Ill. Is Rolling Out Pay-ments to Black Citizens," *Yahoo News*, July 13, 2023, https://news.yahoo.com/how-repa rations-pioneer-evanston-ill-is-rolling-out-payments-to-black-citizens-090000335.html? guccounter=1.

4. HOUSING SOCIALISM FOR THE RICH

1. Erik Gartland, "Chart Book: Funding Limitations Create Widespread Unmet Need for Rental Assistance," Center on Budget and Policy Priorities, February 15, 2022, https://www.cbpp.org/research/housing/funding-limitations-create-widespread-unmet-need-for-rental-assistance.

2. "Families with Children and Non-elderly Adults without Children Have the Greatest Unmet Need for Rental Assistance," Center on Budget and Policy Priorities, 24, https://www.cbpp.org/research/housing/three-out-of-four-low-income-at-risk-renters-do-not-receive-federal-rental-assistance.

3. "About the Gap Report," National Low Income Housing Coalition, https://nlihc.org/gap/about.

4. Gartland, "Chart Book."

5. "Week 54 Household Pulse Survey: February 1–February 13," United States Census Bureau, February 22, 2023, https://www.census.gov/data/tables/2023/demo/hhp/hhp54.html; Matthew Desmond, "Poor Black Women Are Evicted at Alarming Rates, Setting Off a Chain of Hardship," MacArthur Foundation: How Housing Matters, March 2014, https://www.macfound.org/media/files/hhm_research_brief_-_poor_black_women_are_evicted_at_alarming_rates.pdf; "More Older Americans Become Homeless as Inflation Rises and Housing Costs Spike," NPR, November 10, 2022, https://www.npr.org/sections/health-shots/2022/11/10/1135125625/homelessness-elderly-housing-inflation; David Kroman, "Once a Safeguard against Homelessness, Disability Payments Can't Keep Up with the Rent," Crosscut, September 4, 2019, https://crosscut.com/2019/09/once-safeguard-against-homelessness-disability-payments-cant-keep-rent.

6. "A Quick Guide to SNAP Eligibility and Benefits," Center on Budget and Policy Priorities, October 2, 2023, https://www.cbpp.org/research/food-assistance/a-quick-guide-to-snap-eligibility-and-benefits; "Policy Basics: Introduction to Medicaid," Center on Budget and Policy Priorities, April 14, 2020, https://www.cbpp.org/research/health/introduction-to-medicaid.

7. Joe Cortright, "Dr. King: Socialism for the Rich and Rugged Free Enterprise Capitalism for the Poor," CityCommentary, January 21, 2019, https://cityobservatory.org/dr-king-socialism-for-the-rich-and-rugged-free-enterprise-capitalism-for-the-poor/.

8. Sofia Lopez and Sara Myklebust, "Make Them Pay: Corporate Landlords Should Cancel Rent, Mortgages, and Utilities for the Duration of the COVID-19 Pandemic," Action Center on Race and the Economy, May 19, 2020, https://acrecampaigns.org/wp-content/uploads/2020/05/Make-Them-Pay-May-2020.pdf; Hyojung Lee, "Who Owns Rental Properties, and Is It Changing?," Joint Center for Housing Studies of Harvard University, August 18, 2017, http://www.jchs.harvard.edu/blog/who-owns-rental-properties-and-is-it-changing/.

9. Lee, "Who Owns Rental Properties?"

10. "Wall Street and Single Family Rentals," Americans for Financial Reform, January 17, 2018, 30–32, http://ourfinancialsecurity.org/2018/01/afr-report-wall-street-and-single-family-rentals/; Adam Travis, "The Organization of Neglect: Limited Liability Companies and Housing Disinvestment," American Sociological Review 84, no. 1 (January 25, 2019), https://doi.org/10.1177/0003122418821339; Desiree Fields, "Automated Landlord: Digital Technologies and Post-crisis Financial Accumulation," Employment and Planning 54, no. 1 (May 1, 2019), https://doi.org/10.1177/0308518X19846514.

11. Ko Lyn Cheang, "Tenants at Lakeside Pointe Suffered Years of Neglect. Then, Their Homes Caught Fire," Indianapolis Star, November 24, 2021, https://www.indystar.com/story/news/local/marion-county/2021/11/24/indianapolis-apartments-lakeside-pointe-tenants-suffered-neglect-before-fire/8725147002/.

12. "Consumer Expenditures—2021," US Bureau of Labor Statistics, Consumer Expenditure Surveys, 2021, https://www.bls.gov/news.release/cesan.nr0.htm; Thomas Piketty, Emmanuel Saez, and Gabriel Zucman, "Distributional National Accounts: Methods and Estimates for the United States," Quarterly Journal of Economics 133, no.2(May2018):553–609,https://academic.oup.com/qje/article/133/2/553/4430651?login=false.

13. Giacomo Tognini, "Meet the Real Estate Billionaire Who Hates Affordable Housing and Loves Trump and the GOP," Forbes, November 6, 2022, https://www.forbes.com/sites/giacomotognini/2022/11/04/meet-the-real-estate-billionaire-who-hates-affordable-housing-and-loves-trump-and-the-gop/?sh=12644d430dc8.

14. Paul Sullivan, "How Loopholes Help Trump and Other Real Estate Moguls Avoid Taxes," *New York Times*, May 10, 2019, https://www.nytimes.com/2019/05/10/your-money/trump-real-estate-taxes.html.

15. "Bloomberg Billionaires Index—Stephen Ross," *Bloomberg*, https://www.bloom berg.com/billionaires/profiles/stephen-m-ross/?leadSource=uverify%20wall; Jesse Eisinger, Jeff Ernsthausen, and Paul Kiel, "These Real Estate and Oil Tycoons Avoided Paying Taxes for Years," *ProPublica*, December 7, 2021, https://www.propublica.org/article/these-real-estate-and-oil-tycoons-used-paper-losses-to-avoid-paying-taxes-for-years.

16. Eisinger, Ernsthausen, and Kiel, "These Real Estate and Oil Tycoons."

17. Tamar Katz, "Tax the REITs: An Argument to Revoke Single-Family REITs' Tax Exemption," *Columbia Business Law Review*, March 14, 2022, https://journals.library.columbia.edu/index.php/CBLR/announcement/view/509; Nareit Staff, "Sector Spotlight: Residential," *REIT Magazine*, September 15, 2022, https://www.reit.com/news/reit-magazine/september-october-2022/sector-spotlight-residential#:~:text=.

18. "Pass-Through Deduction Benefits Wealthiest, Loses Needed Revenue, and Encourages Tax Avoidance," Center on Budget and Policy Priorities, March 27, 2019, https://www.cbpp.org/research/federal-tax/pass-through-deduction-benefits-wealthiest-loses-needed-revenue-and-encourages#:~:text=.

19. Alex F. Schwartz, *Housing Policy in the United States* (New York: Routledge, 2021), 101.

20. Chuck Marr, "JCT Highlights Pass-Through Deduction's Tilt toward the Top," Center on Budget and Policy Priorities, April 24, 2018, https://www.cbpp.org/blog/jct-highlights-pass-through-deductions-tilt-toward-the-top.

21. Edward Kleinbard, "Congress' Worst Tax Idea Ever," *Hill*, March 25, 2019, https://thehill.com/opinion/finance/434998-congress-worst-tax-idea-ever/.

22. Francine McKenna, "Trump Is Justified in Saying That His Billion-Plus of Tax Losses May Not Have Been Financial," *MarketWatch*, May 8, 2019, https://www.marketwatch.com/story/trump-is-justified-in-saying-that-his-billion-plus-of-tax-losses-may-not-have-been-financial-2019-05-08.

23. Tognini, "Meet the Real Estate Billionaire."

24. Jay Maddox, "Why Multifamily Values Will Continue to Defy Gravity," *Multi-Housing News*, October 13, 2021, https://www.multihousingnews.com/why-multifamily-values-will-continue-to-defy-gravity/.

25. "The Distribution of Household Income, 2016," Congressional Budget Office, July 9, 2019, https://www.cbo.gov/publication/55413.

26. Kathleen Bryant, Samantha Jacoby, and Chuck Marr, "Substantial Income of Wealthy Households Escapes Annual Taxation or Enjoys Special Tax Breaks," Center on Budget and Policy Priorities, November 13, 2019, https://www.cbpp.org/sites/default/files/atoms/files/11-13-19tax.pdf.

27. "Topic No. 409 Capital Gains and Losses," Internal Revenue Service, https://www.irs.gov/taxtopics/tc409.

28. Adam Looney and Kevin B. Moore, "Changes in the Distribution of After-Tax Wealth: Has Income Tax Policy Increased Wealth Inequality?," Finance and Economics Discussion Series, Board of Governors of the Federal Reserve System, August 2015, http://dx.doi.org/10.17016/FEDS.2015.058.

29. Looney and Moore, "Changes in the Distribution."

30. Rebecca Lake, "Buy, Borrow, Die: How the Rich Avoid Taxes," *Yahoo Finance*, January 23, 2023, https://finance.yahoo.com/news/buy-borrow-die-rich-avoid-140004536.html.

31. Doty Pruett Wilson PC Certified Public Accountants, "11 Ways to Significantly Lower Your Taxes as a Real Estate Investor," DPWCPAs, May 19, 2020, https://dpwcpas.com/11-ways-to-significantly-lower-your-taxes-as-a-real-estate-investor/.

32. Joe Lovinger, "Superyachts and Picassos: How Real Estate's Wealthiest Spend Their Millions," *Real Deal*, August 9, 2021, https://therealdeal.com/magazine/national-august-2021/toys-of-the-titans/.

33. Debipriya Chatterjee and Samuel Stein, "421-a at 50: Rising Cost, Diminishing Returns Part 1," Community Service Society, February 2022, https://smhttp-ssl-58547.nexcesscdn.net/nycss/images/uploads/pubs/RisingCost_V9.pdf.

34. "NMHC 2020 Top Owners List," National Multifamily Housing Council, https://www.nmhc.org/research-insight/the-nmhc-50/top-50-lists/2020-top-owners-list/; "Taxpayer Subsidized Evictions: Corporate Landlords Pocket Federal Sweetheart Deals, Subsidies, and Tax Breaks While Evicting Struggling Families," Private Equity Stakeholder Project, January 2021, https://www.jwj.org/wp-content/uploads/2021/01/JWJEDU_Report_TaxpayerSubsidizedEvictions_Jan2021_V4.pdf.

35. "Property Tax Breaks to Lure Businesses Largely Ineffective, Report Says," Lincoln Institute of Land Policy, June 26, 2012, https://www.lincolninst.edu/es/news/press-releases/property-tax-breaks-lure-businesses-largely-ineffective-report-says.

36. "Tax Expenditure of the Week: Tax Free Capital Gains for Primary Residences," Center for American Progress, April 6, 2011, https://www.americanprogress.org/article/tax-expenditure-of-the-week-tax-free-capital-gains-for-primary-residences/; Schwartz, *Housing Policy in the United States*, 6; "An Economic Analysis of the Mortgage Interest Deduction," Congressional Research Service, June 25, 2020, https://sgp.fas.org/crs/misc/R46429.pdf.

37. Matthew Desmond, *Poverty, by America* (New York: Crown, 2023), 99.

38. "Nearly Two-Thirds Say Affordability Factors Are Holding Them Back from Homeownership," *Bankrate*, March 30, 2022, https://www.bankrate.com/pdfs/pr/20220330-march-fsp.pdf.

39. Schwartz, *Housing Policy in the United States*, 337.

40. Richard Rothstein, *The Color of Law: A Forgotten History of How Our Government Segregated America* (New York: Liveright, 2017).

41. Howard Gleckman, "The TCJA Shifted the Benefits of Tax Expenditures to Higher-Income Households," Tax Policy Center, October 26, 2018, https://www.taxpolicycenter.org/taxvox/tcja-shifted-benefits-tax-expenditures-higher-income-households.

42. Jack Caporal, "Average House Price by State in 2023," *Ascent*, May 11, 2023, https://www.fool.com/the-ascent/research/average-house-price-state/ ($436,800 average price); "What Will Homes Be Worth in 10 Years?," National Association of Realtors, October 27, 2020, https://www.nar.realtor/magazine/real-estate-news/economy/what-will-homes-be-worth-in-10-years (49% increase in house prices over ten years).

43. "Most Renters Want to Own a Home; Lifestyle Changes Are Top Motivation to Buy," National Association of Realtors, February 7, 2018, https://www.nar.realtor/newsroom/most-renters-want-to-own-a-home-lifestyle-changes-are-top-motivation-to-buy.

44. Rothstein, *Color of Law*.

45. David Waddington, "Census Bureau Statistics Measure Equity Gaps across Demographic Groups," US Census Bureau, September 14, 2023, https://www.census.gov/library/stories/2021/09/understanding-equity-through-census-bureau-data.html.

46. Scholastica Cororaton, "Single-Family Homeowners Typically Accumulated $225,000 in Housing Wealth over 10 Years," National Association of Realtors, January 7, 2022, https://www.nar.realtor/blogs/economists-outlook/single-family-homeowners-typically-accumulated-225K-in-housing-wealth-over-10-years.

47. Ta-Nehisi Coates, "The Case for Reparations," *Atlantic*, June 15, 2014, https://www.theatlantic.com/magazine/archive/2014/06/the-case-for-reparations/361631/; Brittany Hutson and Miriam Axel-Lute, "Making Homeownership Work Better," *Shelterforce*, March 15, 2022, https://shelterforce.org/2022/03/15/making-homeownership-work-better/.

48. Andre M. Perry, Jonathan Rothwell, and David Harshbarger, "The Devaluation of Assets in Black Neighborhoods," *Brookings*, November 27, 2018, https://www.brookings.edu/research/devaluation-of-assets-in-black-neighborhoods/.

49. Monica Potts, "The Collapse of Black Wealth," *American Prospect*, November 21, 2012, https://prospect.org/civil-rights/collapse-black-wealth/; US House Committee on Financial Services, "Where Have All the Houses Gone? Private Equity, Single Family Rentals, and America's Neighborhoods," 2, 4, https://www.congress.gov/event/117th-congress/house-event/114969/text.

50. Keeanga-Yamahtta Taylor, *Race for Profit: How Banks and the Real Estate Industry Undermined Black Homeownership* (Chapel Hill: University of North Carolina Press, 2019), 253.

51. Alexandra Stevenson and Matthew Goldstein, "Rent-to-Own Homes: A Win-Win for Landlords, a Risk for Struggling Tenants," *New York Times*, August 21, 2016, https://www.nytimes.com/2016/08/22/business/dealbook/rent-to-own-homes-a-win-win-for-landlords-a-risk-for-struggling-tenants.html; Fran Quigley, "Wall Street Is Holding a Gun to the Heads of Mobile Home Residents," *Jacobin*, May 4, 2023, https://jacobin.com/2023/05/mobile-home-park-evictions-rent-wall-street-affordable-housing.

52. Jamie Ross and Kody Glazer, "Overcoming NIMBY Opposition to Affordable Housing," National Low-Income Housing Coalition, 2022, https://nlihc.org/sites/default/files/2022-03/2022AG_2-11_Avoiding-Overcoming.pdf.

53. Rick Perlstein, *The Conservative Politics of Homeownership* (Paris: Cairn, 2007), 59.

54. Cororaton, "Single-Family Homeowners"; Dan Darrah, "We Need Public Housing, Not Affordable Housing," *Jacobin*, April 17, 2022, https://jacobin.com/2022/04/us-canadian-social-housing-affordability-ownership-speculation.

55. Erica York, "Who Benefits from Itemized Deductions?," Tax Foundation, March 7, 2019, https://taxfoundation.org/itemized-deduction-benefit/; Gleckman, "TCJA Shifted."

56. Amee Chew, "Social Housing for All: A Vision for Thriving Communities, Renter Power, and Racial Justice," Center for Popular Democracy, March 2022, 9–14, https://www.populardemocracy.org/socialhousingforall.

57. "Ezra Klein Interviews Jenny Schuetz," *New York Times*, July 19, 2022, https://www.nytimes.com/2022/07/19/podcasts/transcript-ezra-klein-interviews-jenny-schuetz.html.

58. Jenny Schuetz, *Fixer-Upper: How to Repair America's Broken Housing Systems* (Washington, DC: Brookings Institution, 2022), 75.

59. Tim Scott, "Opportunity Zones," accessed June 11, 2024, https://www.scott.senate.gov/issues/opportunity-zones/.

60. Samantha Jacoby," Final Opportunity Zone Rules Could Raise Tax Break's Cost," Center on Budget and Policy Priorities, February 3, 2020, https://www.cbpp.org/blog/final-opportunity-zone-rules-could-raise-tax-breaks-cost.

61. Jesse Drucker and Eric Lipton, "How a Trump Tax Break to Help Poor Communities Became a Windfall for the Rich," *New York Times*, August 31, 2019, https://www.nytimes.com/2019/08/31/business/tax-opportunity-zones.html; Editorial Board, "Opportunity Zones—for Billionaires," *New York Times*, November 6, 2019, https://www.nytimes.com/2019/11/16/opinion/trump-tax-opportunity-zones.html.

62. Samantha Jacoby, "Potential Flaws of Opportunity Zones Loom, as Do Risks of Large-Scale Tax Avoidance," Center on Budget and Policy Priorities, January 11, 2019, https://www.cbpp.org/research/federal-tax/potential-flaws-of-opportunity-zones-loom-as-do-risks-of-large-scale-tax.

63. David C. Ling and Milena Petrova, "The Tax and Economic Impacts of Section 1031 Like-Kind Exchanges in Real Estate," Real Estate Research Consortium, September 2020, https://warrington.ufl.edu/due-diligence/wp-content/uploads/sites/179/2021/04/the-tax-and-economic-impacts-of-section-1031-like-kind-exchanges-in-real-estate.pdf.

64. Jay Maddox, "Why Multifamily Values Will Continue to Defy Gravity," *Multi-Housing News*, October 13, 2021, https://www.multihousingnews.com/why-multifamily-values-will-continue-to-defy-gravity/.

65. "Tax Policy Center, Briefing Book," Urban Institute and Brookings Institution, https://www.taxpolicycenter.org/briefing-book/what-are-largest-tax-expenditures.

66. Roderick Taylor, "New Estate Tax Cut Encourages More Wealthy Individuals to Skirt Capital Gains Tax," Center on Budget and Policy Priorities, May 17, 2018, https://www.cbpp.org/blog/new-estate-tax-cut-encourages-more-wealthy-individuals-to-skirt-capital-gains-tax.

67. Facundo Alvaredo, Bertrand Garbinti, and Thomas Piketty, "On the Share of Inheritance in Aggregate Wealthy: Europe and the USA, 1900–2010," *Economica*, February 3, 2017, http://www.piketty.pse.ens.fr/files/AlvaredoGarbintiPiketty2017.pdf.

68. Sullivan, "How Loopholes Help Trump."

69. Bryant, Jacoby, and Marr, "Substantial Income of Wealthy Households."

70. Chuck Collins, "Updates: Billionaire Wealth, U.S. Job Loss and Pandemic Profiteers," Inequality.org, November 21, 2022, https://inequality.org/great-divide/updates-billionaire-pandemic/; "Eviction Tracking," Eviction Lab, https://evictionlab.org/eviction-tracking/; German Lopez, "Homelessness in America Is Getting Worse," *New York Times*, July 15, 2022, https://www.nytimes.com/2022/07/15/briefing/homelessness-america-housing-crisis.html.

71. Erica Payne and Morris Pearl, *Tax the Rich! How Lies, Loopholes, and Lobbyists Make the Rich Even Richer* (New York: New Press, 2021).

72. "Wyden Unveils Billionaire Tax," US Senate Committee on Finance, October 27, 2021, https://www.finance.senate.gov/chairmans-news/wyden-unveils-billionaires-income-tax.

73. People's Action, *A National Homes Guarantee*, briefing book, September 5, 2019, 15–17, https://homesguarantee.com/wp-content/uploads/Homes-Guarantee-_-Briefing-Book.pdf.

74. Chew, "Social Housing for All."

75. "Vacant Homes v. Homelessness in Cities around the U.S.," United Way CA, March 28, 2023, https://unitedwaynca.org/blog/vacant-homes-vs-homelessness-by-city/.

76. Fran Quigley, "Midterm Voters Send a Message: Housing Is a Human Right," *Common Dreams*, November 20, 2022, https://www.commondreams.org/views/2022/11/20/midterm-voters-send-message-housing-human-right.

77. "Khanna, Porter, and Takano Introduce Bill to Rein in Rent Gouging by Wealthy Corporate Landlords," Congressman Ro Khanna, press release, November 7, 2022, https://khanna.house.gov/media/press-releases/release-khanna-porter-and-takano-introduce-bill-rein-rent-gouging-wealthy; "Brown, Colleagues Introduce Bill to Crack Down on Big Corporate Investors That Buy Up Local Homes, Drive Up Housing Prices," US Senate Committee on Banking, Housing, and Urban Affairs, July 11, 2023, https://www.banking.senate.gov/newsroom/majority/brown-colleagues-introduce-bill-crack-down-big-corporate-investors-buy-up-local-homes-drive-housing-prices.

78. "Municipal Politics: 'Red Vienna'—a Success Story," City of Vienna, accessed June 11, 2024, https://www.wien.gv.at/english/history/commemoration/housing.html.

5. HOW WE FIX THIS—PUMP THE BRAKES ON OUR EVICTION MACHINE

1. Lillian Leung, Peter Hepburn, and Matthew Desmond, "Serial Eviction Filing: Civil Courts, Property Management, and the Threat of Displacement," *Social Forces* 100 (September 2021): 316–44, https://academic.oup.com/sf/article/100/1/316/5903878.

2. "Top Evicting Large Cities in the United States," Eviction Lab, https://evictionlab.org/rankings/#/evictions?r=United%20States&a=0&d=evictionRate&lang=en.

3. "Small Claims Costs and Filing Fees," Washington Township, Marion County, Indiana, accessed June 12, 2024, https://washtwp.org/sccourt-fees.html.

4. Carlos Waters, Jason Reginato, and Lindsey Jacobson, "The Rise of Corporate Landlords in the U.S.," *CNBC*, February 21, 2023, https://www.cnbc.com/video/2023/02/21/the-rise-of-corporate-landlords-in-the-us.html.

5. *AFR Report: Wall Street and Single Family Rentals*, Americans for Financial Reform, January 17, 2018, 15, https://ourfinancialsecurity.org/2018/01/afr-report-wall-street-and-single-family-rentals/; Ko Lyn Cheang and Binghui Huang, "Corporate Landlords Filed 88% of All Evictions in Indianapolis through September," *Indianapolis Star*, October 24, 2021, https://www.indystar.com/story/news/realestate/2021/10/24/indianapolis-eviction-moratorium-top-evictors-during-pandemic/6102198001/.

6. Leung, Hepburn, and Desmond, "Serial Eviction Filing."

7. A brief version of this discussion of the need to reform the eviction court process was originally published in Fran Quigley, "It's Time to Pump the Brakes on the Government Eviction Machine," *Hill*, June 17, 2023, https://thehill.com/opinion/civil-rights/4051899-its-time-to-pump-the-brakes-on-the-government-eviction-machine/.

8. Leung, Hepburn, and Desmond, "Serial Eviction Filing."

9. Philip Garboden and Eva Rosen, "Serial Filing: How Landlords Use the Threat of Eviction," *City and Community* 18, no. 2 (June 1, 2019), https://journals.sagepub.com/doi/10.1111/cico.12387.

10. Garboden and Rosen, "Serial Filing."

11. Kathryn A. Sabbeth, "Eviction Courts," *University of St. Thomas Law Journal* 18 (2022): 359–404, 377–79, 402, https://ir.stthomas.edu/cgi/viewcontent.cgi?article=1542&context=ustlj.

12. Garboden and Rosen, "Serial Filing."

13. Kathryn A. Sabbeth, "Erasing the 'Scarlet E' of Eviction Records," *Appeal*, April 12, 2021, https://theappeal.org/thelab/report/erasing-the-scarlet-e-of-eviction-records/; "The Scarlet E: Unmasking America's Eviction Crisis," WNYC Studios, June 6, 2019, https://www.wnycstudios.org/podcasts/otm/scarlet-e-unmasking-americas-eviction-crisis.

14. "Case Search," Public Courts of Indiana, https://public.courts.in.gov/mycase/#/vw/Search.

15. Sabbeth, "Erasing the 'Scarlet E.'"

16. Suzy Niffenegger, "When No Landlord Will Rent to You, Where Do You Go?," *New York Times*, May 20, 2021, https://www.nytimes.com/2021/05/20/magazine/extended-stay-hotels.html.

17. Steve Nisi, Adam Mueller, and Fran Quigley, "Eviction Trauma: Rethinking an Extreme Remedy to a Contract Dispute," *Res Gestae*, June 2023, 18–22, https://cdn.ymaws.com/www.inbar.org/resource/resmgr/pdfs/June_2023_RG.pdf.

18. Nisi, Mueller, and Quigley, "Eviction Trauma."

19. Nisi, Mueller, and Quigley, "Eviction Trauma."

20. "How Indiana Courts Can Prevent Evictions: Responding to a Looming Public Health and Economic Crisis," Health and Human Rights Clinic, Indiana University McKinney School of Law, Indiana Justice Project, Notre Dame Clinical Law Center, 2022, https://mckinneylaw.iu.edu/practice/clinics/health-human-rights.html.

21. "Marion County (Indiana) Local Court Rules," https://www.in.gov/courts/files/marion-local-rules.pdf.

22. Indiana Code § 32–30–10.5–8.

23. Henry Gomory, Douglas S. Massey, James R. Hendrickson, and Matthew Desmond, "The Racially Disparate Influence of Filing Fees on Eviction Rates," *Housing Policy Debate* 13, no. 6 (May 26, 2023): 1463–83, https://www.tandfonline.com/doi/full/10.1080/10511482.2023.2212662.

24. "Deterring Serial Eviction Filing," Network for Public Health Law, May 2021, 3, https://www.networkforphl.org/wp-content/uploads/2021/05/Fact-Sheet-Deterring-Serial-Eviction-Filing.pdf.

25. Shane Phillips, "We Need Rental Registries Now More Than Ever," *Shelterforce*, December 18, 2020, https://shelterforce.org/2020/12/18/we-need-a-rental-registry-now-more-than-ever/.

26. Jade Vasquez and Sarah Gallagher, "Promoting Housing Stability through Just Cause Eviction Legislation," National Low Income Housing Coalition, May 17, 2022, https://nlihc.org/sites/default/files/Promoting-Housing-Stability-Through-Just-Cause-Eviction-Legislation.pdf; Rachel Cohen, "The Fight to Make It Harder for Landlords to Evict Their Tenants," *Vox*, May 1, 2023, https://www.vox.com/policy/2023/5/1/23697209/landlords-tenants-good-cause-just-cause-eviction-housing.

27. Julieta Cuellar, "Effect of 'Just Cause' Eviction Ordinances on Eviction in Four California Cities," *Princeton Journal of Public and International Affairs*, May 21, 2019, https://jpia.princeton.edu/news/effect-just-cause-eviction-ordinances-eviction-four-california-cities; Vasquez and Gallagher, "Promoting Housing Stability."

28. "Rights of a Mobile Home Owner Threatened with Eviction from a Mobile Home Park," Oregon State Bar, https://www.osbar.org/public/legalinfo/1249_rightsmobilehome.htm; "A Guide to Mobile Home Parks—Renting the Lot," Legal Services Corporation of Delaware, https://www.lscd.com/node/297/mobile-home-parks-renting-lot#non-renewal_and_termination_of_the_rental_agreement_.

29. "The Mobile Home Park Market Review: 49 States in 49 Minutes," Mobile Home University, https://www.mobilehomeuniversity.com/audios/the-mobile-home-park-market-review-49-states-in-49-minutes.

30. "Deterring Serial Eviction Filing," 3.

31. Nada Hussein, Tori Bourret, and Sarah Gallagher, "Eviction Record Sealing and Expungement Toolkit," National Low Income Housing Coalition, April 2023, 5, https://nlihc.org/sites/default/files/2023-04/eviction-record-sealing-and-expungement-toolkit.pdf.

32. Will Jason, "New Coalition Presses Fannie Mae and Freddie Mac to Better Support Underserved Mortgage Markets," Lincoln Institute of Land Policy, October 21, 2021, https://www.lincolninst.edu/publications/articles/2021–10-affordable-housing-underserved-mortgage-markets-coalition.

33. Jasmine Rangel, Jacob Haas, Emily Lemmerman, Joe Fish, and Peter Hepburn, "Preliminary Analysis: 11 Months of the CDC Moratorium," Eviction Lab, August 21, 2021, https://evictionlab.org/eleven-months-cdc/.

34. Russell Engler, "Connecting Self-Representation to Civil Gideon: What Existing Data Reveal about When Counsel Is Most Needed," *Fordham Urban Law Journal* 37, no. 1 (2010): 38, 47.

35. Chief Justice Loretta Rush, "State of the Judiciary: Connecting, Convening, and Collaborating with Our Communities," 2020, https://www.in.gov/courts/supreme/files/soj-2020.pdf.

36. Sandra Park and John Pollock, "Tenants' Right to Counsel Is Critical to Fight Mass Evictions and Advance Race Equity during the Pandemic and Beyond," *ACLU News and Commentary*, January 12, 2021, https://www.aclu.org/news/racial-justice/tenants-right-to-counsel-is-critical-to-fight-mass-evictions-and-advance-race-equity-during-the-pandemic-and-beyond#:~:text=.

37. "National Tenants Bill of Rights—Policy Agenda 2024," National Housing Law Project, June 9, 2024, https://www.nhlp.org/wp-content/uploads/NTBOR-Policy-Final-Updated-6.9.24.pdf.

6. HOW WE FIX THIS—HOUSING FIRST AND BEYOND

1. A version of the discussion of Motels4Now was originally published in Fran Quigley, "Low-Barrier Motel Shelter Is a Success—but Not an Easy One," *Shelterforce*, September 21, 2023, https://shelterforce.org/2023/09/21/low-barrier-motel-shelter-is-a-success-if-a-messy-one/.

2. The statistics about Motels4Now come from interviews with program leadership and the program's reports, some of which are available at their website, "Motels4Now," Our Lady of the Road, accessed June 13, 2024, https://www.olrsb.org/motels4now.

3. "The Case for Housing First," National Low Income Housing Coalition, accessed June 13, 2024, https://nlihc.org/sites/default/files/Housing-First-Research.pdf.

4. Kim Eckart, "Turning Hotels into Emergency Shelter as Part of COVID-19 Response Limited Spread of Coronavirus, Improved Health and Stability," *UW News*, October 7, 2020, https://www.washington.edu/news/2020/10/07/turning-hotels-into-emergency-shelter-as-part-of-covid-19-response-limited-spread-of-coronavirus-improved-health-and-stability/#:~:text=; Leah Robinson, Penelope Schlesinger, and Danya E. Keene, "'You Have a Place to Rest Your Head in Peace': Use of Hotels for Adults Experiencing Homelessness during the Covid-19 Pandemic," *Housing Policy Debate* 32 (August 2022): 837–52, https://www.tandfonline.com/doi/abs/10.1080/10511482.2022.2113816.

5. Rabbi Stephen Lewis Fuchs, "What We Need to Know about Welcoming the Stranger," *Reform Judaism*, November 2016, https://reformjudaism.org/blog/what-we-need-know-about-welcoming-stranger.

6. Alison Bell, Barbara Sard, and Becky Koepnick, "Prohibiting Discrimination against Renters Using Housing Vouchers Improves Results," Center on Budget and Policy Priorities, December 20, 2018, https://www.cbpp.org/research/housing/prohibiting-discrimination-against-renters-using-housing-vouchers-improves-results.

7. Joseph Dits and Jordan Smith, "Funding for Motels4Now Hits a Crossroad," *South Bend Tribune*, February 13, 2023, https://www.southbendtribune.com/story/news/2023/02/13/motels4now-funding-at-risk-for-homeless-in-st-joseph-county/69889581007/.

8. "The 2023 Annual Homeless Assessment Report (AHAR) to Congress," US Department of Housing and Urban Development, December 2023, https://www.huduser.gov/portal/sites/default/files/pdf/2023-ahar-part-1.pdf. For a critique of the estimate see "'Don't Count on It': How the HUD Point-in-Time Count Underestimates the Homelessness Crisis in America," National Law Center on Homelessness and Poverty, 2017, https://homelesslaw.org/wp-content/uploads/2018/10/HUD-PIT-report2017.pdf.

9. "Homelessness: Better HUD Oversight of Data Collection Could Improve Estimates of Homeless Population, GAO-20–433," US General Accounting Office, July 14, 2020, https://www.gao.gov/products/gao-20-433.

10. Rachel Cohen, "What a Landmark New Study on Homelessness Tells Us," *Vox*, July 5, 2023, https://www.vox.com/2023/7/5/23778810/homelessness-california-unsheltered-research.

11. Cohen, "What a Landmark New Study on Homelessness Tells Us."

12. "Housing First: What Is Housing First?," National Alliance to End Homelessness, March 20, 2022, https://endhomelessness.org/resource/housing-first/.

13. "Housing First: What Is Housing First?"

14. "A Home of Your Own: Housing First and Ending Homelessness in Finland," Y-Foundation, 2017, 10, https://www.feantsaresearch.org/download/a_home_of_your_own_lowres_spreads6069661816957790483.pdf.

15. Sam Tsemberis and Ronda F. Eisenberg, "Pathways to Housing: Supported Housing for Street-Dwelling Homeless Individuals with Psychiatric Disabilities," *Psychiatric Services*, April 1, 2000, https://ps.psychiatryonline.org/doi/10.1176/appi.ps.51.4.487.

16. Christopher Swope, "Philip Mangano," *Governing*, 2006, https://www.governing.com/poy/philip-mangano.html; Ben Carson, "We Know How to End Homelessness and Housing Shortages," *USA Today*, December 15, 2017, https://www.usatoday.com/story/opinion/voices/2017/12/15/we-know-how-end-homelessness-and-housing-shortages-ben-carson-column/951456001/.

17. *Making the Most of the American Rescue Plan*, US Department of Housing and Urban Development, August 2021, https://www.usich.gov/resources/uploads/asset_library/USICH_American_Rescue_Plan_Guide.pdf.

18. Christopher Rufo, "Housing First Has Failed: Time to Reform Federal Policy and Make It Work for Homeless Americans," Heritage Foundation, August 4, 2020, https://www.heritage.org/housing/report/the-housing-first-approach-has-failed-time-reform-federal-policy-and-make-it-work; Ned Renikoff, "Why the Right Is Winning Its War on Unhoused People," *Nation*, August 24, 2023, https://www.thenation.com/article/society/unhoused-right-rhetoric-homelessness/.

19. "California Statewide Study of People Experiencing Homelessness," University of California San Francisco Benioff Homelessness and Housing Initiative, June 2023, https://homelessness.ucsf.edu/our-impact/our-studies/california-statewide-study-people-experiencing-homelessness.

20. Robert Pointer, "The 12 Biggest Myths about Homelessness in America," NYU, September 24, 2019, https://www.nyu.edu/about/news-publications/news/2019/september/HomelessQandA.html.

21. Alex Horowitz, Chase Hatchett, and Adam Staveski, "How Housing Costs Drive Levels of Homelessness," Pew Charitable Trusts, August 22, 2023, https://www.pewtrusts.org/en/research-and-analysis/articles/2023/08/22/how-housing-costs-drive-levels-of-homelessness.

22. Rachel M. Cohen, "'Housing First' Works, but It Takes Money, Commitment, and, Well, Housing," *Vox*, December 15, 2022, https://www.vox.com/policy-and-politics/23504323/housing-first-homelessness-houston-homes.

23. "The Case for Housing First," National Low Income Housing Coalition, National Alliance to End Homelessness, CWS, March 2020, https://endhomelessness.org/wp-content/uploads/2020/03/Housing-First-Research-NAEH-NLIHC-Handout.pdf; see also Kontrast At, "Finland Ends Homelessness and Provides Shelter for All in Need," *Scoop.Me*, November 10, 2020, https://scoop.me/housing-first-finland-homelessness/ (reporting 15,000 euros savings per homeless person for the Finnish state under Housing First).

24. Carson, "We Know How to End Homelessness."

25. Sam Tsemberis, Leyla Gulcur, and Maria Nakae, "Housing First, Consumer Choice, and Harm Reduction for Homeless Individuals with a Dual Diagnosis," *American Journal of Public Health* 94, no. 4 (April 2004): 651–56, https://pubmed.ncbi.nlm.nih.gov/15054020/.

26. "Homelessness 101," Coalition for the Homeless (Houston), https://www.homelesshouston.org/houston-facts-info; Editors, "Housing First: Milwaukee County Recognized with Lowest Unsheltered Homeless Population in America," *Milwaukee Independent*, April 12, 2022, https://www.milwaukeeindependent.com/articles/housing-first-milwaukee-county-recognized-lowest-unsheltered-homeless-population-america/; Esteban Hernandez, "Study Shows Effectiveness of Housing-First Program," *Axios*, August 30, 2022, https://www.axios.com/local/denver/2022/08/30/study-denver-effectiveness-housing-first-homelessness; Maria C. Raven, Matthew J. Niedzwiecki, and Margot Kushel, "A Randomized Trial of Permanent Supportive Housing for Chronically Homeless Persons with High Use of Publicly Funded Services," *Health Services Research* 55, no. S2 (October 2020), https://www.hsr.org/node/664701 (Santa Clara).

27. "New Point-in-Time Data Reveals Decrease in Veteran Homelessness," US Department of Housing and Urban Development, November 3, 2022, https://www.hud.gov/press/press_releases_media_advisories/HUD_No_22_227.

28. Cohen, "'Housing First' Works."

29. Kenny Stancil, "In Pursuit of 'Housing Justice for All,' Cori Bush Reintroduces Unhoused Bill of Rights," *Common Dreams*, July 31, 2023, https://www.commondreams.org/news/cori-bush-unhoused-bill-of-rights.

30. "The State of the Nation's Housing," Harvard Joint Center for Housing Studies, 2022, 2, https://www.jchs.harvard.edu/sites/default/files/reports/files/Harvard_JCHS_State_Nations_Housing_2022.pdf; "No Way Home: Tenant Screening Barriers to Housing," Fair Housing Center of Central Indiana, May 2023, 4, https://www.fhcci.org/wp-content/uploads/2023/05/Tenant-Screening-Report-FINAL.pdf.

31. Jenny Schuetz, *Fixer-Upper: How to Repair America's Broken Housing Systems* (Washington, DC: Brookings Institution, 2022), 75.

32. "What Is Single Family Zoning?," Planetizen, https://www.planetizen.com/definition/single-family-zoning#:~:text=.

33. Matthew Desmond, *Poverty, by America* (New York: Crown, 2023), 114.

34. Emily Badger and Quoctrung Bui, "Cities Start to Question an American Ideal: A House with a Yard on Every Lot," *New York Times*, June 18, 2019, https://www.nytimes.com/interactive/2019/06/18/upshot/cities-across-america-question-single-family-zoning.html.

35. Yonah Freemark, Lydia Lo, Eleanor Noble, and Ananya Hariharan, "Cracking the Zoning Code: Understanding Local Land-Use Regulations and How They Can Advance Affordability and Equity," Urban Institute, May 2022, https://apps.urban.org/features/advancing-equity-affordability-through-zoning/#equity.

36. Scholastica Cororaton, "Single-Family Homeowners Typically Accumulated $225,000 in Housing Wealth over 10 Years," National Association of Realtors, January 7, 2022, https://www.nar.realtor/blogs/economists-outlook/single-family-homeowners-typically-accumulated-225K-in-housing-wealth-over-10-years; Dan Darrah, "We Need Public Housing, Not Affordable Housing," *Jacobin*, April 17, 2022, https://jacobin.com/2022/04/us-canadian-social-housing-affordability-ownership-speculation.

37. Randy Shaw, *Generation Priced Out: Who Gets to Live in the New Urban America* (Oakland: University of California Press, 2020).

38. William A. Fischel, *The Homevoter Hypothesis* (Cambridge, MA: Harvard University Press, 2005).

39. "Homeowner Equity Insights—Q1 2023," CoreLogic, June 8, 2023, https://www.corelogic.com/intelligence/homeowner-equity-insights-q1-2023/.

40. William A. Fischel, "An Economic History of Zoning and a Cure for Its Exclusionary Effects," *Urban Studies* 41, no. 2, https://journals.sagepub.com/doi/abs/10.1080/0042098032000165271.

41. Jerusalem Desmas, "60 Percent of Likely Voters Say They Are in Favor of Public Housing. So Why Isn't There More of It?," *Vox*, January 26, 2021, https://www.vox.com/22248779/affordable-housing-public-housing-poll-homelessness-crisis-covid-19-nimby-yimby-zoning; Zoha Qamar, "Americans Want More Affordable Housing—Just Not Nearby," *FiveThirtyEight*, December 16, 2022, https://fivethirtyeight.com/features/americans-want-more-affordable-housing-just-not-nearby/.

42. Desmond, *Poverty, by America*, 96, 115.

43. Village of Euclid v. Ambler Realty Company, 272 U.S. 365 (1926).

44. Desmond, *Poverty, by America*, 114.

45. Stephen Menendian, Samir Gambhir, and Arthur Gailes, "Twenty-First Century Residential Segregation in the United States," Othering and Belonging Institute,

Roots of Structural Racism Project, June 21, 2021, https://belonging.berkeley.edu/roots-structural-racism.

46. Freemark et al., "Cracking the Zoning Code"; Binyamin Applebaum, "California Is Actually Making Progress on Building More Housing," *New York Times*, October 4, 2022, https://www.nytimes.com/2022/10/04/opinion/california-housing-crisis.html; "What Is Single Family Zoning?," *Planitezen*; Thomas J. PlaHovinsak, "Exclusionary Zoning: Policy Design Lessons from the Mount Laurel Decisions," *Housing Policy Debate*, April 24, 2020, https://nlihc.org/sites/default/files/Exclusionary_Zoning_Policy_Design_Lessons_From_the_Mount_Laurel_Decisions.pdf.

47. Luisa Godinez-Puig, Garbiella Garriga, and Yonah Freemark, "Federal and State Dollars Could Be Used to Force Change in Exclusionary Towns," *Shelterforce*, March 23, 2023, https://shelterforce.org/2023/03/23/federal-and-state-dollars-could-be-used-to-force-change-in-exclusionary-towns/.

48. Cecilia Rouse, Jared Bernstein, Helen Knudsen, and Jeffery Zhang, "Exclusionary Zoning: Its Effect on Racial Discrimination in the Housing Market," White House, June 17, 2021, https://www.whitehouse.gov/cea/written-materials/2021/06/17/exclusionary-zoning-its-effect-on-racial-discrimination-in-the-housing-market/.

49. Solomon Greene and Ingrid Gould Ellen, "Breaking Barriers, Boosting Supply: How the Federal Government Can Help Eliminate Exclusionary Zoning," Urban Institute, September 25, 2020, https://www.urban.org/research/publication/breaking-barriers-boosting-supply.

50. "Wall Street and Single Family Rentals," Americans for Financial Reform, January 17, 2018, 30–32, http://ourfinancialsecurity.org/2018/01/afr-report-wall-street-and-single-family-rentals/.

51. People's Action, *A National Homes Guarantee*, briefing book, September 5, 2019, 16, https://homesguarantee.com/wp-content/uploads/Homes-Guarantee-_-Briefing-Book.pdf; Center for Popular Democracy & CPD Action, "2021 Federal Housing Agenda," 2021, 6, https://www.populardemocracy.org/sites/default/files/20210124%20Federal%20Housing%20Agenda.pdf.

52. People's Action, *National Homes Guarantee*, 16.

53. Rachel Cohen, "Could This Obscure Tax Idea Reshape American Housing?," *Vox*, January 5, 2024, https://www.vox.com/24025379/detroit-land-value-tax-lvt-property-tax-housing-vacant-blight.

54. People's Action, *National Homes Guarantee*, 16–17.

55. Olivia Ensign, "The Right to Housing Is on the Ballot in Los Angeles: Voters to Decide on Initiative to Increase Affordable Housing by Taxing Mega Mansions," Human Rights Watch, October 2022, https://www.hrw.org/news/2022/10/13/right-housing-ballot-los-angeles.

56. Michael Leachman and Samantha Waxman, "State 'Mansion Taxes' on Very Expensive Homes," Center on Budget and Policy Priorities, October 1, 2019, https://www.cbpp.org/research/state-budget-and-tax/state-mansion-taxes-on-very-expensive-homes.

57. Leachman and Waxman, "State 'Mansion Taxes.'"

58. "From the Ground Up: Community Centered Policies to Scale Equitable Development," Partners for Dignity & Rights, 2022, 2, 22, https://dignityandrights.org/wp-content/uploads/2022/06/PDR-Ground-Up-Report-Final-Digital-1.pdf.

59. "Wall Street and Single Family Rentals," Americans for Financial Reform; "2021 Federal Housing Agenda," 6.

60. "76% of Low-Income Renters Needing Federal Rental Assistance Don't Receive It," Center on Budget and Policy Priorities, 2019, https://www.cbpp.org/research/housing/three-out-of-four-low-income-at-risk-renters-do-not-receive-federal-rental-assistance.

61. Vincent Reina, Claudia Aiken, and Jenna Epstein, *Exploring a Universal Housing Voucher*, Housing Initiative at Penn, September 21, 2021, https://www.housinginitiative.org/universal-voucher.html.

62. Reina, Aiken, and Epstein, *Exploring a Universal Housing Voucher*.

63. "A Quick Guide to SNAP Eligibility and Benefits," Center on Budget and Policy Priorities, March 3, 2023, https://www.cbpp.org/research/food-assistance/a-quick-guide-to-snap-eligibility-and-benefits; "Policy Basics: Introduction to Medicaid," Center on Budget and Policy Priorities, April 14, 2020, https://www.cbpp.org/research/health/introduction-to-medicaid.

64. "Vice President Joe Biden (D) Housing Plan," National Low Income Housing Coalition, February 24, 2020, https://fcfedbf1-3d28-4722-bcf5-5d4322aac1c2.filesusr.com/ugd/d97bc4_7e450d2227e642b9a9c50cfa70819ed8.pdf; "Ending Homelessness Act of 2023, H.R. 4232, 118th Cong," https://www.congress.gov/bill/118th-congress/house-bill/4232/text; Stancil, "In Pursuit of 'Housing Justice for All.'"

65. Kirk McClure and Alex Schwartz, "The Case for Universal Rental Assistance," *Appeal*, May 15, 2020, https://theappeal.org/rental-assistance-housing-choice-voucher/.

66. Desmond, *Poverty, by America*, 91, n. 21.

67. Mary K. Cunningham, "It's Time to Reinforce the Housing Safety Net by Adopting Universal Vouchers for Low-Income Renters," Urban Institute, April 7, 2020, https://www.urban.org/urban-wire/its-time-reinforce-housing-safety-net-adopting-universal-vouchers-low-income-renters; Stephen Semler, "A New Bill Would Redirect $100 Billion from the Military Budget to Pro-worker Programs," *Jacobin*, June 18, 2022, https://jacobin.com/2022/06/defense-spending-people-over-pentagon-act.

68. Reina, Aiken, and Epstein, *Exploring a Universal Housing Voucher*.

69. J. R. Reed, "Advancing Choice in the Housing Choice Voucher Program: Source of Income Protections and Locational Outcomes," *Stoop*, June 22, 2022, https://furmancenter.org/thestoop/entry/advancing-choice-in-the-housing-choice-voucher-program-source-of-income-protections-and-locational-outcomes; "Source of Income Laws by State, County, and City," National Multifamily Housing Council, 2022, https://www.nmhc.org/research-insight/analysis-and-guidance/source-of-income-laws-by-state-county-and-city/; Alison Bell, Barbara Sard, and Becky Koepnick, "Prohibiting Discrimination against Renters Using Housing Vouchers Improves Results," Center on Budget and Policy Priorities, December 20, 2018, https://www.cbpp.org/research/housing/prohibiting-discrimination-against-renters-using-housing-vouchers-improves-results; "Q: Can Prohibiting Source-of-Income Discrimination Help Voucher Holders?," *Shelterforce*, July 30, 2018, https://shelterforce.org/2018/07/30/q-can-prohibiting-source-of-income-discrimination-help-voucher-holders/.

70. Sarah fit the demographics of voucher holders, which makes blocking discrimination against them all the more appropriate: 78 percent of voucher households are headed by women, and 65 percent of the households are Black or Hispanic; "14–1 Advancing Tenant Protections: Source-of-Income Protections," National Low Income Housing Coalition, February 7, 2023, https://nlihc.org/resource/14-1-advancing-tenant-protections-source-income-protections#:~:text=.

71. Douglas Rice, "Agencies Generally Use All Available Voucher Funding to Help Families Afford Housing," Center on Budget and Policy Priorities, March 4, 2019, https://www.cbpp.org/research/housing/agencies-generally-use-all-available-voucher-funding-to-help-families-afford; "Discrimination against Housing Choice Voucher Holders," Urban Institute, 2018, https://www.urban.org/policy-centers/metropolitan-housing-and-communities-policy-center/projects/housingchoicevoucherdiscrimination.

72. Keith Burbank, "First Study of Its Kind Shows Financial Aid Can Prevent Homelessness," *SFGate*, July 22, 2023, https://www.sfgate.com/news/bayarea/article/first-study-of-its-kind-shows-financial-aid-can-18255390.php; "California Statewide Study of People Experiencing Homelessness," University of California San Francisco Benioff Homelessness and Housing Initiative, June 2023, https://homelessness.ucsf.edu/our-impact/our-studies/california-statewide-study-of-people-experiencing-homelessness.

73. "Week 59 Household Pulse Survey, June 28–July 10," US Census Bureau, July 19, 2023, https://www.census.gov/data/tables/2023/demo/hhp/hhp59.html.

74. "7 Key Trends in Poverty in the United States," Peter G. Peterson Foundation, February 27, 2023, https://www.pgpf.org/blog/2023/02/7-key-trends-in-poverty-in-the-united-states#:~:text=.

75. "7 Key Trends in Poverty."

76. Rick Noack, "See How Much (or How Little) You'd Earn If You Did the Same Job in Another Country," *Washington Post*, March 3, 2015, https://www.washingtonpost.com/news/worldviews/wp/2015/03/03/chart-see-how-much-or-how-little-youd-earn-if-you-did-the-same-job-in-another-country/.

77. Martin Armstrong, "How America's Minimum Wage Compares," *Statista*, January 18, 2024, https://www.statista.com/chart/3501/the-countries-with-the-best-minimum-wages/; "Collective Bargaining," OECD, https://www.oecd.org/els/emp/collective-bargaining.htm.

78. Greg Iacurci, "U.S. Is Worst among Rich Nations for Worker Benefits," *CNBC*, February 4, 2021, https://www.cnbc.com/2021/02/04/us-is-worst-among-rich-nations-for-worker-benefits.html.

79. Rachel Black and Aleta Sprague, "The Rise and Reign of the Welfare Queen," *New America*, September 22, 2016, https://www.newamerica.org/weekly/rise-and-reign-welfare-queen/.

80. Ann C. Foster and Arcenis Rojas, "Program Participation and Spending Patterns of Families Receiving Government Means-Tested Assistance," *Monthly Labor Review*, US Bureau of Labor Statistics, January 2018, https://doi.org/10.21916/mlr.2018.3.

81. Desmond, *Poverty, by America*, 86.

82. Peter Hepburn, Olivia Jin, Joe Fish, Emily Lemmerman, Anne Kat Alexander, and Matthew Desmond, "Preliminary Analysis: Eviction Filing Patterns in 2021," Eviction Lab, March 8, 2022, https://evictionlab.org/us-eviction-filing-patterns-2021/.

83. Sharon Parrott, "Robust COVID Relief Achieved Historic Gains against Poverty and Hardship, Bolstered Economy," Center on Budget and Policy Priorities, June 14, 2022, https://www.cbpp.org/research/poverty-and-inequality/robust-covid-relief-achieved-historic-gains-against-poverty-and-0#:~:text=.

84. Parrott, "Robust COVID Relief."

85. A version of this discussion of the withdrawal of COVID-era government benefits was first published in Fran Quigley, "Letting Go of the Rope," *Common Dreams*, December 10, 2022, https://www.commondreams.org/views/2022/12/10/letting-go-rope-eviction-court.

86. Alexander Herman, "Emergency Rental Assistance Has Helped Stabilize Struggling Renters," Joint Center for Housing Studies of Harvard University, April 6, 2022, https://www.jchs.harvard.edu/blog/emergency-rental-assistance-has-helped-stabilize-struggling-renters.

87. Solomon Greene, T*odd M. Richardson, Jemine A. Bryon, and Richard Cho,* "Rise in Homelessness Averted amidst Worsening Housing Needs in 2021," *PD&R Edge*, August 22, 2023, https://www.huduser.gov/portal/pdredge/pdr-edge-frm-asst-sec-082223.html.

88. "Eviction Tracking," Eviction Lab, https://evictionlab.org/eviction-tracking/.

7. HOW WE FIX THIS—RENT CONTROL

1. "The Rent Is Too Damn High," People's Action, accessed June 13, 2024, https://damnhighrent.com/.

2. "America's Rental Housing 2022," Joint Center for Housing Studies of Harvard University, 2022, 1, https://www.jchs.harvard.edu/sites/default/files/reports/files/Harvard_JCHS_Americas_Rental_Housing_2022.pdf; Alicia Mazzara, "Rents Have Risen More Than

Incomes in Nearly Every State since 2001," Center on Budget and Policy Priorities, December 10, 2019, https://www.cbpp.org/blog/rents-have-risen-more-than-incomes-in-nearly-every-state-since-2001; Madeleine Ngo, "Rising Rent Prices Are Keeping Inflation High," *Vox*, September 14, 2022, https://www.vox.com/policy-and-politics/2022/9/14/23351128/inflation-rent-prices-high.

3. "American Families Face a Growing Rent Burden," Pew Charitable Trusts, April 1, 2018, https://www.pewtrusts.org/-/media/assets/2018/04/rent-burden_report_v2.pdf.

4. HouseCanary, *National Rental Report*, 2022, 5, https://cdn.prod.website-files.com/659c81c0f2b2def2180e9b9f/659dd29d84f3af1b8773a133_HC_Rental-Report_H222_min-1.pdf.

5. Jim Benson, "Indianapolis Rentals amid Surging U.S. Occupancy Rates," Five Star Realty Group, June 27, 2022, https://five-stargroup.com/indianapolis-rentals-amid-surging-u-s-occupancy-rates/.

6. Hyojung Lee, "Who Owns Rental Properties, and Is It Changing?," Joint Center for Housing Studies of Harvard University, August 18, 2017, http://www.jchs.harvard.edu/blog/who-owns-rental-properties-and-is-it-changing/.

7. Heather Little, "Rent Going Up? One Company's Algorithm Could Be Why," *ProPublica*, October 15, 2022, https://www.propublica.org/article/yieldstar-rent-increase-realpage-rent. ("The net effect of driving revenue and pushing people out was $10 million in income," Campo said. "I think that shows keeping the heads in the beds above all else is not always the best strategy.") Mike Leonard, "RealPage, Landlords Face Antitrust Lawsuit over Rent Spike," *Bloomberg Law*, October 19, 2022, https://news.bloomberglaw.com/esg/realpage-major-landlords-face-antitrust-lawsuit-over-rent-spike.

8. "Justice Department Sues RealPage for Algorithmic Pricing Scheme That Harms Millions of American Renters," Office of Public Affairs, US Department of Justice, August 23, 2024, https://www.justice.gov/opa/pr/justice-department-sues-realpage-algorithmic-pricing-scheme-harms-millions-american-renters.

9. Kriston Capps and Sarah Holder, "Wolf of Main Street," *Bloomberg*, March 3, 2022, https://www.bloomberg.com/graphics/2022-evictions-monarch-investment-rental-properties/.

10. "America's Biggest Multifamily and Single-Family Landllords Continue to Reap Huge Profits and Take Advantage of Tenants," Accountable.US, April 10, 2023, https://accountable.us/wp-content/uploads/2023/04/2023-04-10-Updated-Research-On-Housing-Profiteering-FINAL.docx-1.pdf.

11. "Consumer Expenditures—2021," US Bureau of Labor Statistics, September 8, 2022, https://www.bls.gov/news.release/cesan.nr0.htm; Peter J. Mateyka and Jayne Yoo, "Share of Income Needed to Pay Rent Increased the Most for Low-Income Households from 2019 to 2021," US Census, March 2, 2023, https://www.census.gov/library/stories/2023/03/low-income-renters-spent-larger-share-of-income-on-rent.html.

12. Corianne Payton Scally and Dulce Gonzales, "Renters Are More Likely Than Homeowners to Struggle with Paying for Basic Needs," Urban Institute, November 1, 2018, https://www.urban.org/urban-wire/renters-are-more-likely-homeowners-struggle-paying-basic-needs.

13. "Household Pulse Survey, April 2024," US Census Bureau, https://www.census.gov/data/tables/2024/demo/hhp/cycle04.html; "Eviction Tracker," Eviction Lab, https://evictionlab.org/eviction-tracking/#tracker.

14. "Rent Stabilization," State of Oregon Department of Administrative Services, https://www.oregon.gov/das/OEA/Pages/Rent-stabilization.aspx.

15. Patrick Range McDonald, "Update: Big Real Estate Shelled Out Nearly $100 Million to Stop Prop 21," Housing Is a Human Right, January 3, 2021, https://www.housingisahumanright.org/update-big-real-estate-shelled-out-nearly-100-million-to-stop-prop-21/; Vishal Shankar, "CNBC Airs Falsehoods and Parrots Landlord Lobbyists to Trash Rent

Control," Revolving Door Project, March 24, 2023, https://therevolvingdoorproject.org/cnbc-airs-falsehoods-and-parrots-landlord-lobbyists-to-trash-rent-control/.

16. A version of this review of rent control was originally published in Fran Quigley, "Why We Need Rent Control," *Jacobin*, July 20, 2023, https://jacobin.com/2023/07/rent-control-arguments-myths-housing-real-estate.

17. Mary K. Cunningham, "It's Time to Reinforce the Housing Safety Net by Adopting Universal Vouchers for Low-Income Renters," Urban Institute, April 7, 2020, https://www.urban.org/urban-wire/its-time-reinforce-housing-safety-net-adopting-uni versal-vouchers-low-income-renters.

18. Alex Schwartz and Kirk McClure, "Why Building More Homes Won't Solve the Affordable Housing Problem for Those Who Need It the Most," *Conversation*, November 12, 2021, https://theconversation.com/why-building-more-homes-wont-solve-the-affordable-housing-problem-for-the-millions-of-people-who-need-it-most-171100.

19. Bloomberg Editors, "The US Can Solve Its Housing Crisis. It Just Needs to Start Building," *Washington Post*, December 30, 2022, https://www.washingtonpost.com/business/the-us-can-solve-its-housing-crisis-it-just-needs-to-start-building/2022/12/30/4d5b3940-8866-11ed-b5ac-411280b122ef_story.html.

20. For example, see "Rent Board," SF.gov, https://sf.gov/departments/rent-board/about; "Ending Chronic Homelessness Saves Taxpayer Money," National Alliance to End Homelessness, http://endhomelessness.org/wp-content/uploads/2017/06/Cost-Savings-from-PSH.pdf.

21. Amee Chew and Sarah Treuhaft, *Our Homes, Our Future: How Rent Control Can Build Stable, Healthy Communities*, PolicyLink, Center for Popular Democracy, and Right to the City Alliance, 2019, 5, https://www.policylink.org/resources-tools/our-homes-our-future.

22. Chew and Treuhaft, *Our Homes*, 18.

23. "Rental Housing Stock," Harvard Joint Center for Housing Studies, 2017, https://www.jchs.harvard.edu/sites/default/files/03_harvard_jchs_americas_rental_housing_2017.pdf.

24. Allan D. Heskin, Ned Levine, and Mark Garrett, "The Effects of Vacancy Control," *APA Journal* 66, no. 2 (June 2000): 162–76.

25. Manuel Pastor, Vanessa Carter, and Maya Abood, "Rent Matters: What Are the Impacts of Rent Stabilization Measures?," USC Dornsife Program for Environmental and Regional Equity, October 10, 2018, https://dornsife.usc.edu/assets/sites/242/docs/Rent_Matters_PERE_Report_Final_02.pdf; Prasanna Rajasekaran, Mark Treskon, and Solomon Greene, "Rent Control: What Does the Research Tell Us about the Effectiveness of Local Action?," Urban Institute, January 2019, 7, https://www.urban.org/sites/default/files/publication/99646/rent_control._what_does_the_research_tell_us_about_the_effectiveness_of_local_action_1.pdf.

26. Rajasekaran, Treskon, and Greene, "Rent Control"; Lance Freemand and Frank Braconi, "Gentrification and Displacement: New York City in the 1990's," *Journal of the American Planning Association* 70, no. 1 (2004): 39–52.

27. Chew and Treuhaft, *Our Homes*, 21.

28. Matthew Desmond and Carl Gershenson, "Housing and Employment Insecurity among the Working Poor," *Social Problems* 63, no. 1 (2016): 46–67, https://doi.org//10.1093/socpro/spv025; Maya Brennan, Patrick Reed, and Lisa A. Sturtevant, "The Impacts of Affordable Housing on Education: A Research Summary," Center for Housing Policy, November 2014, https://nhc.org/wp-content/uploads/2017/03/The-Impacts-of-Affordable-Housing-on-Education-1.pdf.

29. "Education of Homeless Children and Youth," National Coalition for the Homeless, https://nationalhomeless.org/wp-content/uploads/2014/06/Education-Fact-Sheet.pdf.

30. Emily A. Benfer, Seema Mohapatra, Lindsay F. Wiley, and Ruqaiijah Yearby, "Health Justice Strategies to Combat the Pandemic: Eliminating Discrimination, Poverty, and Health Disparities during and after COVID-19," *Yale Journal of Health Policy, Law, and Ethics* 19, no. 3 (2020): 148–50, https://openyls.law.yale.edu/bitstream/handle/20.500.13051/5966/Benfer_v19n3_122_171.pdf?sequence=2.

31. Mark Paul, "Economists Hate Rent Control. Here's Why They're Wrong," *American Prospect*, May 16, 2023, https://prospect.org/infrastructure/housing/2023-05-16-economists-hate-rent-control/.

32. H. Gibbs Knotts and Moshe Haspel, "The Impact of Gentrification on Voter Turnout," *Social Science Quarterly* 87, no. 1 (2006): 110–21, https://www.jstor.org/stable/42956112; Scott Schieman, "Residential Stability and the Social Impact of Neighborhood Disadvantage," *Social Forces* 83, no. 3 (2005): 1031–64, https://www.jstor.org/stable/3598268.

33. "Should I Stay or Should I Go? Exploring the Effects of Housing Instability and Mobility on Children," Center for Housing Policy, https://mcstudy.norc.org/publications/files/CohenandWardrip_2009.pdf.

34. Jonathan Fisher, David Johnson, Jonathan Latner, Timothy Smeeding, and Jeffrey Thompson, "Estimating the Marginal Propensity to Consume Using the Distributions of Income, Consumption, and Wealth," Washington Center for Equitable Growth, April 19, 2018, https://equitablegrowth.org/working-papers/marginal-propensity-consume/.

35. Elizabeth Kneebone and Emily Garr, "The Suburbanization of Poverty," *Brookings*, January 20, 2010, https://www.brookings.edu/research/the-suburbanization-of-poverty-trends-in-metropolitan-america-2000-to-2008/.

36. "Mapping Out Rental Controls across Europe," *JonesDay*, October 2020, https://www.jonesday.com/en/insights/2020/10/mapping-out-rental-controls-across-europe.

37. Charles Noyes, "Rent Control," CQ Press, October 8, 1941, https://cqpress.sagepub.com/cqresearcher/report/rent-control-cqresrre1941100800#H2_2; Daniel K. Fetter, "The Home Front: Rent Control and the Rapid Wartime Increase in Home Ownership," *Journal of Economic History* 76, no. 4 (2016): 1001–43, https://www.cambridge.org/core/journals/journal-of-economic-history/article/home-front-rent-control-and-the-rapid-wartime-increase-in-home-ownership/171D34C6E02790944799DD9BB808835A; John W. Willis, "Short History of Rent Control Laws," *Cornell Law Review* 36 (Fall 1950): 54.

38. Peter Dreier, "Rent Deregulation in California and Massachusetts," May 14, 1997, https://www.peterdreier.com/wp-content/uploads/2014/04/Rent_Deregulation_In_California_Massachusetts.pdf.

39. Pennell v. City of San Jose, 485 U.S. 1 (1998).

40. 74 Pinehurst LLC v. State of New York, 59 F.4th 557, 569 (2d. Cir, 2023).

41. George Fenton, "Reversing Corporate Tax Cuts to Fund Infrastructure Would Boost Equity and Growth," Center on Budget and Policy Priorities, May 25, 2021, https://www.cbpp.org/blog/reversing-corporate-tax-cuts-to-fund-infrastructure-would-boost-equity-and-growth.

42. Matthew Desmond, *Poverty, by America* (New York: Crown, 2023), 78–79, 137–38.

43. Desmond, 145.

44. Timothy L. Collins, "An Introduction to the New York City Rent Guidelines Board," Rent Guidelines Board, January 2020, 13–26, https://rentguidelinesboard.cityofnewyork.us/wp-content/uploads/2020/01/intro2020.pdf.

45. Todd N. Tucker, "Price Controls: How the U.S. Has Used Them and How They Can Shape Industries," Roosevelt Institute, November 2021, https://rooseveltinstitute.org/wp-content/uploads/2021/11/RI_Industrial-Policy-Price-Controls_Brief-202111.pdf.

46. Bryant Putney, "Price Control in Wartime," CQ Press, 1940, https://library.cqpress.com/cqresearcher/document.php?id=cqresrre1940102400.

47. Daniel Yergin and Joseph Stanislaw, "Nixon, Price Controls, and the Gold Standard," pbs.org, 1997, https://www.pbs.org/wgbh/commandingheights/shared/minitext/ess_nixongold.html.

48. Hadas Their, "To Fight Inflation, Bowman Says We Need Price Controls," *Jacobin*, October 17, 2022, https://jacobin.com/2022/10/jamaal-bowman-inflation-price-controls; Isabella Weber, "Could Strategic Price Controls Help Fight Inflation?," *Guardian*, December 29, 2021, ttps://www.theguardian.com/business/commentisfree/2021/dec/29/inflation-price-controls-time-we-use-it?utm_source=.

49. "Rent Control: Policy Issue," National Apartment Association, accessed June 13, 2024, https://www.naahq.org/rent-control-policy#:~:text=.

50. Eleanor J. Bader, "Rent Is Too Damned High: US Tenants Mobilize to Demand Rent Controls," *Truthout*, November 25, 2022, https://truthout.org/articles/rent-is-too-damned-high-us-tenants-mobilize-to-demand-rent-controls/.

51. Robbie Sequeira, "Some Cities Are Pushing for Rent Control; They Are Meeting Resistance," *Stateline*, August 3, 2023, https://stateline.org/2023/08/03/some-cities-are-pushing-for-rent-control-theyre-meeting-resistance/.

52. "Rent Control," National Multifamily Housing Council, https://www.nmhc.org/industry-topics/affordable-housing/rent-control/.

53. "Top Spenders 2020," Open Secrets, https://www.opensecrets.org/federal-lobbying/top-spenders?cycle=2020; "Why Rent Is Rising in the U.S.," *CNBC*, December 13, 2021, https://www.youtube.com/watch?v=5Ds-_o5oGdk.

54. Walter Block, "Rent Control," EconLib, https://www.econlib.org/library/Enc/RentControl.html#lfHendersonCEE2-145_footnote_nt389.

55. Shankar, "CNBC Airs Falsehoods."

56. Jerusalem Desmas, "I Changed My Mind on Rent Control," *Vox*, December 2, 2021, https://www.vox.com/22789296/housing-crisis-rent-relief-control-supply.

57. Lily Roberts and Ben Olinsky, "Raising the Minimum Wage Would Boost an Economic Recovery—and Reduce Taxpayer Subsidization of Low-Wage Work," Center for American Progress, January 27, 2021, https://www.americanprogress.org/article/raising-minimum-wage-boost-economic-recovery-reduce-taxpayer-subsidization-low-wage-work/.

58. Matthew Castillon, "70% of Workers Are Likely to Quit at Current $7.25 Federal Minimum Wage in 'Brutal' Turnover Cycle," *CNBC*, September 25, 2019, https://www.cnbc.com/2019/09/25/70percent-of-workers-are-likely-to-quit-at-current-federal-minimum-wage.html.

59. "Economists in Support of a Federal Minimum Wage of $15 by 2024," Economic Policy Institute, https://www.epi.org/economists-in-support-of-15-by-2024/.

60. Rajasekaran, Treskon, and Greene, "Rent Control," 7.

61. Roshan Abraham, "Economists Support Nationwide Rent Control in Letter to Biden Admin," *Vice*, August 3, 2023, https://www.vice.com/en/article/5d9yvz/economists-support-national-rent-control-in-letter-to-biden-admin.

62. Patrick Range McDonald, "Top Five Flaws of Stanford University Study on Rent Control," Housing Is a Human Right, January 18, 2023, https://www.housingisahumanright.org/top-five-flaws-of-stanford-university-study-on-rent-control/; Shankar, "CNBC Airs Falsehoods."

63. Val Werness, "Rent Controls: A White Paper Report," National Association of Realtors, March 2017, https://realtorparty.realtor/wp-content/uploads/2017/12/State-Local-Issues-Rent-Control-White-Paper.pdf. The landlord lobby's anti–rent control rhetoric contributes to the few instances where rent control appears to be discouraging new construction. In St. Paul, Minnesota, fewer building permits were issued after a November 2021 vote that created new rent control policies. But HUD data show that the drop in permits actually began almost a year before the vote and well over a year before the policy

ever took effect. As Roshan Abraham wrote for *Shelterforce* and Next City, these data "suggest that developers pulling permits were reacting to the perception of the rent control policy rather than its practical impact." Roshan Abraham, "What Happened to Rent Control in Minneapolis?," Next City, August 24, 2023, https://nextcity.org/urbanist-news/what-happened-to-rent-control-in-minneapolis.

64. Nicole Montojo, Eli Moore, and Stephen Barton, "Opening the Door for Rent Control," Othering and Belonging Institute (UC Berkeley), September 2018, https://belonging.berkeley.edu/opening-door-rent-control; Edward G. Goetz, "Minneapolis Rent Stabilization Study," University of Minnesota Center for Urban and Regional Affairs, September 7, 2021, https://www.cura.umn.edu/research/minneapolis-rent-stabilization-study; Alisa Belinkoff Katz, "People Are Simply Unable to Pay the Rent," UCLA Luskin Center for History and Policy, October 2018, https://luskincenter.pre.ss.ucla.edu/wp-content/uploads/sites/66/2018/09/People-Are-Simply-Unable-to-Pay-the-Rent.pdf; Pastor, Carter, and Abood, "Rent Matters."

65. Chew and Treuhaft, *Our Homes*, 23; "LAS Successfully Defends New York's Rent Reforms, Stabilization Law," Legal Aid Society, February 6, 2023, https://legalaidnyc.org/news/successfully-defends-new-york-rent-reforms-stabilization-law/.

66. J. W. Mason, "Considerations on Rent Control," JWMason.org, November 14, 2019, https://jwmason.org/slackwire/considerations-on-rent-control/.

67. "Rent Report," Rent.com, https://www.rent.com/research/average-rent-price-report/; Mike Leonard, "RealPage, Landlords Face Antitrust Lawsuit over Rent Spike," *Bloomberg Law*, October 19, 2022, https://news.bloomberglaw.com/esg/realpage-major-landlords-face-antitrust-lawsuit-over-rent-spike.

68. Gary Painter, "No, Rent Control Doesn't Always Reduce the Supply of Housing," *Los Angeles Times*, October 31, 2018, https://www.latimes.com/opinion/op-ed/la-oe-painter-rent-control-economist-20181031-story.html.

69. Will Parker, "Aiming at Wealthy Renters, Developers Build More Luxury Apartments Than They Have in Decades," *Wall Street Journal*, January 15, 2020, sec. Real Estate, https://www.wsj.com/articles/aiming-at-wealthy-renters-developers-build-more-luxury-apartments-than-they-have-in-decades-11579084202; Roberto Rodriguez, Liz Haak, and Sue Susman, "NY Must Stop 'Warehousing' of Vacant Affordable Apartments," *City Limits*, October 15, 2020, https://citylimits.org/2020/10/15/opinion-ny-must-act-to-stop-warehousing-of-vacant-affordable-apartments/.

70. John I. Gilderbloom and Lin Ye, "Thirty Years of Rent Control: A Survey of New Jersey Cities," *Journal of Urban Affairs* 29, no. 2 (May 2007): 207–20, https://www.tandfonline.com/doi/abs/10.1111/j.1467-9906.2007.00334.x.

71. Jake Blumgart, "In Defense of Rent Control," *Pacific Standard*, April 1, 2015, https://psmag.com/economics/in-defense-of-rent-control.

72. Dreier, "Rent Deregulation in California and Massachusetts."

73. Tom Acitelli, "Massachusetts Rent Control Repeal Fallout in the 1990's a Lesson for Today," *Curbed Boston*, November 14, 2019, https://boston.curbed.com/2019/11/14/20962932/massachusetts-rent-control-debate-tenants; "The Morning After," *Economist*, April 30, 1998, https://www.economist.com/united-states/1998/04/30/the-morning-after.

74. "Rent Control: Policy Issue," National Apartment Association; "Why Rent Is Rising in the U.S.," *CNBC*.

75. Alex Pareene and Laura Marsh, "The Rent Is Too Damn High," *New Republic*, June 1, 2022, https://newrepublic.com/article/166652/why-is-rent-so-high.

76. Edgar O. Olsen, "What Do Economists Know about the Effect of Rent Control on Housing Maintenance?," *Journal of Real Estate Finance and Economics* 1 (1988): 295–307, https://link.springer.com/article/10.1007/BF00658922#page-1.

77. Werness, "Rent Controls," 86.

78. Schwartz and McClure, "Why Building More Homes Won't Solve the Affordable Housing Problem."

79. Fran Quigley, "A Bold Vision on Housing Is Needed to Win Big Change," Waging Nonviolence, July 31, 2024, https://wagingnonviolence.org/2024/07/bold-vision-housing-needed-to-win-big/. "The Overton Window is based on the premise that elected officials dependent on winning popular elections will never adopt a policy unless it is within the range of options—or window, as it were—that enjoy broad support among the public."

80. Georgia Kromrei, "National Groups Fund NY Landlords' Suit against Rent Law," TheRealDeal, November 13, 2019, https://therealdeal.com/new-york/2019/11/13/national-groups-fund-ny-landlords-suit-against-rent-law/.

81. Brief on file with author.

82. Chew and Treuhaft, Our Homes, 3.

83. "Who Are the Renters in America," USA Facts, February 25, 2021, https://usafacts.org/articles/who-is-renting-in-america-cares-act/.

84. Richard Rothstein, The Color of Law: A Forgotten History of How Our Government Segregated America (New York: Liveright, 2017).

85. Matt Bruenig, "The Problems with Means-Testing Are Real," Jacobin, September 27, 2020, https://jacobin.com/2020/09/means-testing-max-sawicky-universal-programs.

86. Meagan Day, "Targeted Social Programs Make Easy Targets," Jacobin, January 14, 2018, https://jacobin.com/2018/01/targeted-social-programs-make-easy-targets.

87. Rick Shenkman, "When Did Social Security Become the Third Rail of American Politics?," History News Network, https://historynewsnetwork.org/article/10522.

88. Bob Cesca, "Keep Your Goddam Government Hands off My Medicare!" HuffPost, December 6, 2017, https://www.huffpost.com/entry/get-your-goddamn-governme_b_252326.

89. Fran Quigley, "Growing Political Will from the Grassroots," Columbia Human Rights Law Review 41, no. 1 (2009): 13–67.

90. J. Craig Jenkins and Charles Perrow, "Insurgency of the Powerless: Farm Worker Movements (1946–1972)," American Sociological Review 42, no. 2 (1977): 249, 265.

91. "America's Rental Housing 2022," Joint Center for Housing Studies of Harvard University, 2022, 9, https://www.jchs.harvard.edu/sites/default/files/reports/files/Harvard_JCHS_Americas_Rental_Housing_2022.pdf.

92. Michael Kolomatsky, "Which Cities Have More Renters?," New York Times, February 15, 2018, https://www.nytimes.com/2018/02/15/realestate/rent-increases-2017.html; Christopher Mazur, "Homes on the Range: Homeownership Rates Are Higher in Rural America," US Census, December 8, 2016, https://www.census.gov/newsroom/blogs/random-samplings/2016/12/homes_on_the_range.html.

93. Bader, "Rent Is Too Damned High."

94. Bader, "Rent Is Too Damned High"; Samuel Robinson, "Detroiters Want to End Michigan's Ban on Rent Control," Axios, August 18, 2022, https://www.axios.com/local/detroit/2022/08/18/detroiters-end-michigan-ban-rent-control.

95. Kriston Capps, "As Housing Costs Spike, Voters Look for Hope in Rent Control," Bloomberg, November 2021, https://www.bloomberg.com/news/articles/2021-11-04/rent-control-scored-a-big-election-night-victory.

96. Chris Lisinski, "Polls Show Support for Local Option Rent Control," WWLP.com, March 7, 2023, https://www.wwlp.com/news/state-politics/poll-shows-support-for-local-option-rent-control/.

97. Daniel Aldana Cohen, Julian Brave NoiseCat, and Sean McElwee, "Americans Want to Live in a Just Society," Data for Progress, September 25, 2019, https://www.dataforprogress.org/blog/2019/9/25/americans-want-to-live-in-a-just-society.

98. "Lift the Ban Coalition—Who We Are," Lift the Ban, accessed June 14, 2024, https://ltbcoalition.org/.

99. "Mobile Home Rent Stabilization Ordinance," Humboldt Planning and Building, https://humboldtgov.org/2283/Mobile-Home-Rent-Stabilization-Ordinance.

100. Sandra Larson, "How Portland, Maine, Passed Rent Control," *Shelterforce*, November 28, 2022, https://shelterforce.org/2022/11/28/how-portland-maine-passed-rent-control/.

101. Courtney Cooperman, Lena O'Rourke, and David Foster, *Voters Choose Housing*, National Low Income Housing Coalition, December 2022, https://nlihc.org/sites/default/files/2022-12/voters-choose-housing.pdf.

102. Capps, "As Housing Costs Spike."

103. "Executive Order on Protecting Tenants and Stabilizing the American Economy," People's Action Homes Guarantee Campaign, https://peoplesaction.org/wp-content/uploads/2023/01/Updated-Final-1.23-Rent-Regulations-Executive-Order-w-Sign-ons.pdf.

104. "CPD Affiliates Mobilize for National Rent Control," Center for Popular Democracy, March 7, 2019, https://www.populardemocracy.org/blog/cpd-affiliates-mobilize-national-rent-control.

105. "Executive Order on Protecting Tenants," People's Action.

106. Fran Quigley, "Biden Rent Increase Cap Shows the Tenant Union Movement Can Win Nationally," *Common Dreams*, April 17, 2024, https://www.commondreams.org/opinion/biden-rent-increase-cap-tenant.

107. Kristen Broady, Wendy Edelberg, and Emily Moss, "An Eviction Moratorium without Rental Assistance Hurts Smaller Landlords, Too," *Brookings*, 2020, https://www.brookings.edu/blog/up-front/2020/09/21/an-eviction-moratorium-without-rental-assistance-hurts-smaller-landlords-too/.

108. Patrick Range McDonald, "Update: Big Real Estate Shelled Out Nearly $100 Million to Stop Prop 21," Housing Is a Human Right, January 3, 2021, https://www.housingisahumanright.org/update-big-real-estate-shelled-out-nearly-100-million-to-stop-prop-21/.

109. David Brand, "Federal Court Upholds NY Stabilization Laws, Setting Up Possible Supreme Court Showdown," *Gothamist*, February 6, 2023, https://gothamist.com/news/federal-court-upholds-ny-rent-stabilization-laws-setting-up-possible-supreme-court-showdown?mc_cid=.

110. "Rent Control Preemption Act," American Legislative Exchange Council, https://alec.org/model-policy/rent-control-preemption-act/; Maggie Hicks, "Real Estate Industry Groups Spent Millions to Halt the National Eviction Moratorium," *Open Secrets*, August 4, 2021, https://www.opensecrets.org/news/2021/08/real-estate-industry-spent-millions-to-halt-national-eviction-moratorium/.

111. Brittany Johnson, "Is That True? Experts Break Down 'No on Prop. 21' Ad," *KCRA*, October 19, 2021, https://www.kcra.com/article/is-that-true-experts-break-down-no-on-prop-21-ad/34401362.

112. "All About Rent Control," Bungalow, February 1, 2022, https://bungalow.com/articles/all-about-rent-control-what-it-is-how-it-works-and-how-it-impacts-your; Andrew Kliewer, Blair Bean Robertson, and Brianna Rauenzahn, "Constraining Cities," *Regulatory Review*, April 30, 2022, https://www.theregreview.org/2022/04/30/saturday-seminar-constraining-cities/. (Cities are subject to state control under the prevailing interpretation of the US Constitution.)

113. Patricia Cantor, "How Cambridge Lost Rent Control," *Shelterforce*, March 1, 1995, https://shelterforce.org/1995/03/01/25-years-ago-tenants-organized-formed-coalitions-took-to-the-streets-and-won-rent-control-in-massachusetts/; Marcelow Rochabrun and Cezary Podkul, "The Fateful Vote That Made New York City Rents So High," *ProPublica*, December 15, 2016, https://www.propublica.org/article/the-vote-that-made-new-york-city-rents-so-high.

114. Tim Nelson and Ellen Finn, "St. Paul Rolls Back Part of Its New Rent Control Policy," *MPR News*, September 29, 2022, https://www.mprnews.org/episode/2022/09/29/st-paul-rolls-back-part-of-its-new-rent-control-policy.

115. Pennell v. City of San Jose, 485 U.S. 1 (1998).

116. Mark Green, "Rent Destabilization Study II," Office of the Public Advocate, May 18, 1997, http://tenant.net/Alerts/Guide/papers/mgreen2.pdf.

117. Julian Castro, "Corporate Prey: How Corporate Landlords Destabilize Black Homeownership," Thurgood Marshall Institute, https://tminstitutedf.org/corporate-landlords-and-black-neighborhoods/; Mike Leonard, "RealPage, Landlords Face Antitrust Lawsuit over Rent Spike," *Bloomberg Law*, October 19, 2022, https://news.bloomberglaw.com/esg/realpage-major-landlords-face-antitrust-lawsuit-over-rent-spike.

118. "Wall Street and Single Family Rentals," Americans for Financial Reform, January 17, 2018, https://ourfinancialsecurity.org/2018/01/afr-report-wall-street-and-single-family-rentals/; Patrick Range McDonald, "Modern-Day Robber Baron: The Sins of Black-stone CEO Stephen Schwarzman," Housing Is a Human Right, July 29, 2020, https://www.housingisahumanright.org/modern-day-robber-baron-the-sins-of-blackstone-ceo-stephen-schwarzman/; Jeff Ernsthausen, Paul Kiel, and Jesse Eisinger, "These Real Estate and Oil Tycoons Avoided Paying Taxes for Years," *ProPublica*, December 7, 2021, https://www.propublica.org/article/these-real-estate-and-oil-tycoons-used-paper-losses-to-avoid-paying-taxes-for-years.

8. HOW WE FIX THIS—PUBLIC AND SOCIAL HOUSING

1. Unless otherwise indicated, quotes from Ramona Ferreyra are from a telephone interview with the author, December 6, 2022.

2. A version of this discussion of the value of public housing was originally published in Fran Quigley, "Public Housing Works. We Need More of It," *Jacobin*, February 23, 2023, https://jacobin.com/2023/02/public-housing-new-york-affordable-rent-real-estate.

3. "Section 9 Is Public Housing," Save Section 9, accessed June 14, 2024, https://www.savesection9.org/.

4. Bernie Sanders, "News: Sanders and Ocasio-Cortez Rollout Green New Deal for Public Housing Act," Bernie Sanders, U.S. Senator for Vermont, April 19, 2021, https://www.sanders.senate.gov/press-releases/news-sanders-and-ocasio-cortez-rollout-green-new-deal-for-public-housing-act/.

5. Joseph P. Fried, "Nixon's Housing Policy," *New York Times*, September 29, 1973.

6. Howard Husock, "How Public Housing Harms Cities," *City Journal*, Winter 2003, https://www.city-journal.org/article/how-public-housing-harms-cities.

7. Charles Babington, "Some GOP Legislators Hit Jarring Notes in Addressing Katrina," *Washington Post*, September 10, 2005, https://www.city-journal.org/article/how-public-housing-harms-cities.

8. "Next HUD Secretary Clarifies Position on Public Housing," *Washington Post*, December 28, 1976, reprinted at https://www.google.com/books/edition/Nomination_of_Patricia_Roberts_Harris/94lGcMGH7E4C?hl=en&gbpv=1&dq=.

9. Alex Schwartz, *Housing Policy in the United States* (New York: Routledge, 2021), 148.

10. "We Deserve to Have a Place to Live," Human Rights Watch, September 27, 2022, https://www.hrw.org/report/2022/09/27/we-deserve-have-place-live/how-us-underfunding-public-housing-harms-rights-new.

11. Peter Dreier, "Why America Needs More Social Housing," *American Prospect*, April 16, 2018, https://prospect.org/infrastructure/america-needs-social-housing/.

12. Alana Semuels, "The Power of Public Housing," *Atlantic*, September 22, 2015, https://www.theatlantic.com/business/archive/2015/09/public-housing-success/406561/; Matthew Desmond, *Poverty, by America* (New York: Crown, 2023), 144.

13. "We Deserve to Have a Place to Live," Human Rights Watch, September 27, 2022, https://www.hrw.org/report/2022/09/27/we-deserve-have-place-live/how-us-under funding-public-housing-harms-rights-new.

14. Unless otherwise indicated, quotes from Jackson Gandour are from a telephone interview with the author, November 10, 2022.

15. "America's Rental Housing 2022," Joint Center for Housing Studies of Harvard University, 2022, 27, https://www.jchs.harvard.edu/sites/default/files/reports/files/Har vard_JCHS_Americas_Rental_Housing_2022.pdf; "Eviction Tracking," Eviction Lab, https://evictionlab.org/eviction-tracking/.

16. "Resident Characteristics Report," US Department of Housing and Urban Development; Jon Leckie, "Rent Report," rent.com, May 2023, Jon rent.com/research/average-rent-price-report/.

17. "History and Nature of the Federal Procedural Requirements," National Housing Law Project, https://www.nhlp.org/wp-content/uploads/History-of-PH-GP-unedited-for-CW.pdf.

18. Sonya Acosta and Brianna Guerrero, "Long Waitlists for Housing Vouchers Show Pressing Unmet Need for Assistance," Center on Budget and Policy Priorities, October 6, 2021, https://www.cbpp.org/research/housing/long-waitlists-for-housing-vouchers-show-pressing-unmet-need-for-assistance.

19. Matthew Desmond, "Why Poverty Persists in America," *New York Times*, March 9, 2023, https://www.nytimes.com/2023/03/09/magazine/poverty-by-america-matthew-desmond.html?referringSource=articleShare.

20. "Some Trampled in Rush for Dallas Housing Vouchers," *KHOU-TV*, July 14, 2011, https://www.khou.com/article/news/local/texas/some-trampled-in-rush-for-dallas-hous ing-vouchers/285-341123934.

21. Michael A. Stegman, "The Role of Public Housing in a Revitalized National Hous-ing Policy," in *Building Foundations: Housing and Federal Policy*, ed. Denise Di Pasquale (Philadelphia: University of Pennsylvania Press, 1990), 333.

22. "Capital Fund Backlog," National Association of Housing and Redevelopment Officials, accessed June 14, 2024, https://www.nahro.org/wp-content/uploads/2020/04/capital_fund_backlog_One-Pager.pdf.

23. Schwartz, *Housing Policy in the United States*, 151.

24. Francesca Mari, "Imagine a Renters' Utopia: It Might Look Like Vienna," *New York Times*, May 23, 2023, https://www.nytimes.com/2023/05/23/magazine/vienna-social-housing.html?smid=.

25. Amee Chew, "Social Housing for All: A Vision for Thriving Communities, Renter Power, and Racial Justice," Center for Popular Democracy, March 2022, 18, https://www.populardemocracy.org/socialhousingforall.

26. "Policy Basics: Public Housing," Center on Budget and Policy Priorities, 2021, https://www.cbpp.org/research/public-housing.

27. "Public Housing History," National Low Income Housing Coalition, 2019, 4, https://nlihc.org/resource/public-housing-history; "False HOPE: A Critical Assessment of the HOPE VI Public Housing Redevelopment Program," National Housing Law Project, June 2002, https://nhlp.org/files/FalseHOPE.pdf.

28. "Priorities for the Build Back Better Act," National Low Income Housing Coalition, March 15, 2001, https://nlihc.org/sites/default/files/American_Recovery_Plan.pdf.

29. Will Fischer, Sonya Acosta, and Anna Bailey, "An Agenda for the Future of Public Housing," Center on Budget and Policy Priorities, March 11, 2021, 9, n. 14, https://www.cbpp.org/sites/default/files/3-11-21hous.pdf.

30. People's Action, *A National Homes Guarantee*, briefing book, 9, n. 31, https://homesguarantee.com/wp-content/uploads/Homes-Guarantee-_-Briefing-Book.pdf; "Human Rights Watch Report Highlights How HUD and Congress Must Do More to

Protect Public Housing Residents," National Housing Law Project, January 27, 2022, https://www.nhlp.org/wp-content/uploads/HRW-report-statement.pdf.

31. Schwartz, *Housing Policy in the United States*, 6; Richard Florida, "The U.S. Spends Far More on Homeowner Subsidies Than It Does on Affordable Housing," *Bloomberg*, April 17, 2015, https://www.bloomberg.com/news/articles/2015-04-17/the-u-s-spends-far-more-on-homeowner-subsidies-than-it-does-on-affordable-housing.

32. Tatjana Meschede, Jamie Morgan, Andrew Aurand, and Dan Threet, "Misdirected Housing Supports: Why the Mortgage Interest Deduction Unjustly Subsidizes High-Income Households and Expands Racial Disparities," National Low Income Housing Coalition, May 2021, 5–7, https://nlihc.org/sites/default/files/NLIHC-IERE_MID-Report.pdf.

33. Debipriya Chatterjee and Samuel Stein, "421-a at 50: Rising Cost, Diminishing Returns," Community Service Society, February 2022, 5, https://smhttp-ssl-58547.nexcesscdn.net/nycss/images/uploads/pubs/RisingCost_V9.pdf.

34. Ryan Holeywell, "Vienna Offers Affordable and Luxurious Housing," Governing: The States and Localities, February 2013, http://www.governing.com/gov-affordable-luxurious-housing-in-vienna.html; Chew, "Social Housing for All," 23–31; "Public Housing—a Singapore Icon," Housing and Development Board, 2022, https://www.hdb.gov.sg/about-us/our-role/public-housing-a-singapore-icon.

35. Carolin Schmidt, "Strong Tenant Protections and Subsidies Support Germany's Majority-Renter Housing Market," *Brookings*, April 20, 2021, https://www.brookings.edu/essay/germany-rental-housing-markets/.

36. Joseph P. Fried, "Nixon's Housing Policy," *New York Times*, September 29, 1973, https://www.nytimes.com/1973/09/29/archives/nixons-housing-policy-opponents-say-proposal-for-cash-payments-wont.htm; Maggie McCarty, "An Introduction to Public Housing," Congressional Research Service, January 3, 2014, 5–9, https://sgp.fas.org/crs/misc/R41654.pdf.

37. Philip Tegeler, "What Can HUD Do to Expand Public Housing and Community Ownership of Rental Housing?," Poverty and Race Research Action Council, April 2021, 3, http://www.prrac.org/pdf/hud-social-housing-2021.pdf.

38. Sanders, "News: Sanders and Ocasio-Cortez Rollout Green New Deal for Public Housing Act."

39. Rachel M. Cohen, "How State Governments Are Reimagining American Public Housing," *Vox*, August 4, 2022, https://www.vox.com/policy-and-politics/23278643/affordable-public-housing-inflation-renters-home. See also Paul Williams, "Public Housing for All," *Noema*, August 26, 2021. ("A system of public, municipal and state-owned enterprises that build and operate housing presents both an off-ramp from our reliance on rent-seeking investors and laissez-faire 'planning,' and an on-ramp to the socialization of our vast land wealth.")

40. Cohen, "How State Governments Are Reimagining American Public Housing."

41. Keeanga-Yamahtta Taylor, *Race for Profit: How Banks and the Real Estate Industry Undermined Black Homeownership* (Chapel Hill: University of North Carolina Press, 2019), xviii.

42. Samuel Stein, "What Stands in the Way of Affordable Housing?," *Architect's Newspaper*, August 23, 2023, https://www.archpaper.com/2023/08/what-stands-in-the-way-of-affordable-housing/.

43. Bloomberg editors, "The US Can Solve Its Housing Crisis. It Just Needs to Start Building," *Washington Post*, December 30, 2022, https://www.washingtonpost.com/business/the-us-can-solve-its-housing-crisis-it-just-needs-to-start-building/2022/12/30/4d5b3940-8866-11ed-b5ac-411280b122ef_story.html.

44. Yonah Freemark, "Zoning Change," Urban Institute, April 5, 2023, https://www.urban.org/research/publication/zoning-change.

45. "America's Rental Housing 2022," Joint Center for Housing Studies of Harvard University.

46. Rick Jacobus, "Inclusionary Housing: Creating and Maintaining Equitable Communities," Lincoln Institute of Land Policy, 2015, 3, 13, https://www.lincolninst.edu/publications/policy-focus-reports/inclusionary-housing.

47. Peter Coy, "The U.S. Is Finally Trying to Fix Its Money-Laundering Problem," *New York Times*, August 3, 2023, https://www.nytimes.com/2023/08/02/opinion/money-laundering-corruption-treasury.html?smid=.

48. Chuck Collins, "Who Owns the City? Luxury Towers and Supercharged Gentrification," *Nonprofit Quarterly*, May 26, 2021, https://nonprofitquarterly.org/who-owns-the-city-luxury-towers-and-supercharged-gentrification/.

49. Collins, "Who Owns the City?": Chew, "Social Housing for All."

50. Alex Schwartz and Kirk McClure, "Why Building More Homes Won't Solve the Affordable Housing Problem for Those Who Need It the Most," *Conversation*, November 12, 2021, https://theconversation.com/why-building-more-homes-wont-solve-the-affordable-housing-problem-for-the-millions-of-people-who-need-it-most-171100 (citing "Rental Vacancy Rates by Region," US Census, 2021, https://www.census.gov/housing/hvs/files/qtr321/rvr321.jpg); Katherine M. O'Regan and Keren M. Horn, "What Can We Learn about the Low-Income Housing Tax Credit Program by Looking at the Tenants?," *Housing Policy Debate* 23, no. 3 (May 16, 2013): 597–613, https://www.tandfonline.com/doi/abs/10.1080/10511482.2013.772909.

51. Griffin Oleynick, "Beyond YIMBYism: An Interview with Max Holleran," *Commonweal*, January 23, 2023, https://www.commonwealmagazine.org/housing-max-holleran-interview-nimbys-yimbys. See also Allan Mallach, "Is the Solution to Homelessness Obvious?," *Shelterforce*, April 5, 2023, https://shelterforce.org/2023/04/05/is-the-solution-to-homelessness-obvious/. ("Until or unless the federal government provides enough funds so that every homeless person can get a Housing Choice Voucher or the equivalent, we cannot eliminate homelessness. Even when we build new so-called affordable housing with the Low Income Tax Credit or other programs, most homeless people can't afford those units . . . unless they can get housing vouchers. Even with public subsidies for capital costs, we cannot build housing that will rent at levels most homeless people can afford. And even if we increased production of moderately priced housing to the point where some older units filtered down to become more affordable, their rent will not fall below the cost floor a landlord needs to cover their costs and make a reasonable return on their equity investment or make their mortgage payments."); Allan Mallach, "Rents Will Only Go So Low, No Matter How Much We Build," *Shelterforce*, December 13, 2019, https://shelterforce.org/2019/12/13/rents-will-only-go-so-low-no-matter-how-much-we-build/ ("Every landlord has some floor, some minimum amount they need to make—based on their business model—to stay in business. . . . Neither the market nor existing affordable housing programs will solve this problem. The only thing that will is the creation of an entitlement housing allowance to enable all very-low-income families to find basic, decent housing at a price they can afford"); and Peter Cohen, "The Filtering Fallacy," *Shelterforce*, October 21, 2016, https://shelterforce.org/2016/10/12/the-filtering-fallacy/.

52. Chew, "Social Housing for All"; Gianpaolo Baiocchi and H. Jacob Carlson, "Housing Is a Social Good," *Boston Review*, June 2, 2021, https://bostonreview.net/articles/housing-is-a-social-good/; People's Action, *National Homes Guarantee*, 2.

53. Chew, "Social Housing for All"; Baiocchi and Carlson, "Housing Is a Social Good"; People's Action, *National Homes Guarantee*, 2.

54. Baiocchi and Carlson, "Housing Is a Social Good"; People's Action, *National Homes Guarantee*, 2; "PH 4.2, Social Rental Housing Stock," OECD, https://www.oecd.org/els/family/PH4-2-Social-rental-housing-stock.pdf, 1.

55. Chew, "Social Housing for All"; Baiocchi and Carlson, "Housing Is a Social Good"; People's Action, *National Homes Guarantee*, 2; Peter Gowan and Ryan Cooper, "Social Housing in the United States," People's Policy Project, 2018, 27, www.peoplespolicy project.org/wp-content/uploads/2018/04/SocialHousing.pdf.

56. Chew, "Social Housing for All"; Baiocchi and Carlson, "Housing Is a Social Good"; People's Action, *National Homes Guarantee*, 2; Gowan and Cooper, "Social Housing in the United States," 27.

57. James A. Crowder Jr., Chris Schildt, and Rick Jacobus, *Our Homes, Our Communities: How Housing Acquisition Strategies Can Create Affordable Housing, Stabilize Neighborhoods, and Prevent Displacement*, PolicyLink, 2021, 6, 14, https://www.policylink.org/sites/default/files/pl_Our-Homes_050321_a.pdf.

58. Emily Thaden, Kim Graziani, and Annie Stup, "Land Banks and Community Land Trusts: Not Synonyms or Antonyms. Complements," *Shelterforce*, 2016, https://shelterforce.org/2016/11/09/land-banks-community-land-trusts-not-synonyms-or-antonyms-complements/; Chew, "Social Housing for All," 22.

59. All-In Cities, "Tenant/Community Opportunity to Purchase," PolicyLink, https://allincities.org/toolkit/tenant-community-opportunity-to-purchase; Jenny Reed, "DC's First Right Purchase Program Helps to Preserve Affordable Housing and Is One of DC's Key Anti-displacement Tools," DC Fiscal Policy Institute, September 24, 2013, https://www.dcfpi.org/wp-content/uploads/2013/09/9-24-13-First_Right_Purchase_Paper-Final.pdf; Associates and NYU Furman Center, "Rights of First Refusal," Local Housing Solutions, 2021, https://localhousingsolutions.org/housing-policy-library/rights-of-first-refusal/.

60. Julie Gilgoff, "The California SHIMBY Movement—Social Housing in My Backyard," *California Western Law Review* 60 (2023–2024), https://papers.ssrn.com/sol3/papers.cfm?abstract_id=4789072.

61. Amanda Abrams, "Lessons from the Last Housing Crisis: How to Get Control of Properties," *Shelterforce*, 2020, https://shelterforce.org/2020/09/17/lessons-from-the-last-housing-crisis/.

62. For an example of cooperative housing see Erik Forman, "How Unions Can Solve the Housing Crisis," *In These Times*, October 2018, https://inthesetimes.com/features/unions-housing-crisis-labor-coop-apartments-new-york-homeless-rent-control.html.

63. Chew, "Social Housing for All," 31.

64. Baiocchi and Carlson, "Housing Is a Social Good"; People's Action, National *Homes Guarantee*, 2.

65. Emily Thaden and Greg Rosenberg, "Outperforming the Market: Delinquency and Foreclosure Rates in Community Land Trusts," Lincoln Institute of Land Policy, 2010, https://www.lincolninst.edu/publications/articles/outperforming-market.

66. Holeywell, "Vienna Offers Affordable and Luxurious Housing." (Because public housing is so expansive in Vienna, developers of unsubsidized units still must provide good prices and high quality to prospective tenants in order to remain competitive. "The city—without having direct control of the property market—has managed to keep the cost of new residential property down.")

67. Julie Lawson and Hannu Ruonavaara, *Land Policy for Affordable and Inclusive Housing: An International Review*, SmartLand, 2020, 33, https://smartland.fi/wp-content/uploads/Land-policy-for-affordable-and-inclusive-housing-an-international-review.pdf.

68. Chew, "Social Housing for All," 4; Gowan and Cooper, "Social Housing in the United States," 29.

69. People's Action, *National Homes Guarantee*, 2.

70. Claudia Copeland, Linda Levine, and William J. Mallett, "The Role of Public Works Infrastructure in Economic Recovery," Congressional Research Service, September 21, 2011, 12–15, https://sgp.fas.org/crs/misc/R42018.pdf; Gowan and Cooper, "Social

Housing in the United States," 29. ("One major benefit of an ongoing government investment in municipal housing is an increase in job security for people involved in municipal housing construction—while the supply of housing being built may vary somewhat over time, it need not do so to the same extent that any individual private developer's workload fluctuates.")

71. Dianne Enriquez, "A System That Makes Housing a Commodity Can't Serve Human Needs, *Jacobin,* 2021, https://jacobin.com/2021/07/housing-evictions-covid-19-crisis-homelessness-organize-policy; "2021 Federal Housing Agenda," Center for Popular Democracy & CPD Action, January 2021, 8, https://www.populardemocracy.org/sites/default/files/20210124%20Federal%20Housing%20Agenda.pdf; People's Action, *National Homes Guarantee,* 14. The City of Evanston, Illinois, has a local reparations program focused on building intergenerational wealth among Black residents through homeownership: "Evanston Local Reparations," City of Evanston, accessed June 14, 2024, https://www.cityofevanston.org/government/city-council/reparations. ("Reparations, and any process for restorative relief, must connect between the harm imposed and the City. The strongest case for reparations by the City of Evanston is in the area of housing, where there is sufficient evidence showing the City's part in housing discrimination as a result of early City zoning ordinances in place between 1919 and 1969, when the City banned housing discrimination.")

72. People's Action, *National Homes Guarantee,* 14; Baiocchi and Carlson, "Housing Is a Social Good': Chew, "Social Housing for All," 30–31.

73. Desmond, *Poverty, By America,* 144.

74. Chew, "Social Housing for All," 13.

75. Holeywell, "Vienna Offers Affordable and Luxurious Housing"; Gowan and Cooper, "Social Housing in the United States," 29; Joanna Kusiak, "Socialization: A Democratic, Affordable, and Lawful Solution to Berlin's Housing Crisis," Rosa Luxemburg Stiftung, January 2021, 3–4, https://www.rosalux.de/fileadmin/rls_uploads/pdfs/Policy_Paper/PolicyPaper_1-2021_EN.pdf.

76. "National Land Bank Map," Center for Community Progress, https://communityprogress.org/resources/land-banks/national-land-bank-map/; "Housing Trust Funds," Local Housing Solutions, https://localhousingsolutions.org/housing-policy-library/housing-trust-funds/.

77. Crowder, Schildt, and Jacobus, *Our Homes, Our Communities.*

78. Will Peischel, "How a Brief Socialist Takeover in North Dakota Gave Residents a Public Bank," *Vox,* October 1, 2019, https://www.vox.com/the-highlight/2019/9/24/20872558/california-north-dakota-public-bank; "California Public Banking Option Act (AB 1177) Passes the State Legislature," California Public Banking Alliance, September 11, 2021, https://californiapublicbankingalliance.org/news/california-public-banking-option-act-ab-1177-passes-the-state-legislature/; "Finance Our Future," Pathways to a People's Economy, accessed June 14, 2024, https://peopleseconomy.org/create-and-strengthen-banks-community-capital-vehicles-and-financial-institutions-that-prioritize-the-communities-they-serve/; Thomas Hanna, "Buyouts, Not Bailouts: Public Banks as a Solution to the Next Crisis," *openDemocracy,* August 28, 2019, https://www.opendemocracy.net/en/oureconomy/buyouts-not-bailouts-public-banks-solution-next-crisis/; "From the Ground Up: Community Centered Policies to Scale Equitable Development," Partners for Dignity & Rights, 2022, 30–31, https://dignityandrights.org/wp-content/uploads/2022/06/PDR-Ground-Up-Report-Final-Digital-1.pdf.

79. Crowder, Schildt, and Jacobus, *Our Homes, Our Communities*; Laura Waxmann, "S.F. Supervisors Approve $20M in Prop. I Revenue for Rent Relief, Affordable Housing," *San Francisco Business Times,* March 23, 2021, https://www.bizjournals.com/sanfrancisco/news/2021/03/23/prop-i-sf-rent-reliefaffordable-housing.html.

80. Julie Gilgoff, "Giving Tenants the First Opportunity to Purchase Their Homes," *Shelterforce*, 2020, https://shelterforce.org/2020/07/24/giving-tenants-the-first-opportu nity-to-purchase-their-homes/; Reed, "DC's First Right Purchase Program"; Noah Arroyo, "SF Tenants Set to Gain New Powers in Negotiations with Landlords," *San Francisco Public Press*, February 17, 2022, https://www.sfpublicpress.org/sf-tenantsto-gain-new-powers-in-negotiations-with-landlords/; Patrick Range McDonald, "The Righteous Battle for Rent Control in St. Paul and Minneapolis," Housing Is a Human Right, December 31, 2021, https://www.housinghumanright.org/the-righteous-battle-for-rent-control-in-st-paul-and-minneapolis/; Roxana Kopetman, "Santa Ana's Rent Control Law Is on after Efforts to Repeal It Fail," *Orange County Register*, November 22, 2021, https://www.ocregister.com/2021/11/22/santa-anas-rent-control-law-is-on-after-efforts-to-repeal-it-fail/. ("Hard" rent control restricts increases based on a formula usually tied to inflation, no matter who the occupant is. "Weak" rent control is limited to the tenure of the tenant, allowing rents to be reset when the occupants change.); Gowan and Cooper, "Social Housing in the United States"; "From the Ground Up," Partners for Dignity & Rights.

81. Cohen, "How State Governments Are Reimagining American Public Housing." See also Williams, "Public Housing for All."

82. Cohen, "How State Governments Are Reimagining American Public Housing."

83. Cohen, "How State Governments Are Reimagining American Public Housing."

84. Democracy Collaborative, "Community Land Trusts (CLTs)," Community-Wealth. org, June 21, 2012, https://community-wealth.org/strategies/panel/clts/index.html; Miriam Axel-Lute, "Understanding Community Land Trusts," *Shelterforce*, 2021, https://shelterforce.org/2021/07/12/understanding-community-land-trusts/.

85. Axel-Lute, "Understanding Community Land Trusts."

86. Axel-Lute, "Understanding Community Land Trusts."

87. Axel-Lute, "Understanding Community Land Trusts."

88. "Roots & Branches: A Gardener's Guide to the Origins and Evolution of the Community Land Trust," Center for Community Land Trust Innovation, November 2019, accessed June 14, 2024, http://cltroots.org/the-guide/early-hybrids-breeding-and-seed ing-the-clt-model/georgia-seedbed; Audrea Lim, "We Shall Not Be Moved: Collective Ownership Gives Power Back to Poor Farmers," *Harper's Magazine*, July 2020, https://harpers.org/archive/2020/07/we-shall-not-be-moved-collective-ownership-black-farmers/.

89. Crowder, Schildt, and Jacobus, *Our Homes, Our Communities*; Ko Lyn Cheang, "As Indy Grapples with Gentrification, Affordable Housing Advocates Turn to Bold Solution," *Indianapolis Star*, May 19, 2022, https://www.indystar.com/story/news/real-estate/2022/05/19/indianapolis-gentrification-affordable-housing-community-land-trust/7371740001/.

90. Brenda Torpy, "Champlain Housing Trust," International Center for Community Land Trusts, 2015, https://cltweb.org/case-studies/champlain-housing-trust/.

91. Karen Narefsky, "The Case for Public Housing," *Dissent*, November 2015, https://www.dissentmagazine.org/online_articles/case-for-public-housing-vienna-chicago. (Narefsky calls for social housing that "would have to be built at a large scale, beyond that at which local community land trusts can operate. But I hope that the community land trust movement can provide an example of the kind of housing we need.")

92. David Zahniser, "L.A. Leaders Weigh a New Idea to Halt Rent Hikes: Force Landlords to Sell Their Buildings," *Los Angeles Times*, February 3, 2020, https://www.latimes.com/ homeless-housing/story/2020-02-03/la-me-eminent-doman-proposalrent-hikes. For a discussion of land value tax, which unlike traditional property tax schemes disincentivizes owners keeping property vacant or undeveloped, see Jerusalem Desmas, "Tax the Land: One Radical Idea to Solve America's Housing Crisis," *Vox*, March 4, 2022, https://www.vox.com/policy-and-politics/22951092/land-tax-housing-crisis.

93. "AHF Praises Newsom for Signing Bill to Convert Buildings into Affordable Housing," *BusinessWire*, September 30, 2022, https://www.businesswire.com/news/home/20220929006027/en/AHF-Praises-Newsom-for-Signing-Bill-to-Convert-Buildings-into-Affordable-Housing.

94. "Congresswoman Rashida Tlaib Introduces Bill to Repeal Controversial Opportunity Zones," Representative Rashida Tlaib, November 22, 2019, https://tlaib.house.gov/media/press-releases/congresswoman-rashida-tlaib-introduces-bill-repeal-controversial-opportunity; "Where Have All the Houses Gone? Private Equity, Single Family Rentals, and America's Neighborhoods," Committee on Financial Services, https://www.congress.gov/event/117th-congress/house-event/114969.

95. Gianpaolo Baiocchi and H. Jacob Carlson, "The Case for a Social Housing Development Authority," Urban Democracy Lab, November 2020, https://urbandemos.nyu.edu/wp-content/uploads/2020/11/SHDA-whitepaper-Nov2020.pdf.

96. Baiocchi and Carlson, "Housing Is a Social Good."

97. "Rep. Omar Reintroduces Homes for All, Manufactured Housing Legislation," Ilhan Omar, press release, March 24, 2022, https://omar.house.gov/media/press-releases/rep-omar-reintroduces-homes-all-manufactured-housing-legislation; People's Action, *National Homes Guarantee*, 8.

98. Gianpaolo Baiocchi, H. Jacob Carlson, Ruthy Gourevitch, and Daniel Aldana Cohen, "Homes Act: Analysis of Legislative Impact," Climate & Community Institute, September 2024, https://climateandcommunity.org/research/homes-act-analysis-of-legislative-impact/; Alexandria Ocasio-Cortez and Tina Smith, "Our Solution to the Housing Crisis," *New York Times*, September 18, 2024, https://www.nytimes.com/2024/09/18/opinion/aoc-tina-smith-housing.html.

99. "HoUSed," National Low Income Housing Coalition, https://nlihc.org/housed.

9. LESSONS FROM OTHER COUNTRIES AND OUR OWN HISTORY

1. Francesca Mari, "Imagine a Renters' Utopia: It Might Look Like Vienna," *New York Times*, May 23, 2023, https://www.nytimes.com/2023/05/23/magazine/vienna-social-housing.html?smid=.

2. A version of my discussion of the Vienna success with social housing was originally published in Fran Quigley, "We Should Look to Vienna for Answers to Our Housing Crisis," *Jacobin*, October 29, 2023, https://jacobin.com/2023/10/red-vienna-public-affordable-housing-homelessness-matthew-yglesias.

3. "The System of Limited For-Profit Housing in Austria: Cost-Rents, Revolving Funds, and Economic Impacts," CIRIEC Working Paper, May 2022, https://www.housinginternational.coop/wp-content/uploads/2022/07/CIRIEC-WORKING-PAPER_Limited-Profit-Housing-Associations-in-Austria_May2022-1.pdf; "Vienna's Unique Social Housing Program," US Department of Housing and Urban Development, January 13, 2014, https://www.huduser.gov/portal/pdredge/pdr_edge_featd_article_011314.html#:~:text=.

4. Mari, "Imagine a Renters' Utopia."

5. Mari, "Imagine a Renters' Utopia."

6. Peter Dreier, "Why America Needs More Social Housing," *American Prospect*, April 16, 2018, https://prospect.org/infrastructure/america-needs-social-housing/.

7. Kathrin Gaál and Karin Ramser, "Social Housing in Vienna," City of Vienna, https://socialhousing.wien/. See also H. Jacob Carlson and Gianpaolo Baiocchi, "Social Housing: How a New Generation of Activists Is Reinventing Housing," *Shelterforce*, June 30, 2023, https://shelterforce.org/2023/06/30/social-housing-how-a-new-generation-of-activists-are-reinventing-housing/; "City of Vienna: Human Rights Council Resolution

39/7 on Local Government and Human Rights," UN Office of the High Commissioner for Human Rights, February 12, 2019, ttps://www.ohchr.org/sites/default/files/Documents/Issues/LocalGvt/Local/20190212Vienna.pdf.

8. "Vienna's Unique Social Housing Program," US Department of Housing and Urban Development.

9. Dreier, "Why America Needs More Social Housing."

10. Gaál and Ramser, "Social Housing in Vienna."

11. Mirko Lorenz, "How Vienna Found a Unique Model for Low Rent," Datawrapper, May 25, 2023, https://blog.datawrapper.de/how-vienna-found-a-unique-model-for-low-rent/.

12. "The World's Most Livable Cities in 2023," *Economist*, June 21, 2023, https://www.economist.com/graphic-detail/2023/06/21/the-worlds-most-liveable-cities-in-2023.

13. "76% of Low-Income Renters Needing Federal Rental Assistance Don't Receive It," Center on Budget and Policy Priorities, 2019, https://www.cbpp.org/research/housing/three-out-of-four-low-income-at-risk-renters-do-not-receive-federal-rental-assistance; "2022 Annual Homeless Assessment Report (AHAR) to Congress," US Department of Housing and Urban Development, December 19, 2022, https://www.huduser.gov/por tal/sites/default/files/pdf/2022-ahar-part-1.pdf. For a critique of the estimate see "'Don't Count on It': How the HUD Point-in-Time Count Underestimates the Homelessness Crisis in America," National Law Center on Homelessness and Poverty, 2017, https://homelesslaw.org/wp-content/uploads/2018/10/HUD-PIT-report2017.pdf.

14. Veronika Duma and Hanna Lichtenberger, "Remembering Red Vienna," *Jacobin*, February 10, 2017, https://jacobin.com/2017/02/red-vienna-austria-housing-urban-planning.

15. Jake Blumgart, "Most Livable City: How Vienna Earned Its Place in Housing History," CityMonitor, June 22, 2023, https://citymonitor.ai/housing/red-vienna-how-aus trias-capital-earned-its-place-in-housing-history; "Municipal Housing" in Vienna, City of Vienna, https://socialhousing.wien/tools/municipal-housing-in-vienna.

16. Gaál and Ramser, "Social Housing in Vienna."

17. Blumgart, "Most Livable City."

18. Meagan Day, "We Can Have Beautiful Public Housing," *Jacobin*, November 13, 2018, https://jacobin.com/2018/11/beautiful-public-housing-red-vienna-social-housing.

19. Gaal and Ramser, "Social Housing in Vienna."

20. "Municipal Politics—'Red Vienna'—a Success Story," City of Vienna, accessed June 14, 2024, https://www.wien.gv.at/english/history/commemoration/housing.html.

21. "How Much Does the Austrian State Spend on Housing?," Die Gemeinnutzigen (analysis of Eurostat, Cofog data, 2020). On file with the author.

22. "Urban Development and Land Policy," City of Vienna, accessed June 14, 2024, https://socialhousing.wien/tools/urban-development-and-land-policy.

23. Mari, "Imagine a Renters' Utopia."

24. "Sonnwendviertel—a New Urban Quarter," City of Vienna, accessed June 14, 2024, https://socialhousing.wien/best-practice/planning-urban-development/sonnwend viertel-a-new-urban-quarter.

25. "A Home of Your Own: Housing First and Ending Homelessness in Finland," Y-Foundation, 2017, 11, 24, https://www.feantsaresearch.org/download/a_home_of_your_own_lowres_spreads6069661816957790483.pdf; Jon Henley, "'It's a Miracle': Helsinki's Radical Solution to Homelessness," *Guardian*, June 3, 2019, https://www.theguardian.com/cities/2019/jun/03/its-a-miracle-helsinkis-radical-solution-to-homelessness.

26. "Home of Your Own," Y-Foundation, 10. (Section 19 of the Constitution of Finland includes the following provisions: "Those who cannot obtain the means necessary for a life of dignity have the right to receive indispensable subsistence and care. Everyone shall be guaranteed by an Act the right to basic subsistence in the event of unemployment, illness, and disability and during old age as well as at the birth of a child or the loss of a

provider. . . . The public authorities shall promote the right of everyone to housing and the opportunity to arrange their own housing.")

27. Peter Gowan and Ryan Cooper, "Social Housing in the United States," People's Policy Project, 2018, 20, www.peoplespolicyproject.org/wp-content/uploads/2018/04/SocialHousing.pdf.

28. Julie Lawson and Hannu Ruonavaara, "Land Policy for Affordable and Inclusive Housing: An International Review" SmartLand, 2020, 32, https://smartland.fi/wp-content/uploads/Land-policy-for-affordable-and-inclusive-housing-an-international-review.pdf.

29. Penelope Colston, "The Finnish Secret to Happiness? Knowing When You Have Enough," *New York Times*, April 1, 2023, https://www.nytimes.com/2023/04/01/world/europe/finland-happiness-optimism.html?referringSource=articleShare.

30. "Public Housing—a Singapore Icon," Housing and Development Board, 2022, https://www.hdb.gov.sg/about-us/our-role/public-housing-a-singapore-icon; Tien-Foo Sing, I-Chun Tsai, and Ming-Chi Chen, "Price Dynamics in Public and Private Housing Markets in Singapore," *Journal of Housing Economics* 15, no. 4 (December 2006): 305–20, https://ideas.repec.org/a/eee/jhouse/v15y2006i4p305-320.html.

31. "Public Housing—a Singapore Icon," Housing and Development Board.

32. Abhas Jha, "'But What about Singapore?' Lessons from the Best Public Housing Program in the World," *World Bank Blogs*, January 31, 2018, https://blogs.worldbank.org/sustainablecities/what-about-singapore-lessons-best-public-housing-program-world.

33. Fran Quigley, "Social Housing Can Work: An Interview with Alex Lee and Stanley Chang," *Jacobin*, May 13, 2024, https://jacobin.com/2024/05/social-housing-policy-california-hawaii.

34. "South-South Cooperation—FUCVAM, Uruguay," Building and Social Housing Foundation, accessed June 14, 2024, https://www.world-habitat.org/wp-content/uploads/2016/03/Report-South-South-co-operation-FUCVAM-WEB-5MB.pdf.

35. Day, "We Can Have Beautiful Public Housing."

36. John Harris, "The End of Council Housing," *Guardian*, January 4, 2016, https://www.theguardian.com/society/2016/jan/04/end-of-council-housing-bill-secure-tenancies-pay-to-stay.

37. Ösgård, Anton, "Sweden's Collective Bargaining for Rents Must Be Defended," *Jacobin*, July 12, 2021, https://jacobin.com/2021/07/sweden-left-party-social-democrats-housing-crisis; "About Us: Introducing the Swedish Union of Tenants," Swedish Union of Tenants, accessed June 14, 2024, http://www.iut.nu/wp-content/uploads/2017/03/A-Introduction-to-the-Swedish-Union-of-Tenants.pdf.

38. Gowan and Cooper, "Social Housing in the United States," 23, 25.

39. Gowan and Cooper, "Social Housing in the United States."

40. Gowan and Cooper, "Social Housing in the United States."

41. "Rep. Omar Reintroduces Homes for All, Manufactured Housing Legislation," Ilhan Omar, press release, March 24, 2022, https://omar.house.gov/media/press-releases/rep-omar-reintroduces-homes-all-manufactured-housing-legislation.

42. Raina Lipsitz, "To House the People, Expropriate the Landlords," *Conversationalist*, August 12, 2021, https://conversationalist.org/2021/08/12/to-house-the-people-expropriate-the-landlords/.

43. Alexander Vasudevan, "Berlin's Vote to Take Property from Big Landlords Could Be a Watershed Moment," *Guardian*, September 29, 2021, https://www.theguardian.com/commentisfree/2021/sep/29/berlin-vote-landlords-referendum-corporate; Lipsitz, "To House the People"; Joanna Kusiak, "Socialization: A Democratic, Affordable, and Lawful Solution to Berlin's Housing Crisis," Rosa Luxemburg Stiftung, January 2021, https://www.rosalux.de/fileadmin/rls_uploads/pdfs/Policy_Paper/PolicyPaper_1-2021_EN.pdf.

44. Bill Davies, Charlotte Snelling, Ed Turner, and Susanne Marquardt, "Lessons from Germany: Tenant Power in the Rental Market," Institute for Public Policy Research, 2017, https://www.ippr.org/publications/lessons-from-germany-tenant-power-in-the-rental-market; Matt Phillips, "Most Germans Don't Buy Their Homes, They Rent: Here's Why," *Quartz*, January 23, 2014, https://qz.com/167887/germany-has-one-of-the-orlds-lowest-homeownership-rates/.

45. Sarah Abramsky, "Other Countries Know Housing Is a Human Right. Why Doesn't America?," *Nation*, July 28, 2023, https://www.thenation.com/article/politics/housing-homelessness-europe-america/.

46. Quigley, "Social Housing Can Work."

47. Chuck Collins, "Who Owns the City? Luxury Towers and Supercharged Gentrification," *Nonprofit Quarterly*, May 26, 2021, https://nonprofitquarterly.org/who-owns-the-city-luxury-towers-and-supercharged-gentrification/.

48. Peter Coy, "The U.S. Is Finally Trying to Fix Its Money-Laundering Problem," *New York Times*, August 3, 2023, https://www.nytimes.com/2023/08/02/opinion/money-laundering-corruption-treasury.html?smid=.

49. Fran Quigley, "Tell Me How It Ends: The Path to Nationalizing the U.S. Pharmaceutical Industry," *University of Michigan Journal of Law Reform* 53 (2020): 755, https://papers.ssrn.com/sol3/papers.cfm?abstract_id=3496795.

50. Franklin D. Roosevelt, "State of the Union Message to Congress," January 11, 1944.

51. "Eleanor Roosevelt and the Universal Declaration of Human Rights," Eleanor Roosevelt Papers Project, Columbian College of Arts & Sciences, accessed June 14, 2024, https://erpapers.columbian.gwu.edu/eleanor-roosevelt-and-universal-declaration-human-rights.

52. "The Right to Adequate Housing Fact Sheet No. 21 / Rev. 1," Office of the United Nations High Commissioner for Human Rights, 2014, 1, 3–9, https://www.ohchr.org/sites/default/files/Documents/Publications/FS21_rev_1_Housing_en.pdf.

53. Universal Declaration of Human Rights, G.A. Res. 217, U.N. GAOR, 3d Sess., pt. 1, art. 25(1), U.N. Doc. A/810 (1948).

54. "The Universal Declaration of Human Rights and Its Relevance for the European Union," European Parliamentary Research Service, November 2018, https://www.europarl.europa.eu/RegData/etudes/ATAG/2018/628295/EPRS_ATA(2018)628295_EN.pdf.

55. International Covenant on Economic, Social and Cultural Rights, opened for signature December 16, 1966, art. 11(1), 993 U.N.T.S. 3, 5 (entered into force January 3, 1976).

56. International Covenant on Economic, Social and Cultural Rights.

57. Franklin D. Roosevelt, "Radio Address on the Election of Liberals," November 4, 1938, https://www.presidency.ucsb.edu/documents/radio-address-the-election-liberals.

58. "Status of Ratification Interactive Dashboard," United Nations Human Rights Office of the High Commissioner, https://indicators.ohchr.org/.

59. Vienna Convention on the Law of Treaties (VCLT), adopted May 22, 1969, G.A. Res. 2166 (XXI), 2287 (XXII), 1155 U.N.T.S. 331, U.N. Doc. A/CONF.39/11/Add.2, art. 18.

60. Lindsey v. Normet, 405 U.S. 56 (1972).

61. Eric Tars, "Housing as a Human Right," National Law Center on Homelessness & Poverty, 2019, 1–14, https://nlihc.org/sites/default/files/AG-2019/01-06_Housing-Human-Right.pdf.

62. "General Comments No. 4 and 24: The Right to Adequate Housing," CESCR, U.N. Doc. E/1992/23 (1991), para. 7.

63. Tars, "Housing as a Human Right."

64. "Country Info," Housing Rights Watch, November 22, 2012, 1–21, https://www.housingrightswatch.org/content/country-info; Arthur Acolin, "The Public Sector Plays

a Significant Role in Supporting French Renters," Brookings Institution, April 20, 2021, https://www.brookings.edu/essay/france-rental-housing-markets/. (More than 40 percent of French renters live in public housing.)

65. "Homelessness," Scottish Government, accessed June 14, 2024, https://www.gov.scot/policies/homelessness/.

66. Finland Constitution, amended 2011, https://www.constituteproject.org/constitution/Finland_2011.pdf?lang=en_.

67. Ella Hancock, "Helsinki Still Leading the Way to Ending Homelessness," World Habitat, October 6, 2022, https://world-habitat.org/news/our-blog/helsinki-is-still-leading-the-way-in-ending-homelessness-but-how-are-they-doing-it/.

68. Svilena Iotkovska, "Athens Takes Another Step towards Eliminating Homelessness," TheMayor.Eu, March 12, 2021, https://www.themayor.eu/en/a/view/athens-takes-another-step-towards-eliminating-homelessness-7408.

69. Gaál and Ramser, "Social Housing in Vienna."

70. Tars, "Housing as a Human Right."

71. Joanne Goldblum and Colleen Shaddox, *Broke in America: Seeing, Understanding, and Ending U.S. Poverty* (Dallas: BenBella, 2021), 55.

72. Housing Act of 1949 (Title V of P.L. 81–171).

73. Tars, "Housing as a Human Right."

74. "From Wrongs to Rights: The Case for Homeless Bill of Rights Legislation," National Law Center on Homelessness & Poverty, 2013, 6, https://homelesslaw.org/wp-content/uploads/2018/10/Wrongs_to_Rights_HBOR.pdf; Brian Eason, "Indy Council Creates 'Homeless Bill of Rights,'" *Indianapolis Star*, March 3, 2015, https://www.usatoday.com/story/news/nation/2015/03/03/indy-council-creates-homeless-bill-rights/24333503/.

75. Tars, "Housing as a Human Right."

76. H.R. 3772—Housing Is a Human Right Act of 2023, US Congress, https://www.congress.gov/bill/118th-congress/house-bill/1708/text.

77. "Building a Housing Justice Framework," Urban Institute, 2022, 5, https://www.urban.org/sites/default/files/2022-08/Building%20a%20Housing%20Justice%20Framework.pdf.

78. Jerusalem Demsas, "The Housing Crisis Is the Top Concern for Urban Residents," *Vox*, September 16, 2021, https://www.vox.com/2021/9/16/22674410/housing-crisis-homelessness-poll.

79. Alan Jenkins, "American Ideals and Human Rights: Findings from New Public Opinion Research by the Opportunity Agenda," Opportunity Agenda, November 2008, 447, https://www.researchgate.net/publication/254595501; "YouGov Survey: Views on Homelessness," YouGov, 2022, 69, https://docs.cdn.yougov.com/lmomgy9cc2/crosstabs_Views%20on%20Homelessness.pdf. (Seventy-two percent of Americans think housing is a basic human right.)

80. Jenkins, "American Ideals and Human Rights."

81. Daniel Aldana Cohen and Mark Paul, "The Case for Social Housing," Data for Progress and the Justice Collaborative Institute, November 2020, 6, https://www.filesforprogress.org/memos/the-case-for-social-housing.pdf.

82. "Post," President Joe Biden @POTUS (Tweet), March 10, 2021, https://x.com/POTUS/status/1369834567411109891.

83. Sonali Kolhatkar, "How to Make Housing as a Human Right a Reality," *Portside*, April 4, 2022, https://portside.org/2022-04-04/how-make-housing-human-right-reality.

84. Tars, "Housing as a Human Right."

85. Nicholas Kristof, "It's Easy to Feel Righteous in the Trump Era. Liberals, Beware," *New York Times*, June 17, 2023, https://www.nytimes.com/2023/06/17/opinion/trump-conservatives-liberals.html?action=.

10. RELIGIOUS TRADITIONS AND THE HUMAN RIGHT TO HOUSING

1. Rabbi Spiegel, telephone interview with the author, February 14, 2023.

2. Jeffrey M. Jones, "How Religious Are Americans?," Gallup, December 2021, https://news.gallup.com/poll/358364/religious-americans.aspx.

3. Jones, "How Religious Are Americans?"

4. Regretfully, it is outside the scope of this chapter to review the many other impactful religious traditions with their own strong legacies pointing toward the embrace of a human right to housing. For further reading on this topic please see James Taylor and Richard Kearney, eds., *Hosting the Stranger: Between Religions* (New York: Continuum, 2011), https://www.google.com/books/edition/Hosting_the_Stranger_Between_Religions/rnvjBAAAQBAJ?hl=en.

5. Many thanks to Jack Quigley, Ben Keele, and Andreanna Kalasountas for their help researching the connections between religious traditions and the human right to housing.

6. Taylor and Kearney, *Hosting the Stranger*.

7. Jones, "How Religious Are Americans?"

8. Aaron Zitner, "America Pulls Back from Values That Once Defined It, WSJ-NORC Poll Finds," *Wall Street Journal*, March 27, 2023, https://www.wsj.com/articles/americans-pull-back-from-values-that-once-defined-u-s-wsj-norc-poll-finds-df8534cd.

9. Jonathan Evans, "U.S. Adults More Religious Than Western Europeans," Pew Research Center, September 5, 2018, https://www.pewresearch.org/short-reads/2018/09/05/u-s-adults-are-more-religious-than-western-europeans/; "The Role of Religion in Politics," AP-NORC, August 2018, https://apnorc.org/projects/the-role-of-religion-in-politics/. (Fifty-seven percent of adults say religion should have "a lot/some" influence on poverty policies.)

10. Cathrine O'Dell, "'Motels4Now' Project Near Notre Dame Offers Housing for South Bend Homeless People," *National Catholic Reporter*, August 11, 2023, https://www.ncronline.org/news/motels4now-project-near-notre-dame-offers-housing-south-bend-homeless-people.

11. Fran Quigley, "With Post-pandemic Eviction Crisis Looming, Catholics Must Insist on Housing for All," *National Catholic Reporter*, July 2021, https://www.ncronline.org/news/justice/post-pandemic-eviction-crisis-looming-catholics-must-insist-housing-all.

12. Nadia Miriam, "Black Congregations Are Developing Housing on Church Land," *Shelterforce*, January 17, 2023, https://shelterforce.org/2023/01/17/black-churches-become-affordable-housing-developers/.

13. "Letter to Majority Leader Schumer, Minority Leader McConnell, Speaker McCarthy, and Minority Leader Jeffries," National Low Income Housing Coalition, April 25, 2023, https://nlihc.org/sites/default/files/Sign_On_Letter.pdf.

14. Some of the discussion of St. Martin's housing advocacy was originally published in Fran Quigley, "How Activists Are Making the Right to Housing a Reality," *Waging Nonviolence*, October 7, 2022, https://wagingnonviolence.org/2022/10/how-activists-are-making-right-to-housing-reality/.

15. Kay Miller, telephone interview with the author, September 13, 2022.

16. Christine McTaggart, "Disciple: Culture Shift," Episcopal Diocese of North Carolina, accessed June 15, 2024, https://www.episdionc.org/blog/disciple-culture-shift/.

17. Apryl Lewis, telephone interview with the author, September 9, 2022.

18. Andrea Palumbo, telephone interview with the author, July 23, 2022.

19. "People of Faith: Frederick Douglass," Faith Project Inc., PBS, 2003, https://www.pbs.org/thisfarbyfaith/people/frederick_douglass.html; "People of Faith: Sojourner Truth," Faith Project Inc., PBS, 2003, https://www.pbs.org/thisfarbyfaith/people/sojourner_truth.html; Charles H. Lippy and Peter W. Williams, *Encyclopedia of Religion in America* (Washington, DC: Sage, 2010).

20. Fran Quigley, *Religious Socialism: Faith in Action for a Better World* (Maryknoll, NY: Orbis, 2021), 15–25.

21. Lippy and Williams, *Encyclopedia of Religion in America.*

22. Lippy and Williams, *Encyclopedia of Religion in America.*

23. Lippy and Williams, *Encyclopedia of Religion in America.*

24. Gary Dorrien, *Breaking White Supremacy: Martin Luther King Jr. and the Black Social Gospel* (New Haven, CT: Yale University Press, 2018), 1–23.

25. Lippy and Williams, *Encyclopedia of Religion in America.*

26. Lippy and Williams, *Encyclopedia of Religion in America*; Sara Fritz, "U.S. Churches Will Launch Campaign against Apartheid," *Los Angeles Times*, January 14, 1986, https://www.latimes.com/archives/la-xpm-1986-01-14-mn-27824-story.html.

27. Simone Campbell, *A Nun on the Bus: How All of Us Can Create Hope, Change, and Community* (San Francisco: Harper One, 2014).

28. "Circle of Protection," Members of Circle of Protection Steering Committee, November 2017, https://circleofprotection.us/wp-content/uploads/2017/11/circle-of-protection-letter-to-congress-november-1-2017.pdf; Jack Jenkins, "Faith Groups Launch Major Push to Stop GOP Health Care Repeal," *ThinkProgress*, July 2017, https://thinkprogress.org/faith-groups-push-obamacare-e200406c21ad/.

29. "40 Faith Organizations Send Message to Healthcare Markup Committees," Network Lobby for Catholic Social Justice, March 2017, https://networklobby.org/wp-content/uploads/2017/03/FaithLeaderPrinciplesGOPHealthcareMarkup.pdf; Fran Quigley, "Faith in Medicare for All," *Canopy Forum*, December 2, 2019, https://canopyforum.org/2019/12/02/faith-in-medicare-for-all-by-fran-quigley/.

30. Fran Quigley, "How a Baptist Pastor Developed Canada's Single-Payer System," *Sojourners*, March 2019, https://sojo.net/magazine/march-2019/pastor-developed-Canada-single-payer-healthcare-universal.

31. Janet Somerville, "Why Christians Should Stay Involved in Canada's Health Care Debate," Canadian Council of Churches, May 2005, https://www.councilofchurches.ca/wp-content/uploads/2013/12/health_somerville_christian_involvement.pdf.

32. Quigley, "How a Baptist Pastor Developed Canada's Single-Payer System."

33. Julie Bressler, "Praying with Your Feet," Reform Judaism, July 2, 2009, https://reformjudaism.org/blog/praying-your-feet.

34. Assia Loutfi, "10 Muslims Who Won a Nobel Prize Because of Their Remarkable Contributions," *Mvslim*, April 2018, https://mvslim.com/10-muslims-won-a-nobel-prize-because-of-their-remarkable-contributions/.

35. Quigley, *Religious Socialism*, 49–151.

36. Quigley, 62–66.

37. Quigley, 62–66.

38. Clarence Williams and *Washington Post* staff, "An Oral History of the March on Washington, 60 Years after MLK's Dream," *Washington Post*, August 25, 2023, https://www.washingtonpost.com/history/interactive/2023/march-on-washington-60th-anniversary-memories/.

39. "Civil Rights," JoachimPrinz.com, accessed June 15, 2024, http://www.joachimprinz.com/civilrights.htm.

40. Bayard Rustin, "10 Demands of the March on Washington," *American Historama*, https://www.american-historama.org/1945-1989-cold-war-era/10-demands-of-the-march-on-washington.htm.

41. Southern Christian Leadership Conference Committee, "The Question of Poverty," Poor People's Campaign, Spring 1968, https://www.crmvet.org/docs/6805_ppc_demands.pdf.

42. Michael Karp, "The St. Louis Rent Strike of 1969: Transforming Black Activism and American Low-Income Housing," *Journal of Urban History* 40, no. 4 (2013), https:// journals.sagepub.com/doi/abs/10.1177/0096144213516082; "St. Louis Civil Rights Leader Dies, Southeast Missourian," Associated Press, May 12, 2002, https://www.semissourian. com/story/73400.html.

43. Karp, "St. Louis Rent Strike of 1969."

44. Quigley, "With Post-pandemic Eviction Crisis Looming."

45. Mark Colville, telephone interviews with the author, July 20, 2022, and December 11, 2023.

46. The St. Luke's response was part of a local Catholic legacy of responses to housing crises. Religious groups, including many Catholic parishes, played key roles in the robust New York City tenant rights movements of the twentieth century. See Ronald Lawson, ed., *The Tenant Movement in New York City, 1904–1984* (New Brunswick, NJ: Rutgers University Press, 1986), 4, 156–57, 209, 221, 234.

47. McKenzie and Del Santo quotes come from two interviews: Corey Sorenson, "CT Affordable Housing Interview," November 15, 2023, https://www.youtube.com/ watch?v=o-TvxonqUYo, and "Just in Time Interviews: Tiny Homes," *New Haven Independent*, November 22, 2023, https://www.youtube.com/watch?v=yCWjGqoxlE8.

48. Sonya Acosta and Erik Gartland, "Families Wait Years for Housing Vouchers Due to Inadequate Funding," Center on Budget and Policy Priorities, July 22, 2021, https://www.cbpp.org/research/housing/families-wait-years-for-housing-vouchers-due-to-inadequate-funding.

49. Brooke Griffin, "How the Housing Crisis Is Affecting Thousands in New Haven," *Fox61 News*, August 9, 2023, https://www.fox61.com/article/news/local/new-haven-county/new-haven/new-haven-connecticut-housing-crisis-section-8/520-f42eb 404-26eb-469d-bab6-f9e4509e4286.

50. Mark Zaretsky, "New Haven Moves in on Tent City," *New Haven Register*, March 16, 2023, https://www.nhregister.com/news/article/new-haven-moves-tent-city-clear-encamp ment-1-17843219.php.

51. Zaretsky, "New Haven Moves in on Tent City."

52. "Study Shows Involuntary Displacement of People Experiencing Homelessness May Cause Significant Spikes in Mortality, Overdoses, and Hospitalizations," National Health Care for the Homeless Council, April 10, 2023, https://nhchc.org/media/press-releases/study-shows-involuntary-displacement-of-people-experiencing-homelessness-may-cause-significant-spikes-in-mortality-overdoses-and-hospitalizations/.

53. "Study Shows," National Health Care for the Homeless Council.

54. Jenny Schuetz, *Fixer-Upper: How to Repair America's Broken Housing Systems* (Washington, DC: Brookings Institution, 2022), 75.

55. "Just in Time Interviews: Tiny Homes."

56. Luke 2:7.

57. Luke 9:58.

58. *Under the Bridge: The Criminalization of Homelessness*, Bigger Vision, film, 2015.

59. Matthew 25:35.

60. Luke 4:18.

61. Luke 10:37. Of course, this is just one example of many similar admonitions throughout the Old and New Testaments. As Anglican priest Tish Harrison Warren has written, "Throw a dart at the Bible and you are likely to hit a verse about the need to aid the vulnerable, to care for orphans and widows, to love the 'least of these.'" Tish Harrison Warren, "The Culture War That More Christians Should Be Fighting," *New York Times*, July 3, 2022, https://www.nytimes.com/2022/07/03/opinion/economic-justice-culture-war.html? referringSource=articleShare.

62. Luke 16:19–31.

63. Matthew 19:24.

64. Acts 2:44–45.

65. Acts 4:34–35.

66. James 2:15–17.

67. David Bentley Hart, "Are Christians Supposed to Be Communists?," *New York Times*, November 4, 2017, https://www.nytimes.com/2017/11/04/opinion/sunday/chris tianity-communism.html.

68. Alan Keith-Lucas, *The Poor You Will Have with You Always* (Palos Heights, IL: North American Association of Christians in Social Work, 1989), 7.

69. Saint Basil, *Homilia VII*, 1, 3, and 4, MPG, T. XXXI, cols. 280–81, 288, 289–92.

70. Na Zhao, "Eye on Housing: Nation's Stock of Second Homes," National Association of Homebuilders, October 2020, https://eyeonhousing.org/2020/10/nations-stock-of-second-homes-2/; "The State of Homelessness in America," Council of Economic Advisors, September 2019, https://www.nhipdata.org/local/upload/file/The-State-of-Home lessness-in-America.pdf.

71. John C. Cort, *Christian Socialism: An Informal History* (Maryknoll, NY: Orbis Books, 2020), 47.

72. Saint Jerome, Carta 120, PL, 22, col. 984, http://www.tertullian.org/fathers/jerome_hedibia_2_trans.htm.

73. Saint Augustine of Hippo, Sermo 50: Sermo Contra Manichaeos: De Eo Quod Scriptum Est in Aggeo Propheta: "Meum Est Aurum et Meum Est Argentum" Non sunt divitiae nec verae nec vestrae, http://www.monumenta.ch/latein/text.php?tabelle=August inus&rumpfid=Augustinus,%20Sermones,%2010,%20%20%2050&level=4&domain=&lang= 0&id=&hilite_id=&links=&inframe=1.

74. Keith-Lucas, *Poor You Will Have with You Always*, 19.

75. Keith-Lucas, 17–18.

76. Saint Thomas Aquinas, *Summa Theologica¸ Second Part of the Second Part, Question 66, Article 7, Response.*

77. Keith-Lucas, *Poor You Will Have with You Always*, 17–18.

78. Gary Dorrien, *Breaking White Supremacy: Martin Luther King Jr. and the Black Social Gospel* (New Haven, CT: Yale University Press, 2018), 472.

79. Cort, *Christian Socialism*, 19.

80. "About Us," National Council of Jewish Women, accessed June 15, 2024, https://www.ncjw.org/about/.

81. Rabbi Stephen Lewis Fuchs, "What We Need to Know about Welcoming the Stranger," Reform Judaism, November 2016, https://reformjudaism.org/blog/what-we-need-know-about-welcoming-stranger.

82. Marianne Moyaert, "Biblical, Ethical and Hermeneutical Reflections on Narrative Hospitality," in Taylor and Kearney, *Hosting the Stranger*, 98–99.

83. Jill Jacobs, "Judaism and the Homeless," *My Jewish Learning*, https://www.my jewishlearning.com/article/judaism-and-the-homeless/.

84. Fran Quigley, "Rabbi Michael Knopf: Jewish Tradition and Healthcare as a Human Right," *Faith in Healthcare*, August 27, 2019, https://faithinhealthcare.org/fhc/rabbi-michael-knopf-jewish-tradition-healthcare-human-right.

85. Jacobs, "Judaism and the Homeless."

86. Aryeh Cohen, "Justice, Wealth, Taxes: A View from the Perspective of Rabbinic Judaism," *Journal of Religious Ethics* 43, no. 3 (September 2015): 409–31, 415, 423, https://www.jstor.org/stable/24586126.

87. Daniel Walkowitz, "The Jewish Working Class in America," *Oxford Research Encyclopedia—American History*, November 29, 2021, https://oxfordre.com/american history/display/10.1093/acrefore/9780199329175.001.0001/acrefore-9780199329175-e-935.

88. Lawson, *Tenant Movement in New York City*, 109, 143.

89. "Civil Rights and Economic Justice," Union for Reform Judaism, May 1968, https://urj.org/what-we-believe/resolutions/civil-rights-and-economic-justice.

90. Rabbi Jonah Dov Pesner, telephone interview with the author, October 14, 2022.

91. Moyaert, "Biblical, Ethical and Hermeneutical Reflections," 163, n. 5.

92. Moyaert, 97.

93. Quran 107:1.

94. Quran 51:19.

95. Jacobs, "Judaism and the Homeless."

96. Taylor and Kearney, *Hosting the Stranger*, 136.

97. "Rights of Citizens in an Islamic State," Alukah, April 7, 2012, http://en.alukah.net/Society_Reform/0/1141/.

98. "Zakat: Purifying and Blessing Your Wealth," Islamic Relief Worldwide, May 24, 2016, https://islamic-relief.org/news/zakat/#:~:text=.

99. Brian Merchant, "Guaranteeing a Minimum Income Has Been a Utopian Dream for Centuries," *Vice*, November 14, 2013, https://www.vice.com/en/article/z4mbg3/guaranteeing-a-minimum-income-has-been-a-utopian-dream-for-centuries.

100. Quigley, *Religious Socialism*, 125.

101. Quran, lesson 104:1–5.

102. "Cairo Declaration on Human Rights in Islam," University of Minnesota Human Rights Library, August 1990, http://hrlibrary.umn.edu/instree/cairodeclaration.html#:~:text=.

103. Quigley, "Faith in Medicare for All."

104. "Rep. Omar Reintroduces Homes for All, Manufactured Housing Legislation," Ilhan Omar, press release, March 24, 2022, https://omar.house.gov/media/press-releases/rep-omar-reintroduces-homes-all-manufactured-housing-legislation.

105. Quigley, *Religious Socialism*, 125–26.

106. Kenneth K. Inada, "The Buddhist Perspective on Homelessness," in *Human Rights in Religious Traditions*, ed. Arlene Swidler (New York: Pilgrims, 1982), 66–76, 70, http://hongwanjihawaii.com/wp-content/uploads/2016/05/homelessness_hawaii_buddhism_2016_final.pdf.

107. Inada, "Buddhist Perspective on Homelessness."

108. Quigley, *Religious Socialism*, 146–66.

109. Ed Haliwell, "Of Course the Dalai Lama's a Marxist," *Guardian*, July 2011, https://www.theguardian.com/commentisfree/belief/2011/jun/20/dalai-lama-marxist-buddhism.

110. Inada, "Buddhist Perspective on Homelessness."

111. "Buddhistdoor View: Resolving the Hetupratyaya of Homelessness," *Buddhistdoor Global*, September 4, 2021, https://www.buddhistdoor.net/features/buddhistdoor-view-resolving-the-hetupratyaya-of-homelessness/.

112. Devin Watkins, "U.S. Catholics, Buddhists Helping Poor and Homeless Together," *Vatican News*, September 13, 2018, https://www.vaticannews.va/en/church/news/2018-09/catholics-buddhists-usa-green-affordable-housing.html.

113. Lawrence E. Adams, *Going Public: Christian Responsibility in a Divided America* (Ada, MI: Brazos, 2002), 13, 57; "Metro Atlanta Center Helps Formerly Incarcerated People with Jobs, Housing, Therapy," Inner-City Muslim Action Network, April 14, 2023, https://www.imancentral.org/updates/atlanta-center-helps-18663/.

114. Peter W. Peters, "Housing: A Human Right as a Norm for Housing First," accessed June 15, 2024, https://static1.squarespace.com/static/513e08bfe4b0b5df0ec24cda/t/5adf86ab88251b04dc42e690/1524598443966/.

115. Adams, *Going Public*, 13, 57; "Faith-Based Programs Still Popular, Less Visible," Pew Research Center, November 2009, https://www.pewresearch.org/religion/2009/11/16/faith-based-programs-still-popular-less-visible/; Fran Quigley, "The Limits of Philanthropy:

Time to End the Charitable Tax Deduction," *Commonweal*, January 2015, https://www.commonwealmagazine.org/limits-philanthropy.

116. Alexis de Toqueville, *Democracy in America* (1835; New York: Library of America, 2012, trans. Arthur Goldhammer), 595. ("The Americans make associations to give entertainments, to found seminaries, to build inns, to construct churches, to diffuse books, to send missionaries to the antipodes; in this manner they found hospitals, prisons, and schools. If it is proposed to inculcate some truth or to foster some feeling by the encouragement of a great example, they form a society. . . . I have often admired the extreme skill with which the inhabitants of the United States succeed in proposing a common object for the exertions of a great many men and in inducing them voluntarily to pursue it.")

117. "CAF World Giving Index," October 2019, 7, https://www.cafonline.org/docs/default-source/about-us-publications/caf_wgi_10th_edition_report_2712a_web_101019.pdf.

118. Frank Greve, "Poor Americans Are Country's Most Charitable Demographic," *Philanthropy News Digest*, May 2009, https://philanthropynewsdigest.org/news/poor-americans-are-country-s-most-charitable-demographic.

119. "These Countries Spend the Most, and the Least, on Social Benefits," World Economic Forum, February 10, 2021, https://www.weforum.org/agenda/2021/02/social-spending-highest-lowest-country-comparison-oecd-france-economics-politics-welfare/.

120. Ronald Reagan, "Address to the Nation on the Program for Economic Recovery, September 24, 1981," University of Texas, http://www.reagan.utexas.edu/archives/speeches/1981/92481d.htm.

121. Chris Roberts, "The Great Eliminator: How Ronald Reagan Made Homelessness Permanent," *SF Weekly*, June 2016, https://www.sfweekly.com/news/the-great-eliminator-how-ronald-reagan-made-homelessness-permanent/.

122. "State of Homelessness: 2023 Edition," National Alliance to End Homelessness, 2023, https://endhomelessness.org/homelessness-in-america/homelessness-statistics/state-of-homelessness/.

123. Janet Poppendieck, *Sweet Charity? Emergency Food and the End of Entitlement* (New York: Penguin, 1999), 5.

124. U.S.C. § 170(b)(1)(A). The deduction for charitable contributions has existed since 1917. *See* War Revenue Act of 1917, ch. 63, § 1201(2), 40 Stat. 330.

125. Rob Reich, "A Failure of Philanthropy: American Charity Shortchanges the Poor, and Public Policy Is Partly to Blame," *Stanford Social Innovation Review*, Winter 2005, https://www.giarts.org/sites/default/files/Failure-of-Philanthropy.pdf.

126. "Briefing Book," Tax Policy Center, May 2020, https://www.taxpolicycenter.org/briefing-book/what-are-largest-tax-expenditures; Mary K. Cunningham, "It's Time to Reinforce the Housing Safety Net by Adopting Universal Vouchers for Low-Income Renters," Urban Institute, 2020, https://www.urban.org/urban-wire/its-time-reinforce-housing-safety-net-adopting-universal-vouchers-low-income-renters.

127. Robert Reich, "Toward a Political Theory of Philanthropy," in *Giving Well: The Ethics of Philanthropy*, ed. Patricia Illingworth, Thomas Pogge, and Leif Wenar (New York: Oxford University Press, 2011), 184; "Robust COVID Relief Achieved Historic Gains against Poverty and Hardship, Bolstered Economy," Center on Budget and Policy Priorities, February 24, 2022, https://www.cbpp.org/research/poverty-and-inequality/robust-covid-relief-achieved-historic-gains-against-poverty-and.

128. Quigley, "With Post-pandemic Eviction Crisis Looming."

129. Mvenner, "Pope Francis Wants to Attack Structures That Perpetuate Inequality. As St. Augustine Puts It, Charity Is No Substitute for Justice Withheld," Catholic Network US, August 25, 2018, https://catholicnetwork.us/2018/08/25/pope-francis-wants-to-attack-structures-that-perpetuate-inequality-as-st-augustine-put-it-charity-is-no-substitute-for-justice-withheld/.

130. John D. Mason, "Biblical Teaching and the Objectives of Welfare Policy in the U.S.," *Faith and Economics* 22 (Fall 1993): 7–30, https://christianeconomists.org/wp-con tent/uploads/2020/06/1993-Fall-Mason.pdf.

131. Gary Scott Smith, "Creating a Cooperative Commonwealth," *Anglican and Episco-pal History* 62, no. 3 (1993): 404–5.

132. Saint Basil, *Homilia VII*, 1, 3, and 4, MPG, T. XXXI, cols. 280–81, 288, 289–92.

133. Miroslav Volf, *A Public Faith: How Followers of Christ Should Serve the Common Good* (Ada, MI: Brazos, 2011).

134. John Paul II, *Evangelium Vitae*. Francis, 9/16/13.

135. "Compendium of the Social Doctrine of the Church," Pontifical Coun-cil for Justice and Peace, Vatican.va, accessed June 15, 2024, https://www.vatican.va/roman_curia/pontifical_councils/justpeace/documents/rc_pc_justpeace_doc_20060526_compendio-dott-soc_en.html.

136. "Make the Most of the Pope's Visit with Your Member of Congress," National Alli-ance to End Homelessness, October 2015, https://endhomelessness.org/blog/make-the-most-of-the-popes-visit-with-your-member-of-congress/.

137. "A Message on Homelessness: A Renewal of Commitment," Evangelical Lutheran Church in America, accessed June 15, 2024, https://www.elca.org/Faith/Faith-and-Society/Social-Messages/Homelessness.

138. "Advocate for Policies Supporting Nutrition, Healthcare, and Housing as Human Rights, Resolution No. 2018-C041," Episcopal Archive, accessed June 15, 2024, https://www.episcopalarchives.org/cgi-bin/acts/acts_resolution.pl?resolution=2018-C041.

139. "Social Principles: The Social Community, 2016," United Methodist Church, accessed June 15, 2024, https://www.umc.org/en/content/social-principles-the-social-community.

140. "Sec. 51 of Doctrines and Covenants," Church of Jesus Christ, accessed June 15, 2024, https://www.churchofjesuschrist.org/study/manual/doctrine-and-covenants-teacher-manual-2017/lesson-20-doctrine-and-covenants-51-56?lang=eng.

141. Cori Bush, "Rep. Cori Bush: I Slept on the Capitol Steps Because I've Been Evicted Three Times in My Life," *CNN Opinion*, August 6, 2021, https://www.cnn.com/2021/08/06/opinions/sleep-on-capitol-steps-for-eviction-moratorium-motivation-cori-bush/index.html.

142. Cori Bush (@RepCori), Twitter, December 2, 2021, 6:38 pm, https://twitter.com/RepCori/status/1466552258120884224.

143. Melissa Cedillo, "Catholic Members of Congress Cite Faith in Eviction Moratorium Fight, Victory," *National Catholic Reporter*, August 2021, https://www.ncronline.org/news/coronavirus/catholic-members-congress-cite-faith-eviction-moratorium-fight-victory.

144. Jonah Dov Pesner, "Speak Up, Judge Righteously, Stand with the Poor: The Jewish Imperative for Social Justice," in *Spirit and Capital in an Age of Inequality*, ed. Robert P. Jones and Ted A. Smith (New York: Routledge, 2018).

145. Jacobs, "Judaism and the Homeless."

146. "Rep. Omar Reintroduces Homes for All."

147. Cort, *Christian Socialism*, 56.

11. BUILDING A MOVEMENT

1. Anna Rose, "Bill Moyer's Movement Action Plan," Commons Social Change Library 2012, https://commonslibrary.org/resource-bill-moyers-movement-action-plan/.

2. Anton Osgard, "Sweden's Collective Bargaining for Rents Must Be Defended," *Jacobin*, July 12, 2021, https://jacobin.com/2021/07/sweden-left-party-social-democrats-housing-crisis; Joanna Kusiak, "Socialization: A Democratic, Affordable, and Lawful Solution to Berlin's Housing Crisis," Rosa-Luxemburg-Stiftung, January 2021, https://www.rosalux.de/fileadmin/rls_uploads/pdfs/Policy_Paper/PolicyPaper_1-2021_EN.pdf;

Melissa Garcia-Lamarca, "From Occupying Plazas to Recuperating Housing: Insurgent Practices in Spain," *International Journal of Urban and Regional Research* 41, no. 1 (January 29, 2017): 37–53, https://onlinelibrary.wiley.com/doi/10.1111/1468-2427.12386; Veronika Duma and Hanna Lichtenberger, "Remembering Red Vienna," *Jacobin*, February 10, 2017, https://jacobin.com/2017/02/red-vienna-austria-housing-urban-planning.

3. Ronald Lawson, ed., *The Tenant Movement in New York City, 1904–1984* (New Brunswick, NJ: Rutgers University Press, 1986).

4. Bayard Rustin, "10 Demands of the March on Washington," American Historama, https://www.american-historama.org/1945-1989-cold-war-era/10-demands-of-the-march-on-washington.htm; Southern Christian Leadership Conference Committee, "The Question of Poverty," Poor People's Campaign, Spring 1968, https://www.crmvet.org/docs/6805_ppc_demands.pdf; Michael Karp, "The St. Louis Rent Strike of 1969: Transforming Black Activism and American Low-Income Housing," *Journal of Urban History* 40, no. 4 (2013), https://journals.sagepub.com/doi/abs/10.1177/0096144213516082.

5. "St. Louis Civil Rights Leader Dies, Southeast Missourian," Associated Press, May 12, 2002, https://www.semissourian.com/story/73400.html.

6. John Atlas, "The Rise and Fall of the National Tenants Union," *Shelterforce*, November 22, 2022, https://shelterforce.org/2022/11/22/the-rise-and-fall-of-the-national-tenants-union/.

7. Lillian M. Ortiz, "Tenant Power: Organizing for Rent Strikes and Landlord Negotiations," *Shelterforce*, July 30, 2018; Fran Quigley, "Midterm Voters Send a Message: Housing Is a Human Right," *Common Dreams*, November 30, 2022, https://www.commondreams.org/views/2022/11/20/midterm-voters-send-message-housing-human-right; Tyler Walicek, "Amid Eviction Crisis, Organizers Win Right to Legal Representation for Tenants," *Real News Network*, July 26, 2022, https://therealnews.com/amid-eviction-crisis-organizers-win-right-to-legal-representation-for-tenants.

8. Amee Chew, "Social Housing for All: A Vision for Thriving Communities, Renter Power, and Racial Justice," Center for Popular Democracy, March 2022, 18, https://www.populardemocracy.org/socialhousingforall; Loretta Graceffo, "'You Only Get What You're Organized to Take'—Lessons from the National Union of the Homeless," *Waging Nonviolence*, October 8, 2021, https://wagingnonviolence.org/2021/10/national-union-of-the-homeless/; Pamela Yates and Peter Kinoy, *Takeover* (film), Skylight Pictures Production, 1991, https://freespeech.org/stories/takeover-full-documentary; Maansi Shah, "What Happened When Activists Took Over Vacant Homes in Los Angeles," *Next City*, January 21, 2021, https://nextcity.org/urbanist-news/what-happened-whenactivists-took-over-vacant-homes-in-los-angeles; Sam Levin, "'This Is Life or Death': Homeless Families Reclaim Vacant Homes to Survive Virus Outbreak," *Guardian*, March 24, 2020, https://www.theguardian.com/world/2020/mar/24/this-is-life-or-death-homeless-families-reclaim-vacant-homes-to-survive-virus-outbreak; Noah Arroyo, "SF Tenants Set to Gain New Powers in Negotiations with Landlords," *San Francisco Public Press*, February 17, 2022, https://www.sfpublicpress.org/sf-tenantsto-gain-new-powers-in-negotiations-with-landlords/; Steve King, "Mom's House," Oakland CLT, accessed June 15, 2024, https://oakclt.org/portfolio-items/moms-house/.

9. "After 2.5 Year Rent Strike, ACCE Members Claim Victory after the Owner Officially Sells Building to the Oakland Community Land Trust!!!!," Alliance of Californians for Community Empowerment Action, August 12, 2022, https://www.acceaction.org/29th_ave_victory.

10. H. Jacob Carlson and Gianpaolo Baiocchi, "Social Housing: How a New Generation of Activists Is Reinventing Housing," *Shelterforce*, June 30, 2023, https://shelterforce.org/2023/06/30/social-housing-how-a-new-generation-of-activists-are-reinventing-housing/; Dianne Enriquez, "A System That Makes Housing a Commodity Can't Serve Human Needs," *Jacobin*, July 15, 2021, https://jacobin.com/2021/07/

housing-evictions-covid-19-crisis-homelessness-organize-policy; Chew, "Social Housing for All," 38–39.

11. "HoUSed," National Low Income Housing Coalition, accessed June 14, 2024, https://nlihc.org/housed.

12. Nick Blumberg, "Housing Advocates Stage Tent Encampment in City Hall during Mayor's Budget Address," *WTTW News*, October 3, 2022, https://news.wttw.com/2022/10/03/housing-advocates-stage-tent-encampment-city-hall-during-mayor-s-budget-address.

13. Alcynna Lloyd, "Renter Activists Crashed a DC Landlords Conference to Protest 'Corrupt Greed' and Rising Rents," *Business Insider*, September 15, 2022, https://www.businessinsider.com/activists-crash-dc-corporate-landlords-meeting-to-protest-rent-increases-2022-9; Justin Walker and Maddie McQueen, "'Housing Is a Human Right' Tenants Chant Marching to City Hall," *36NewsNow*, October 13, 2022 (arguing for a tenants bill of rights in Lexington, Kentucky), https://www.wtvq.com/update-housing-is-a-human-right-tenants-chant-marching-to-city-hall/.

14. "More Than 525 Organizations and Leaders Form Diverse Housing Coalition in California," Housing Is a Human Right, November 15, 2018, https://www.housinghumanright.org/500-organizations-leaders-formed-diverse-housing-coalition-california/; Arielle Stevenson, "St. Pete City Council Moves Closer to Putting Rent Control on the Ballot," *Creative Loafing*, August 4, 2022, https://www.cltampa.com/news/st-pete-city-council-moves-closer-to-putting-rent-control-on-the-ballot-13918801; Samuel Robinson, "Detroiters Want to End Michigan's Ban on Rent Control," *Axios*, August 18, 2022, https://www.axios.com/local/detroit/2022/08/18/detroiters-end-michigan-ban-rent-control; DaShawn Brown and Almiya White, "Merck County Pushes Federal Action against Corporate Landlords as Families Get Priced Out," *WSOC-TV*, August 23, 2022, https://www.wsoctv.com/news/local/meck-county-pushes-federal-action-against-corporate-landlords-families-get-priced-out/mdc57v7zx5bzvgmczozqdk5fxq/; Fran Quigley, "Philadelphia Renters Calling Out Government-Subsidized Landlord on Poor Conditions," *Common Dreams*, June 8, 2024, https://www.commondreams.org/opinion/philly-renters-fighting-together. For an excellent review of the current literature and debate about rent control see Jerusalem Desmas, "I Changed My Mind on Rent Control," *Vox*, December 2, 2021, https://www.vox.com/22789296/housing-crisis-rent-relief-control-supply.

15. Keeanga-Yamahtta Taylor, "How Real Estate Segregated America," *Dissent*, Fall 2018, https://www.dissentmagazine.org/article/how-real-estate-segregated-america-fair-housing-act-race.

16. Some of my reporting on the work of the Louisville Tenants Union has been published in Fran Quigley, "Louisville's Multiracial Tenant Union Is at the Forefront of a Growing National Movement," *Waging Nonviolence*, March 10, 2023, https://wagingnonviolence.org/2023/03/louisville-tenant-union-at-forefront-of-growing-national-movement/; Fran Quigley, "Tenants Push Biden for Rent Control on All Government-Backed Housing," *Waging Nonviolence*, July 11, 2023, https://wagingnonviolence.org/2023/07/tenants-push-biden-for-rent-control-government-backed-housing/; and Fran Quigley, "Governments Fund Gentrification. But We Can Stop It," *Jacobin*, March 17, 2024, https://jacobin.com/2024/03/government-gentrification-urban-renewal-racism.

17. Accounts of Louisville Tenants Union activity and quotes from its leaders come from the author's reporting and interviews from November 2022 to July 2024, unless otherwise noted.

18. Yasmine Jumaa and Jacob Munoz, "Supply in Demand: Here's Why Some in Louisville Continue to Struggle to Find Affordable Housing," *Louisville Public Media*, September 28, 2022, https://www.lpm.org/news/2022-09-28/supply-in-demand-heres-why-some-in-louisville-continue-to-struggle-to-find-affordable-housing.

19. David Harten, "Louisville Collegiate School Denied Request to Demolish Afford-able Apartments," *MSN News*, September 14, 2022, https://www.msn.com/en-us/news/us/louisville-collegiate-school-denied-request-to-demolish-affordable-apartments/ar-AA18pUt2.

20. Darcy Costello, "Lawyers in Breonna Taylor Case Had Ties to City's Gentrifica-tion Plan, Records Show," *Courier-Journal*, July 5, 2020, https://www.courier-journal.com/story/news/crime/2020/07/05/lawyers-breonna-taylor-case-connected-gentrification-plan/5381352002/.

21. Yasmine Jumaa, "Louisville Public Housing Residents Protest Conditions: 'Nobody's Coming to Help Us,'" *Louisville Public Media*, March 16, 2022, https://www.lpm.org/news/2022-03-16/louisville-public-housing-residents-protest-conditions-nobodys-coming-to-help-us.

22. Michael L. Jones, "Louisville Public Housing Manager under Fire to Cede Con-trol of Some Units," *LEO Weekly*, April 6, 2022, https://www.leoweekly.com/2022/04/louisville-public-housing-manager-under-fire-to-cede-control-of-some-units/.

23. John P. Wise, "Mark Handy, Ex-LMPD Detective Whose Lies Sent Innocent Men to Prison Released Early from Jail," *WAVE 3 News*, May 28, 2021, https://www.wave3.com/2021/05/28/mark-handy-ex-lmpd-detective-whose-lies-sent-innocent-men-prison-released-early-jail/.

24. Josh Poe, "Louisville's Eviction Crisis Is Being Ignored," Root Cause Research Center, November 22, 2019, https://www.rootcauseresearch.org/post/louisville-s-eviction-crisis-is-being-ignored.

25. WHAS 11 News Staff, "WHAS11 I-Team Investigates 'Louisville's Worst Landlord,'" *WHAS11 News*, November 22, 2016, https://www.whas11.com/article/money/consumer/whas11-i-team-investigates-louisvilles-worst-landlord/417-356575888.

26. Emma Austin, "CT Associates Ends Management of Louisville Public Hous-ing Complexes," *Courier Journal*, October 26, 2022, https://www.courier-journal.com/story/news/local/2022/10/26/ct-associates-ends-management-louisville-public-housing-complexes/69588962007/.

27. Maressa Burke, "New Directions Tenants Union Protest Unlivable Conditions," *WAVE3*, October 11, 2022, https://www.wave3.com/2022/10/11/new-direction-tenants-union-protest-unlivable-conditions/.

28. Alexis Jones, "'How Dare You Treat People Like That': West Louisville Tenants Pro-test Living Conditions," *WHAS News*, October 11, 2022, https://www.whas11.com/article/news/local/new-directions-housing-tenants-protest-conditions-russell-apartments/417-aecd4e9f-e734-4535-a281-07cb03c1d7e0.

29. "Public Housing: History," National Low Income Housing Coalition, October 17, 2019, https://nlihc.org/resource/public-housing-history.

30. "The Problem," HBN Assembly, accessed June 15, 2024, https://www.hbnassembly.org/hbno.

31. Emily Badger, Quoctrung Bui, and Robert Gebeloff, "The Neighborhood Is Mostly Black. The Home Buyers Are Mostly White," *New York Times*, April 27, 2019, https://www.nytimes.com/interactive/2019/04/27/upshot/diversity-housing-maps-raleigh-gentrification.html.

32. "Housing and Community Development Expenditures," Urban Institute, accessed June 15, 2024, https://www.urban.org/policy-centers/cross-center-initiatives/state-and-local-finance-initiative/state-and-local-backgrounders/housing-and-community-development-expenditures.

33. Justin Dorazio, "Localized Anti-displacement Policies," Center for American Progress, September 26, 2022, https://www.americanprogress.org/article/localized-anti-displacement-policies/.

34. "Russell: What Is the Right to Remain? Part 3," Root Cause Research Center, March 16, 2020, https://www.rootcauseresearch.org/post/russell-what-is-the-right-to-remain-part-3; "Housing Needs Assessment," LouisvilleKy.gov, accessed June 15, 2024, https://louisvilleky.gov/government/housing/housing-needs-assessment.

35. "Affirmatively Furthering Fair Housing, Article 80," Boston Planning and Development Agency, accessed June 15, 2024, https://www.bostonplans.org/housing/affirmatively-furthering-fair-housing-article-80.

36. Poe wrote about his background in a compelling article in *Shelterforce*: Josh Poe, "Tenant Unions Are How We Win in the South," *Shelterforce*, September 1, 2023, https://shelterforce.org/2023/09/01/tenants-unions-are-how-we-win-in-the-south/.

37. "The White House Must Act Now to Ensure Tenants' Rights," Homes Guarantee, https://homesguarantee.com/white-house/.

38. "The White House Blueprint for a Renters' Bill of Rights," January 2023, White House.gov, https://www.whitehouse.gov/wp-content/uploads/2023/01/White-House-Blueprint-for-a-Renters-Bill-of-Rights-1.pdf.

39. Tara Raghuveer, telephone interview with the author, February 2024.

40. Poe, "Louisville's Eviction Crisis Is Being Ignored."

41. "Louisville Apartment Complex Goes Days without Water," *WHAS-11*, August 8, 2022, https://www.whas11.com/video/news/local/louisville-apartment-complex-goes-days-with out-water/417-a28ffbb7-a149-4456-ac96-9483cae212df.

42. "Dougherty Mortgage Provides $8.2 Million Fannie Mae Green Loan for Multifamily Property in Louisville," *REBusiness Online*, December 11, 2019, https://rebusinessonline.com/dougherty-mortgage-provides-8-2m-fannie-mae-green-loan-for-multifamily-property-in-louisville/.

43. "Biden-Harris Administration Announces New Actions to Protect Renters and Promote Rent Affordability," White House, January 25, 2023, https://www.whitehouse.gov/briefing-room/statements-releases/2023/01/25/fact-sheet-biden-harris-administra tion-announces-new-actions-to-protect-renters-and-promote-rental-affordability/.

44. Laurie Goodman, Karan Kaul, and Michael Neal, "The CARES Act Eviction Moratorium Covers All Federally Financed Rentals—That's One in Four US Rental Units," Urban Institute, April 2, 20220, https://www.urban.org/urban-wire/cares-act-eviction-moratorium-covers-all-federally-financed-rentals-thats-one-four-us-rental-units.

45. Katy O' Donnell, "White House Prepares New Tenant Protections, Alarming Industry," *Politico*, January 18, 2023, https://www.politico.com/news/2023/01/18/white-house-new-tenant-protections-00077686.

12. "NO HOUSING, NO PEACE"

1. "Group Protests Rent to Be Canceled Outside Mecklenburg County Courthouse," *WBTV*, September 1, 2020, https://www.wbtv.com/2020/09/01/group-protests-rent-be-canceled-outside-mecklenburg-county-courthouse/.

2. "Mold on Furniture and Cabinets, Broken Air Conditioners, and Rats," *WCCB Charlotte*, October 2, 2018, https://www.wccbcharlotte.com/2018/10/02/mold-on-furni ture-and-cabinets-broken-air-conditioners-and-rats/?jwsource=cl; Lauren Lindstrom, "'Don't Close Your Eyes to Them': Displaced Tenants Urge City Action on Lake Arbor," *Charlotte Observer / WBTV*, August 27, 2019, https://www.wbtv.com/2019/08/27/dont-close-your-eyes-them-displaced-tenants-urge-city-action-lake-arbor/.

3. Fran Quigley, "Philadelphia Renters Calling Out Government-Subsidized Landlord on Poor Conditions," *Common Dreams*, June 8, 2024, https://www.commondreams.org/opinion/philly-renters-fighting-together.

4. Quotes from Apryl Lewis and other Action NC activists are from interviews with the author in September 2022, unless otherwise noted. Some of the discussion of Action

NC work was originally published in Fran Quigley, "How Activists Are Making the Right to Housing a Reality," *Waging Nonviolence*, October 7, 2022, https://wagingnonviolence. org/2022/10/how-activists-are-making-right-to-housing-reality/.

5. "Consumer Expenditures in 2020: Home (Report No. 1082)," US Bureau of Labor Statistics, December 2021, https://www.bls.gov/opub/reports/consumer-expenditures/ 2020/home.htm.

6. Emily Stewart, "The Housing Crisis Is a Homelessness Crisis, Too," *Vox*, September 16, 2021, https://www.vox.com/2021/9/16/22674410/housing-crisis-homelessness-poll.

7. Alan Jenkins and Kevin Shaw Hsu, "American Ideals and Human Rights: Findings from New Public Opinion Research by the Opportunity Agenda," *Fordham Law Review* 77 (2008): 439–59, https://www.researchgate.net/publication/254595501.

8. A discussion of the successful housing votes in the 2022 elections was originally published in Fran Quigley, "Midterm Voters Send a Message: Housing Is a Human Right," *Common Dreams*, November 20, 2022, https://www.commondreams.org/views/ 2022/11/20/midterm-voters-send-message-housing-human-right.

9. Samuel King, "Kansas City Voters Pass $175 Million in Bonds for Affordable Housing and Convention Center," *KCUR*, November 8, 2022, https://www.kcur.org/ politics-elections-and-government/2022-11-08/kansas-city-voters-pass-175-million-in-bonds- for-affordable-housing-and-convention-center.

10. Jacob Myers, "Columbus Voters Approving Affordable Housing, Infrastruc- ture Bonds," *Columbus Dispatch*, November 9, 2022, https://www.dispatch.com/story/ news/local/2022/11/09/columbus-voters-approving-affordable-housing-infrastructure- bonds/69605995007/.

11. Janie Hair, "Rent Stabilization Measures Win in US Midterm Election," Associated Press, November 16, 2022, https://apnews.com/article/2022-midterm-elections-inflation- florida-california-ef325d98687bbc08f2900b230a155852.

12. "Affordable Housing Wins on Ballots in the High Country," *Sky-Hi News*, Novem- ber 18, 2022, https://www.skyhinews.com/news/affordable-housing-wins-on-ballots-in- the-high-country/.

13. Holden Walter-Warner, "Hamptons, North Fork Pass Affordable Housing Fund," *TheRealDeal*, November 9, 2022, https://therealdeal.com/tristate/2022/11/09/hamptons- north-fork-pass-affordable-housing-fund/.

14. Sonja Isger, "Election Results: Palm Beach County Passes Affordable Hous- ing Bond," *Palm Beach Post*, November 9, 2022, https://www.palmbeachpost.com/ story/news/politics/elections/2022/11/09/election-results-palm-beach-county-afford able-housing-bond-2022-florida/10564837002/; Estephany Escobar, "Charlotte Voters Approve $50 million Affordable Housing Bond," *Spectrum News*, November 18, 2022, https://spectrumlocalnews.com/nc/charlotte/news/2022/11/18/affordable-housing-bond-#:~: text=; Andrew Jones, "As $70M Buncombe Bond Referendum Gets Green Light from Voters, How Much Will You Pay?," *Asheville Citizen Times*, November 8, 2022, https:// www.citizen-times.com/story/news/local/2022/11/09/buncombe-bond-referendum-passes- vote-election-2022/69631559007/.

15. Hair, "Rent Stabilization Measures Win."

16. Alex Schultz, "San Francisco Voters Back Prop. M, a Vacancy Tax on Landlords," *SFGATE*, November 15, 2022, https://www.sfgate.com/politics/article/san-francisco- voters-vacancy-tax-17584082.php.

17. Max Rameau and Shareef El-Mubarak, "Real Estate Industry Spends Big to Crush LA Mansion Tax," *MR Online*, October 31, 2022, https://mronline.org/2022/10/31/real- estate-industry-spends-big-to-crush-la-mansion-tax/; "Los Angeles, California, Propo- sition ULA, Tax on $5 Million House Sales Initiative (November 2022)," Ballotpedia, https://ballotpedia.org/Los_Angeles,_California,_Proposition_ULA,_Tax_on_%245_ Million_House_Sales_Initiative_(November_2022).

18. "Woodlawn Preservation Ordinance," City of Chicago, https://www.chicago.gov/city/en/depts/doh/supp_info/woodlawn-housing-ordinance.html.

19. Fran Quigley, "Three Big Things: The Presidential Election and Housing, Justice Department Sues for Rent-Pricing Collusion, and Labor and Housing," *Housing Is a Human Right Newsletter*, August 30, 2024, https://housingisahumanright.substack.com/p/three-big-things-the-presidential.

20. Rachel Siegel, "Biden Administration to Cap Rent Increases for Some Affordable Housing Units," *Washington Post*, March 29, 2024, https://www.washingtonpost.com/business/2024/03/29/biden-rent-housing/.

21. Sharon Wilson, "Harris' Misguided Rent Control Proposal," National Multifamily Housing Council, August 1, 2024, https://www.nmhc.org/news/nmhc-news/2024/harris-misguided-rent-control-proposal/; and "Rent Caps Are the Easy Way Out," National Apartment Association, July 11, 2024, https://www.naahq.org/rent-caps-are-easy-way-out.

22. Fran Quigley, *If We Can Win Here: The New Front Lines of the Labor Movement* (Ithaca, NY: Cornell University Press, 2015).

23. Kaitlyn Henderson, "The Crisis of Low Wages in the U.S.," Oxfam, March 21, 2022, https://www.oxfamamerica.org/explore/research-publications/the-crisis-of-low-wages-in-the-us/.

24. Matthew Desmond, *Poverty, by America* (New York: Crown, 2023), 51.

25. Katherine Guyot and Richard V. Reeves, "Unpredictable Work Hours and Volatile Incomes Are Long-Term Risks for American Workers," *Brookings*, August 18, 2020, https://www.brookings.edu/articles/unpredictable-work-hours-and-volatile-incomes-are-long-term-risks-for-american-workers/.

26. David Leonhardt, "The Racial Wage Gap Is Shrinking," *New York Times*, June 19, 2023, https://www.nytimes.com/2023/06/19/briefing/juneteenth-racial-wage-gap.html; "The Basic Facts about Women and Poverty," *American Progress*, August 3, 2020, https://www.americanprogress.org/article/basic-facts-women-poverty/.

27. Daniel Costa, "Employers Increase Their Profits and Put Downward Pressure on Wages and Labor Standards by Exploiting Migrant Workers," Economic Policy Institute, August 27, 2019, https://www.epi.org/publication/labor-day-2019-immigration-policy/; Nan Wu, "Immigrants Punch above Their Weight as Taxpayers," *Immigration Impact*, April 14, 2022, https://immigrationimpact.com/2022/04/14/immigrants-as-taxpayers-2022/.

28. Dan Burns, "U.S. Union Membership Hits Fresh Record Low," Reuters, January 23, 2024, https://www.reuters.com/markets/us/us-union-membership-rate-hits-fresh-record-low-2023-labor-dept-2024-01-23/.

29. Lawrence Mishel, "The Enormous Impact of Eroded Collective Bargaining on Wages," Economic Policy Institute, April 8, 2021, https://www.epi.org/publication/eroded-collective-bargaining/.

30. Justin McCarthy, "U.S. Approval of Labor Unions at Highest Point since 1965," Gallup, August 30, 2022, https://news.gallup.com/poll/398303/approval-labor-unions-highest-point-1965.aspx.

31. A discussion of labor unions' ties with tenant unions was originally published in Fran Quigley, "Unions and Tenant Organizations Are Natural Allies," *Jacobin*, June 3, 2024, https://jacobin.com/2024/06/labor-tenants-unions-organizing-solidarity.

32. Sarah Lazare, "The Chicago Teachers Union Wants to End Student Homelessness at the Bargaining Table," *Nation*, March 25, 2024, https://www.thenation.com/article/activism/chicago-teachers-union-homelessness/.

33. Benjamin Oreskes, "L.A. to Vote on 'Mansion Tax' to Raise Money for Housing," *Los Angeles Times*, September 30, 2022, https://www.latimes.com/california/story/2022-09-30/mansion-tax-la-ballot-measure.

34. Mathilde Lind Gustavussen, "Tenants Are Forcing Bay Area Landlords to the Bargaining Table," *Jacobin*, April 12, 2024, https://jacobin.com/2024/04/berkeley-tenants-union-at-home-organizing/#:~:text=.

35. "Winning Rent Stabilization in Minneapolis and St. Paul," SEIU Local 26, https://www.seiu26.org/winning-rent-stabilization-in-minneapolis-and-st-paul, accessed August 31, 2024.

36. "UNITE Here Local 11: Housing!," https://www.unitehere11.org/housing/.

37. Ty Moore, "UFCW Local Leads Fight to Win Washington's Strongest Tenant Protections," *LaborNotes*, February 12, 2024, https://labornotes.org/2024/02/ufcw-local-leads-fight-win-washingtons-strongest-tenant-protections; "Endorsements," Tacoma for All, accessed May 29, 2024, https://www.tacoma4all.org/endorsers.

38. Steven Greenhouse, "U.S. Unions Target the Housing Affordability Crisis as Their 'Biggest Issue,'" *Guardian*, February 16, 2024, https://www.theguardian.com/society/2024/feb/16/unions-affordable-housing.

39. "Investing in Communities the Union Way," AFL-CIO HIT, Housing Investment Trust, accessed May 29, 2024, https://www.aflcio-hit.com/about/.

40. Peter Dreier, "We Must Strengthen the Labor-Housing Coalition," *Shelterforce*, June 8, 2023, https://shelterforce.org/2023/06/08/we-must-strengthen-the-labor-housing-coalition/.

41. Alexander Kolokotronis, "What Is Workforce Housing?," Research for a Better Connecticut, March 10, 2024, https://abetterct.org/what-is-workforce-housing-cooperatives-are-one-answer/.

42. Sam Sachs, "Rent Has 'Exceeded Income Gains by 325%' in Past 37 Years, Researchers Tell U.S. Senate," *WFLA.com*, August 3, 2022, https://www.wfla.com/news/national/rent-has-exceeded-income-gains-by-325-in-past-37-years-researchers-tell-us-senate/.

43. Rachel M. Cohen, "How Housing Activists and Unions Found Common Ground in California," *Vox*, August 21, 2023, https://www.vox.com/policy/2023/8/21/23831121/housing-yimbys-affordable-rent-unions-california.

44. "Blackstone Comes to Collect: How America's Largest Landlord and Wall Street's Highest Paid CEO Are Jacking Up Rents and Ramping Up Evictions," *Private Equity Stakeholder Project*, March 25, 2023, https://pestakeholder.org/reports/blackstone-comes-to-collect-how-americas-largest-landlord-and-wall-streets-highest-paid-ceo-are-jacking-up-rents-and-ramping-up-evictions/#:~:text=; Adam Brinklow, "Wall Street Firm Tapping Public Worker Funds for Anti–Rent Control Campaign," *Curbed San Francisco*, October 24, 2018, https://sf.curbed.com/2018/10/15/17980380/prop-10-rent-control-housing-wall-street-blackstone.

45. Tobias Burns, "Labor Unions Call for Repeal of Trump Tax Cuts," *Hill*, May 21, 2024, https://thehill.*com*/business/4675525-labor-unions-call-for-repeal-of-trump-tax-cuts/.

46. "Public Pension Assets—Quarterly Update Q4 2023," *NASRA*, https://www.nasra.org/content.asp?admin=Y&contentid=200#:~:text=.

47. Fran Quigley, "Governments Fund Gentrification. But We Can Stop It," *Jacobin*, March 17, 2024, https://jacobin.com/2024/03/government-gentrification-urban-renewal-racism.

48. Matthew Royer, "AFSCME Local 3299, Community Members Call on UC to Divest from Blackstone," *Daily Bruin*, February 14, 2024, https://dailybruin.com/2024/02/14/afscme-local-3299-community-members-call-on-uc-to-divest-from-blackstone.

49. Unless otherwise noted, the statements of Connecticut tenants and union members were provided during telephone interviews with the author in May 2024.

50. Anton Osgard, "Sweden's Collective Bargaining for Rents Must Be Defended," *Jacobin*, July 12, 2021, https://jacobin.com/2021/07/sweden-left-party-social-democrats-housing-crisis.

51. Veronika Duma and Hanna Lichtenberger, "Remembering Red Vienna," *Jacobin*, February 10, 2017, https://jacobin.com/2017/02/red-vienna-austria-housing-urban-planning.

CONCLUSION

1. Ko Lyn Cheang and Binghui Huang, "Corporate Landlords Filed 88% of All Evictions in Indianapolis through September," *Indianapolis Star*, October 24, 2021, https://www.indystar.com/story/news/realestate/2021/10/24/indianapolis-eviction-moratorium-top-evictors-during-pandemic/6102198001/.

2. Jesse Eisinger, Jeff Ernsthausen, and Paul Kiel, "These Real Estate and Oil Tycoons Avoided Paying Taxes for Years," *ProPublica*, December 7, 2021, https://www.propublica.org/article/these-real-estate-and-oil-tycoons-used-paper-losses-to-avoid-paying-taxes-for-years.

3. Rachel M. Cohen, "A Bold New Federal Experiment in Giving Renters Cash," *Vox*, September 12, 2023, https://www.vox.com/2023/9/12/23864165/affordable-housing-voucher-program-hud-federal-government-section-8.

4. "Los Angeles, California, Proposition ULA, Tax on $5 Million House Sales Initiative (November 2022)," Ballotpedia, https://ballotpedia.org/Los_Angeles,_California,_Proposition_ULA,_Tax_on_%245_Million_House_Sales_Initiative_(November_2022).

5. Taylor Branch, *Parting the Waters: America in the King Years 1954–63* (New York: Simon & Schuster, 1989), 129–136 (explaining the critical role played by E. D. Nixon and Jo Ann Robinson in Montgomery).

6. Henry Mayer, *All on Fire: William Lloyd Garrison and the Abolition of Slavery* (New York: Norton, 2000).

Index

Action NC, 114–115, 153, 155

Acts of Apostles, 123–124, 134

Affordable housing: federally subsidized housing, 16, 33–45, 68, 163–165; human right to housing, 107–111, 154; privatization of, 16–20; public support for, 5, 19, 86, 137, 153–156; US investment historically, 13–16, 24–25. *See also* public housing, social housing, universal housing vouchers

American Anti-Slavery Society, 116

American Housing Act of 1937, 14, 88, 90, 158

American Housing Act of 1949, 13, 20, 29, 92, 110

American Legislative Exchange Council (ALEC), 86

American Muslim Healthcare Professionals, 130

American Rescue Plan of 2021, 70

Amistad Catholic Worker Community, 119–122

Apollo Global Management, 11

Aquinas, Thomas, 124–125

Armounfelder, Eliana, 58–59

Arthur, Jecorey, 141–142, 145

Athens, 110

Austria, 91, 100–101, 137

Austrian Social Democratic Party, 102–103

Bach, Victor, 15

Baiocchi, Gianpaolo, 16, 98

Ballot measures supporting housing, 5, 19, 86, 137, 154–155, 158

Bank of America, Countrywide Financial, 27

Bargaining for the Common Good, 158–159

Baril, Rob, 161–162

Belgium, 106

Bellamy, Jessica, 140, 143–147

Berlin, 106

Biden, Joe, 62–63, 66, 68, 111, 147, 149–150

Blackstone, 11, 19, 78, 159–160

Boden, Paul, 14, 110

Boffo, Leonard, 116

Bowron, Josh, 114

Breitner Taxes (Vienna), 103

Brookings Institution, 27, 42, 65, 85, 122

Brothers Karamazov, 60

Brown, Jasmine, 150

Brown-Jackson, Ketanji, 22

Buddhism and Housing, 130–131

Buffett, Warren, 11

Bush, Cori, 64, 134

Cairo Declaration on Human Rights in Islam, 129–130

Capital gains taxes on real estate income, 37–38

CARES Act, 58

Carlson, H. Jacob, 16, 98

Carlyle Group, 11

Carson, Ben, 62, 64

Carter, Jimmy, 17, 88, 108

Catholic Charities USA, 114, 119

Catholicism and Housing, 115–116, 134

Catholic Worker, 57–60, 114, 119–122

Cebul, Brent, 29

Center for American Progress, 145

Center for Popular Democracy, 45, 75, 85, 135, 153

Center on Budget and Policy Priorities, 38, 43–44, 70

Chang, Stanley, 14–15, 20, 105–106

Chew, Amee, 75, 83

Chicago Teachers Union, 158

Chile, social housing, 106

Christianity and Housing, 123–125, 134

Church of Jesus Chris of Latter Day Saints, 134

Clean Hands requirement for evictions, 53, 148

Clinton, Bill, 17, 70, 90

Cohen, Aryeh, 128

Cohen, Daniel Aldana, 15

Colville, Mark, 119–123

Committee on Economic, Social, and Cultural Rights, 109

Community Development Block Grants, 85

Community Land Trusts (CLT's), 97–98

Community Opportunity to Purchase Act (COPA), 95, 97–98

www.ingramcontent.com/pod-product-compliance
Lightning Source LLC
Chambersburg PA
CBHW030405270326
41926CB00009B/1269